How to Build a Beowulf

Scientific and Engineering Computation

Janusz Kowalik, editor

How to Build a Beowulf

A Guide to the Implementation and Application of PC Clusters

Thomas L. Sterling
John Salmon
Donald J. Becker
Daniel F. Savarese

The MIT Press
Cambridge, Massachusetts
London, England

Second printing, 1999

Library of Congress Cataloging-in-Publication Data

Sterling, Thomas Lawrence.
How to build a Beowulf: a guide to the implementation and application of PC clusters / Thomas L. Sterling, John Salmon, Donald J. Becker, and Daniel F. Savarese.
   p. cm.—(Scientific and Engineering Computation)
  Includes bibliographical references and index.
  ISBN 0-262-69218-X (pbk.: alk. paper)
  1. Parallel computers. 2. Electronic Data Processing—Distributed processing. 3. Beowulf clusters (Computer systems). I. Salmon, John (John Kennedy), 1960— . II. Becker, Donald J. III. Savarese, Daniel F. IV. Title. V. Series.
QA76.58.S854 1998
004'.36—dc21

98-37596
CIP

This book was set in LATEX by the authors and was printed and bound in the United States of America.

To James R. Fischer

Contents

Series Foreword

The world of modern computing potentially offers many helpful methods and tools toscientists and engineers, but the fast pace of change in computer hardware, software, and algorithms often makes practical use of the newest computing technology difficult. The Scientific and Engineering Computation series focuses on rapid advances in computing technologies and attempts to facilitate transferring these technologies to applications in science and engineering. It will include books on theories, methods, and original applications in such areas as parallelism, large-scale simulations, time-critical computing, computer-aided design and engineering, use of computers in manufacturing, visualization of scientific data, and human-machine interface technology.

The series will help scientists and engineers to understand the current world of advanced computation and to anticipate future developments that will impact their computing environments and open up new capabilities and modes of computation.

This volume is about the increasingly successful distributed/parallel system called Beowulf. Beowulf is a cluster of PCs interconnected by network technology running Linux operating system and employing the message-passing method for parallel computation. Key advantages of this approach to parallel computation are (a) high performance for low price, (b) system scalability, and (c) rapid adjustment to new technological advances.

The book provides a complete description of the Beowulf hardware, software, programming, and selected applications. It can be used as an academic textbook, as well as a practical guide for designing and implementing Beowulf for those in science and industry who need a powerful system but are reluctant to purchase an expensive system such as MPP or vector machine.

As any other alternative parallel system the Beowulf system has technical challenges created by relatively large communication latencies. To perform well Beowulf must run suitable algorithms characterized by infrequent communication and medium to large granularity of parallel tasks. Fortunately there are many practical large-scale problems that satisfy this requirement. The book provides detailed examples illuminating the algorithmic performance and scalability of Beowulf.

Janusz S. Kowalik

Foreword

You have just picked up a most interesting book. To understand how interesting it is, you have to take a short trip with me back in time.

It is September of 1968. You are in Philadelphia, and you are going to study computer science at a major university. The computer system you are going to work on costs in the neighborhood of several million dollars. The computer's time is scheduled twenty-four hours a day, for its time is even more valuable than your own. The concept of shutting the operating system down to allow you to practice writing an operating system is not even considered. If you (the lowly student or researcher) wish to practice writing an operating system, you use a hardware emulator (written in software) that runs on top of the hugely expensive computer system.

Time moves on. It is now 1977, and some of the first microcomputers are coming out. They are still relatively expensive, and they have very small memories and disks. While students can work on writing device drivers and other small additions to various "sample" operating systems, having the entire source code for an industry-capable operating system and hardware that would be capable of solving "real" problems is still not in the grasp of the average student.

Now it is 1994. "PC" hardware has become much more sophisticated, and a new operating system is beginning to make its presence known. The source code for this operating system is available over the Internet, and large numbers of people are working with it, improving it, and fashioning it for a commercial market. Yet there is still something missing, for while the hardware for "simple" tasks is within the realm of the average user (or even wealthy college student), there are a class of problems that are designated for those awesome systems known as "supercomputers"—systems that still cost many millions of dollars to build, beyond the reach of all but a few of the most prestigious universities and laboratories.

Meanwhile, at a small user-conference in San Francisco, two men present their talk on how to break up large programs and split them across a series of workstations. The talk goes largely unnoticed, but the work goes on.

Finally, in 1997 the world begins to take notice of the work of these people. Words like "Beowulf" are tossed around, and "cheap supercomputers." While these "cheap supercomputers" can be made out of any of several operating systems, the one started by a young Finnish university student pulls out ahead, and the term "Extreme Linux" makes its way into the jargon. At the 1997 Supercomputer conference, three systems vie for the coveted Gordon Bell Award for price/performance in a supercomputer. All three are these Beowulf systems, and all three run the Linux operating system.

This in itself would be interesting, but there is more.

> *A university in Sao Paulo, Brazil builds a 125-unit Beowulf system running Linux. Their goal: real-time animated graphics. A side goal is to develop a technique to analyze a mammogram in 1/120th the time it takes a workstation to come to the same conclusions, ten minutes instead of twenty hours.*
>
> *A research group in New Mexico uses a 16-node Beowulf system to research collisions of the earth with asteroids.*
>
> *A research group outside Chicago recognizes that a Beowulf system is the most cost effective (and with their budget, the only) way they can update their computer systems to handle the load of their supercollider.*

But the epitome of Beowulf study comes from a national lab in Oakridge, Tennessee, where they build an "Extreme Linux" system from cast-off personal computers, no longer in use when their owners were upgraded to new, more powerful machines.

They call this system the "Stone Soupercomputer," and for the first time it is demonstrated that any university, any college, any high school, even a grade school can build a system that allows its students to practice this distributed programming, to practice programming a "Soupercomputer," to solve problems that would have taken days and weeks in minutes.

As I write this, a high school in Nashua, New Hampshire, is assembling its own Extreme Linux system. Made from donated computers, these students will learn to build, program, and system-administer this very powerful system. Perhaps they will even help contribute algorithms and ideas on how to make the system work better and faster. And if it happens in Nashua, it will probably happen all over the world.

The world can no longer afford to have all of the expertise in computer science reside in elite places. We have problems to solve, and the world needs to contribute to solving them. With the combination of the Internet, Open Source operating systems and software, inexpensive "PC" hardware, and concepts like the Beowulf systems, any person from any country can now contribute to the development of these technologies. We hope to find and acknowledge the next "Albert Einstein" of computer science, whether he or she comes from the United States, from Brazil, from Korea, from China, or from any other country.

With this book, you should be able to build your own "Soupercomputer." I thank Thomas Sterling and his coauthors for writing it, and for allowing me the opportunity to add this small introduction.

Carpe Diem.

Jon "maddog" Hall
Executive Director
Linux International
January 1999

Preface

How to Build a Beowulf has the principal objective of enabling, facilitating, and accelerating the adoption of the Beowulf model of distributed computing for real-world applications. Beowulfs use commodity hardware components and open source software components to deliver supercomputer levels of performance at an astonishingly low price. This book is targeted to a diverse readership and is intended to serve in multiple roles. It can be used by small groups to quickly bring up such systems for direct application. It can be used by college laboratories as a basis for practical courses in parallel computing systems. And it can be used by potential future users of Beowulf systems to evaluate their needs against the strengths and weaknesses of the approach. Finally, it can be used by the general technical reader to gain an overview of an important and rapidly growing field of parallel and high performance computing.

A book of this nature is challenged by the success its subject matter. *How to Build a Beowulf* concerns a topic that is undergoing rapid advancement. Many of the technologies on which Beowulf-class systems depend are experiencing such growth that hard data cannot help but become progressively out of date. On one hand, *Beowulf,* the book, provides specific information about devices and components available at the time of writing. On the other hand, it also places that information in a technological context that transcends a single generation of components. Where the technological trends are clear, the book also has information about systems that will soon be available. Much of the power of Beowulf is generation independent. It is safe to say that there will always be one or more mass-market microprocessors and operating systems to run on them, and that there will always be one or more commercial networks with which they can be integrated. As long as those predictions remain true, the ideas in this book will continue to be useful.

In crafting *How to Build a Beowulf,* we have had to cope with the enormous quantity of relevant material. At each level in the system structure of a Beowulf cluster, from the hardware all the way up to the applications, there are multiple choices for implementation. There are several choices of processor or network topology at the hardware level, more than one alternative for the Unix-based operating system, several possible ways to perform message passing, a range of possibilities for managing the ensemble, and alternatives to algorithm design. The total space of possible instances would demand scores of volumes and indeed their documentation takes up at least that many reference works under separate title. Within the restrictions of time and space allotted to *How to Build a Beowulf,* we have chosen a depth-first approach. We show at least one complete and detailed path from the basic available elements that comprise a Beowulf system to achieving a fully executing parallel application on a Beowulf. Additional information is provided about some of the alternatives and references are made to yet more approaches. In this sense, we have chosen to make this work narrow but complete rather than exhaustive but shallow.

How to Build a Beowulf grew out of a series of tutorials given by the authors and their colleagues in 1997 and 1998. These very successful full-day events were presented at several technical conferences as well as at one of our home institutions, Caltech. The tutorials mixed hardware, software and a little theater (nodes were assembled on stage, and there was always some drama when they were powered up for the first time) and attendees received a set of notes that summarized the talks. These notes gained wider distribution, until eventually, the MIT Press approached the authors suggesting that the widespread demand for practical information about Beowulfs could be satisfied by a book. You are now holding that book.

Acknowledgments

This book is dedicated to James R. Fischer of the NASA Goddard Space Flight Center, for his vision, commitment to applied research, and professional management, without which the Beowulf Project and its many contributions would not have occurred. Jim established the goals addressed by the initial Beowulf Project and recognized the innovation and opportunity that the Beowulf model represented. And it was he who supported the Beowulf project through a period when its long-term potential value was not always recognized by others. This book is a direct consequence of Jim Fischer's contributions and the authors wish to convey their personal appreciation to him through this dedication.

The genesis and evolution of this book has benefitted from the contributions and assistance of many. It is not possible to adequately credit everyone responsible for this accomplishment. We would like to cite several major efforts without which Beowulf would not have been possible and ask those responsible for these many contributions to accept our respect and appreciation. These initiatives, research projects, development efforts, and companies include: Linux, the GNU project, BSD, Cygnus Solutions, IEEE 802 Working Group, Red Hat Software, Extreme Linux, MPI, and PVM. We would like to thank our colleagues on the Beowulf project at the NASA Goddard Space Flight Center, USRA Center of Excellence in Space Data and Information Sciences, the California Institute of Technology Center for Advanced Computing Research, and the NASA Jet Propulsion Laboratory, including Phil Merkey, Dan Ridge, Chance Reschke, John Dorband, Clark Mobarry, Jason Crawford, Jan Lindheim, Paul Angelino, Joe Fouché, Chris Stein, Tom Gottschalk, Sharon Brunett, Tom Cwik, Dan Katz, John Lou, Ping Wang, Paul Springer, and Jeff Edlund, as well as Mike Warren at the Los Alamos National Laboratory. As this book is a direct consequence of the series of workshops conducted at CCC'97, SC'97, Hot Chips'97, Caltech, and HPDC'98, we would like to recognize those who directly contributed to their success in addition to those already cited, including: Jack Dongarra, David Bailey, Al Geist, Rusty Lusk, Chip Chapman, Madeline Crain, and Nick Kerbis. We wish to thank Sarah Emery for her assistance with the preparation of the book and Mike MacDonald for his detailed corrections of much of the body of the text. Paul Angelino deserves special recognition for providing much of the PC hardware assembly information and for being an instrumental part of making the "Beowulf Tutorial" a success at the various conferences at which it has been given. The authors wish to thank Jon Hall for his foreword to this book. We also convey our most sincere thanks to Doug Sery of MIT Press, for his infinite patience and continuing guidance.

T. Sterling would like to convey his personal appreciation to Jon Mangan for his continuous professional contributions throughout the course of this writing. T. Sterling would also like to thank Kevin Mahoney for his advice and support as well as Scott Brown for his focused perspective. J. Salmon would like to thank Lynn Salmon for cheerfully learning more than she ever wanted to know about how to build a Beowulf. D. Savarese thanks his parents and sister for sacrificing some of their time with him over the holidays so he could work on this book.

1 Introduction

Beowulf was the legendary sixth-century hero from a distant realm who freed the Danes of Heorot by destroying the oppressive monster Grendel. As a metaphor, "Beowulf" has been applied to a new strategy in high performance computing that exploits mass-market technologies to overcome the oppressive costs in time and money of supercomputing, thus freeing scientists, engineers, and others to devote themselves to their respective disciplines. Beowulf, both in myth and reality, challenges and conquers a dominant obstacle, in their respective domains, thus opening the way to future achievement.

You are about to engage in an experience that only a few years ago would have been impossible. You are going to learn how to build and use a supercomputer. And you are going to find out how to do so quickly, at low cost, and with facilities readily available to most small academic or industrial groups. In short, you are about to enter the world of what *Science* magazine has called "Do-it-yourself Supercomputing" or what much of the high performance computing community refers to as "Beowulf PC Clusters," "Beowulf-class Systems," or simply "Beowulfs."

A Beowulf-class system is a cluster of mass-market commodity off the shelf (M^2COTS) PCs interconnected by low cost local area network (LAN) technology running an open source code Unix-like operating system and executing parallel applications programmed with an industry standard message passing model and library. Today, Beowulf-class systems are installed and operational at sites all over the world. These systems range from a few nodes with sustained performance of hundreds of Megaflops to more than a hundred nodes achieving tens of Gigaflops. The most powerful of these systems are among the top 500 list of the highest performance computers in the world. Beowulfs can be found in universities, national laboratories, industrial groups, government installations, undergraduate dormitories, and small entrepreneurial start-up companies. They are even beginning to show up in mainstream commercial and business concerns. Beowulfs are applied to a wide range of applications and workloads. Many of the computing problems performed using Beowulfs have come from the domains of science and engineering, the primary users of supercomputers and massively parallel processors (MPPs). But other problems have involved data-oriented computations for databases, information archiving and retrieval, and education. Beowulfs are used in many academic laboratories as test beds for teaching concepts in parallel computer systems, software, measurement, and application. They are also used as development platforms for application codes that are eventually migrated to bigger MPPs.

Beowulf-class computers are simply the best price/performance systems available today for many high end applications. This cost advantage often can be as much as an order of magnitude over commercial systems of comparable capabilities. This level of cost benefit has also been achieved for sustained performance for many, but not all, important classes of applications. Recognition of the dramatic improvement possible through Beowulf systems was received by a combined team of NASA and Los Alamos researchers who were awarded the 1997 Gordon Bell Prize for Price/Performance. The Los Alamos team again won the Gordon Bell Prize in 1998 for a second Beowulf-class machine. With an order of magnitude price/performance superiority, Beowulfs open entirely new modes of system usage, making them available in areas previously without access to high end computing. Not since the advent of the minicomputer in the mid-1960s or the microprocessor in the mid-1970s has there been such a wealth of new opportunities.

1.1   A Brief History

In 1993, most of the conditions necessary for the emergence of PC clusters were in place. The Intel 80386 processor was a major performance advance over its 80286 predecessor, DRAM densities and costs were such that 8 MBytes was within budget, disk drives of a hundred MBytes or more were available for PC configurations, Ethernet (10 Mbps) interface controllers were available for PCs, and hubs (not switches) were cheap enough to consider using for small cluster configurations. In addition, an early version of Linux was undergoing rapid evolution, and PVM was achieving stature as the first major cross-platform parallel programming message passing model to achieve wide acceptance. Also, substantial experience had been gained by the high performance computing (HPC) community in programming MPPs due in part to the Federal High Performance Computing and Communication (HPCC) Program. At the same time, a number of universities were engaging in efforts to apply workstation clusters to real problems and develop software tools to facilitate their use.

What was missing was the opportunity to bring these still relatively weak system components together to address real problems. The NASA HPCC Program Earth and Space Sciences Project at the Goddard Space Flight Center had just such a problem. It required a single-user science station for holding, manipulating, and displaying large data sets produced as output by grand challenge applications running on MPPs. It had to cost no more than a high end scientific workstation (< \$50K), store at least 10 GBytes of data, and provide high bandwidth from secondary storage to the system display console. An initial requirement for near 1 Gflops peak performance was also specified. An analysis of commercial systems at that time showed that existing systems with the required capabilities would cost 10 to 20 times too much.

Scientists at Goddard proposed a radical solution: the use of mass-market computing components, employed in parallel. Initial studies showed that all requirements could be met except for the 1 Gflops performance figure. However, one billion operations per second (not necessarily floating point) could be achieved and this was sufficient to meet the project's goals. The only missing component was the networking software technology which would have to be developed in-house. The Beowulf project was officially inaugurated in Fall of 1993 and the initial team was formed by early 1994.

In late 1994, the first Beowulf system, Wiglaf, Beowulf's trusted aide, was operational. This was a 16-processor system with 66 MHz Intel 80486 processors, which were quickly replaced with 100 MHz DX4 processors. Even with this early technology, Beowulf was able to compete with such contemporary MPPs as the Intel Paragon and TMC CM-5 on problems suitable to its architecture. Sustained performance of 4.6 Mflops per node (74 Mflops total) was achieved for certain compute intensive applications. The second Beowulf, Hrothgar, named for the king of Danes and builder of Heorot incorporating newer technology, was completed and operational by the end of 1995. Its 16 Intel Pentium-based PCs and Fast Ethernet delivered 17.5 Mflops sustained performance per node (280 Mflops total). By the end of 1996, the third generation Beowulfs, Hyglac at the Jet Propulsion Laboratory (JPL) and Loki at Los Alamos National Laboratory (LANL), were operational based on Pentium Pro processors. These achieved greater than a Gflops sustained performance, winning the Gordon Bell Prize in 1997 for price/performance. These machines were demonstrated at Supercomputing'96 and were connected to produce a 32-node Beowulf with a rather peculiar network topology. Without optimizations specific to the combined system, together they achieved a performance of just over 2 Gflops sustained throughput. In 1997, larger systems were being assembled and applied, achieving sustained performance of over 10 Gflops on multiple applications with one to two hundred processors. In 1998, Beowulfs based on the high performance DEC Alpha family of microprocessors were being implemented at a number of sites culminating in Avalon at LANL which achieved a sustained performance over 48 Gflops, placing it 113th on a popular list of the world's 500 most powerful computers[1] in November 1998.

Today, Beowulf-class systems of small, moderate, and even large scale have become commonplace, with many more planned for the near future, even beyond a

---

[1] http://www.top500.org/

thousand processors. But at this time, there is no single source of information covering the wide range of related topics to provide guidance to future Beowulf implementors and users, alike. This book is offered to at least begin to fill that gap.

1.2   The Beowulf Book

How to Build a Beowulf is an introduction to Beowulf-class computing system implementation and application. Its purpose is simply to provide the basic information required to build, operate, and apply a Beowulf-class PC cluster at performance levels comparable to those of supercomputers of earlier years. The number of ways to do this are enormous and cannot be covered by a single volume. Indeed, every chapter could (and is) represented in the literature by its own book or books. Instead, this book chooses a single complete path from concept to computation, from parts to processing. At the many branch points, alternative paths are highlighted and discussed, but not pursued. You will learn about Linux, but not about the highly capable open source BSD operating systems. You will learn about MPI, but not about PVM which predated it and has many valuable features. You will learn in detail about building networks with Ethernet but only a small amount about the high bandwidth Myrinet network and ATM. Nonetheless, by the end of this book, you will know how to implement and apply Beowulf technology and you will have a clear understanding of alternative approaches you may consider pursuing as well.

We have chosen a bottom-up approach to the vertically integrated sequence of topics that make up the realm of a Beowulf. It could have been presented the other way, perhaps even more elegantly. But there is a degree of discomfort working with levels of abstraction and not touching the ground until the very end. It was decided to avoid this and start with feet firmly planted on the ground of tangible hardware. But before we do that, before we focus on the trees, we thought we should give you a sense of the lay of the land and show you the entire forest. Chapter 2 therefore provides a brief glimpse of all aspects of what it takes to make and use a Beowulf. This overview is intended to provide the conceptual framework in which all the layers of abstraction fit and interrelate. Through the overview chapter, you should acquire a sense of where we are headed and how each step will lead to the next.

Chapter 3, describing single-node hardware, presents a detailed view of a Beowulf node, i.e., a PC. Although one approach is to just go out and buy a pile of turnkey PCs, this does not release you from the necessity of understanding their internals. First of all, you have to choose the components that go into your PC, even if someone else builds it for you. You may find it necessary to replace or install additional elements into your Beowulf nodes, change various jumpers on motherboards, or upgrade the system at some future time. Therefore, the hardware chapter takes the view that you are going to assemble your own nodes from separately selected and acquired subsystems. In so doing, the range of choices, the operational characteristics, and the installation requirements of the primary constituent elements will be discussed in detail. By the time you have finished this chapter, you will be able to assemble a complete PC or make any modifications/enhancements/repairs necessary throughout the lifetime of the Beowulf system.

If you are an experienced user of Unix workstations from Sun Microsystems, SGI and others, then you will be comfortable with Linux even if you have never used it before. It is often a surprise to the first time user of Linux on a current generation PC just how good a Linux based PC can be in direct comparison to a Unix workstation. If you come from the Microsoft Windows or Mac OS worlds, then you are entirely comfortable with PCs but may be put off by the different paradigm of Linux. Things like command lines may seem primitive to you if you have become accustomed in the menu-driven mind set even if you are aware of the old MS-DOS days. Chapter 4, introducing Linux, is written to do for single-node software what the preceding chapter did for single-node hardware. It is intended to give you the basics of everything you need to know to make it happen and make it useful. There is no way that a single chapter can make you a Unix system administrator, but enough information is provided to install and initialize a Linux system, to boot and bring up a full user environment, and to manage files and launch tasks, as well as retrieve output, printed or otherwise. By the time you have finished this chapter, you will be able to set up and run a PC workstation with Linux.

But a room full of PCs, even those enlightened enough to be hosting Linux, does not in itself make a Beowulf. They require a system area network and the software to manage them as a single entity (or at least a loose federation). Chapter 5 discusses the network hardware and network software, respectively. When the Beowulf project first began, 10 Mbps Ethernet was just inexpensive enough to use for this purpose and just capable enough to be worth doing. Now, networks a hundred times faster are available and will soon be cost effective. The hardware discussion covers this range of capabilities with a focus on Ethernet technology but also includes mention of other network types. The software sections discuss the interface between the Linux operating system and the network hardware including some typical but powerful Linux commands that provide the user with direct access to the network. Upon completion of this chapter, you will be able to assemble a fully integrated network of PCs.

A Beowulf is a complex system of subsystems in hardware and software. Managing an ensemble of such diversity and complexity can be daunting. Unfortunately, it is in this area that additional applied research and advanced development is needed. Fortunately, current tools are good enough to make effective use of Beowulfs and much of the required research is being carried out at a number of institutions. Chapter 6 on managing ensembles is offered to familiarize the Beowulf user with the challenges and available tools for assisting in supervising the operation of a Beowulf cluster.

A parallel computer like a Beowulf needs parallel programs to use it effectively. Chapter 7 discusses the parallel programming in general terms, and then focuses on the easiest and most accessible approach to exploiting the parallelism of a Beowulf system: process-level parallelism. One simply runs many copies of the same program with different inputs or data sets to achieve throughput many times greater than what could be achieved by a single processor. This method of exploiting parallelism works for well some very large problems including rendering and data reduction. Scripts to automatically load-balance process-level parallelism are provided.

Things are more complicated when a single application must run in parallel to address a single problem. Application programs rarely need the full generality of the sockets interface provided by the Linux operating system and opt instead for the message passing model provided by the MPI library. Chapter 8 introduces the basics of MPI and discusses parallel data structures as well as some strategies which can be used to parallelize existing applications. A one-dimensional cellular automaton is used as an example of a regular problem which is well-suited to MPI. By the time you have completed this chapter you will be able to write, compile, load, launch, and execute message passing applications in MPI.

There is more to parallel programming than just knowing MPI as there is more to programming in general than just learning the syntax of Fortran. An entire methodology exists for organizing data and computational tasks to achieve efficient parallel execution. Clearly, this is another area that has been represented in many full text books. Chapter 9 gives the reader an idea of the more general issues in parallel programming by implementing, and carefully analyzing two different parallel sorting functions. By the time you have completed this chapter, you will have expanded your knowledge of parallel algorithms, and more importantly, you will have the tools to develop and analyze parallel algorithms of your own.

There are a number of issues and practical concerns that we wish to share with you as a result of our experience with this form of parallel computing. In Chapter 10 we bring this book to a close by discussing a number of the aspects of Beowulf implementation and usage that are of practical concern. Also in this chapter is our expectation of the direction and future impact we anticipate for Beowulf-class computing and the barriers that must be overcome to achieve its full potential. However, regardless of what the future may bring, this book is about an exciting reality and capability that is in your hands through its pages. We thank you for joining with us in sharing this opportunity. Now let us show you how to build a Beowulf.

2 Overview of Beowulf Systems

2.1 What Is a Beowulf?

A Beowulf is a collection of personal computers (PCs) interconnected by widely available networking technology running any one of several open-source Unix-like operating systems. Beowulf programs are usually written in C or FORTRAN, adopting a message passing model of parallel computation but other open, standards based approaches are possible, including process level parallelism, shared memory (OpenMP, BSP), other languages (Java, LISP, FORTRAN90), and other communication strategies (RPC, RMI, CORBA). This definition, albeit a bit lengthy, captures the complete essence of the factors contributing to what makes a system a Beowulf.

The PCs benefit from the economy of scale of the mass production of millions of microprocessors, memory chips, input/output (I/O) controllers, and motherboard chip sets as well as the mass production of the systems in which the components are incorporated—the complete personal computers found in offices, labs, and homes. These same PCs are the constituent elements of Beowulf high performance parallel computers. Beowulfs, with no special hardware development costs or lead times, exploit the exceptional (almost extraordinary) cost effectiveness of these complete systems. "Parts by dawn, processing by dusk" is an apt description of the Beowulf revolution. While many commercial massively parallel processors (MPPs) use the same processor, memory, and controller chips that are employed by both PCs and Beowulfs, they also must incorporate custom "glue" (internal communications networks, packaging, advanced compiler technologies, etc.), that greatly increase cost and development time. Consequently, the advantages of using mass-market commodity-off-the-shelf (M^2COTS) components in these systems is significantly reduced. Beowulfs use *only* mass-market components and are not subject to the delays and costs associated with custom parts and custom integration.

The interconnection networks that allow processors to work together also benefit from the same mass-market economy that provides low-cost processing. Derived from technology developed over many years to provide robust, scalable, high bandwidth local area networks (LANs), the system area network (SAN) integrating the processors of a Beowulf is implemented with COTS communications subsystems including network interface controllers and switches. Among those available, Ethernet in its various configurations and capacities is the technology most widely used. A Beowulf system of a hundred nodes or more may be integrated by a system area network derived from Fast Ethernet LAN technology at a total cost of about a quarter of that of the entire system.

In most cases, a Beowulf node will include one to four microprocessors, 128 to 512 MBytes of memory, 8 to 40 GBytes of EIDE disk storage, one or more 100 Mbps Fast Ethernet network interface controllers (NIC), and ancillary devices.

It is the job of the operating system to manage all of these resources and coordinate the user software that employs them. Beowulfs have evolved from the scientific computing community, although their applications have extended far beyond that somewhat narrow realm. For many years, Unix has been the operating system of choice for scientific computing systems ranging from scientific workstations and servers to supercomputers and MPPs.

Because of the need for an operating system on every processor, the per node cost of a Beowulf operating system should be very low. Furthermore, early development of Beowulf systems required extending existing PC operating systems, for example to support new devices. Ongoing research on topics in such areas as faster messaging protocols, and distributed shared-memory would be impossible without the ability to examine and modify source code of the operating system itself. For these reasons, Beowulf employs low cost/no cost versions of Unix, principally Linux and FreeBSD for which source code is widely available at no additional cost.

For most environments, the primary objective of installing a Beowulf is to perform real-world applications much faster than workstations or small servers and to do so much cheaper than MPPs of comparable complexity and performance. The framework we have described so far is missing the crucial logical interface between the application programmer and the parallel system resources. The need to harness system concurrency demands another layer of logical structure to match the physical communications layer. Among the possible models of parallel computation, message passing has been widely adopted because of its close association with the physical attributes of a multiprocessor system architecture. Message passing supports a framework of communicating sequential processes. One or more such processes runs on each processor. These processes interact via messages conveyed between them by the physical network. The application programming interface (API) is a combination of a conventional sequential language and a set of standardized library calls to perform the interprocess communications. For example, programs written in the C programming language with calls to the MPI libraries have been run on commercial multiprocessors, workstation clusters, and Beowulfs.

Implicit in the definition and description of what makes a Beowulf is the exploitation of industry and community standards both for hardware and software. Such interface standards enable interoperability of components developed by independent organizations. At the hardware level, SCSI and EIDE protocols permit many vendors to supply compatible disk drives. The ISA and PCI bus standards per-

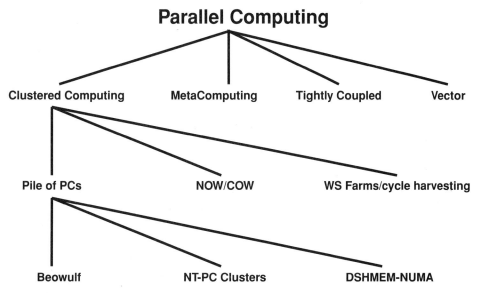

Figure 2.1
One possible classification scheme for parallel computing based on degree of coupling.

mit manufacturers to develop a variety of controllers and functional units with the confidence that they will effectively cooperate with other elements of the system. Similar interface standards in the PC world enable third party memory vendors to supply compatible SIMMs and DIMMs. External interfaces such as RS-232, parallel ports, Ethernet, video and so forth have led to mass-market conditions that drive prices down as availability and reliability go up. With this ensured base of hardware capability, software also benefits from common frameworks, many of them open, to provide robustness and interoperability. Programming languages represented the first such cross-platform standards. The IEEE POSIX specification has guaranteed base-level functionality among Unix-like operating systems supplied by multiple sources. More recently, community-wide acceptance of libraries like MPI and PVM have extended compatibility to multiple processor configurations including MPPs, workstation clusters, Beowulfs, and other PC clusters. Beowulf relies upon the existence, acceptance, growth, and evolution of community standards in hardware and software to provide low cost solutions to high end computing problems.

2.2   A Taxonomy of Parallel Computing

Beowulf-class computing systems are part of a large family of parallel computer architectures. Indeed, different hierarchical taxonomies of parallel computers are possible depending on the primary issues chosen to distinguish among them. Here, degree-of-coupling is applied loosely to reflect a combination of bisection bandwidth and worst case communication latency. At the top level of this taxonomy from most loosely coupled to most tightly coupled are meta-computers, clustered computing, multiprocessors, and vector based systems. Meta-computers harness widely separated computer systems by means of wide area networks with latencies, i.e., the time lapse between sending and receiving a message, measured in the tens of milliseconds. Clusters are loosely coupled collections of stand-alone computing elements, usually in the same location and administrative domain, with latencies between 10 to 100 microseconds. MPPs comprise many processors tightly connected within the same unit exhibiting latencies of between half a microsecond and 5 microseconds. Vector computers pipeline computations so that the effective latency between successive operand sets can be measured in the tens of nanoseconds.

Of these systems, clusters, with a history that goes back to almost the dawn of digital electronic computing, are directly relevant to Beowulf. Clusters comprise essentially independent and self supporting systems that are networked to provide a means of interaction. Clusters differ from meta-computing in that they are relatively local, under the same administrative domain, and incorporate a dedicated network. Clusters can be implemented with networks of servers, workstations, or PCs. Another form of clustering is the use of an existing local area network of desktop computers which can be used collectively when the computers are not serving their respective users. Known alternatively as "cycle harvesting" or "workstation farms", this form of cluster can provide a valuable resource under certain circumstances. Within the family of clusters, Beowulfs fall under clusters of PCs, also referred to as "piles of PCs."

PC clusters are subdivided into additional groups, one of which is Beowulf-class systems. Another group is NT-clusters using PCs but running the Microsoft Windows NT operating system. Yet another type of PC cluster employs specialty networks such as SCI or that from the Princeton SHRIMP project, providing hardware support for distributed shared memory. Although identified as a single category of PC clusters, Beowulf systems themselves exhibit wide diversity in configuration and operation.

2.3   Benefits of Beowulf

In addition to the significant price/performance advantage of Beowulf-class systems, Beowulfs provide several other important advantages, ranging from rapid inclusion of COTS technology advances to widely-used APIs and programming languages.

Ironically, in today's dynamic technology market it is the low end systems that first incorporate the latest and highest performance devices. This is because they represent the largest market share and will provide the largest early return on investment. Since Beowulfs require no development lead time, as soon as the latest advances in chip technology are incorporated into the mass-market PCs they can be immediately included in Beowulf configurations. It takes much longer for the same devices to find their way into commercial MPPs. Thus, an advantage of the Beowulf model is rapid response to technology trends.

One of the greatest obstacles hindering the acceptance and application of high performance parallel computing systems is that every manufacturer produced its own particular architecture. Not only were these architectures not compatible between manufacturers, but almost routinely, different generations from the same vendor would be largely incompatible with one another, despite claims to the contrary, e.g., the switch in architecture from the Thinking Machines CM-2 to the CM-5. The problem of disparate architectures is aggravated by the high mortality rate of companies producing MPPs, resulting in no follow-on machines and lost application software investment. Examples include Thinking Machine Corp., Kendall Square Research, Alliant and others. Beowulfs, however, are not susceptible to the vagaries of commercial offerings and corporate mortality. They are assembled from subsystems that can be acquired from multiple vendors who make mass-market systems. Thus an advantage of Beowulfs is that they are not subject to the whims of a single source.

There is no specific, fixed Beowulf system architecture. A broad range of processor nodes and system topologies are possible and can be optimized on-site and at the last minute. They can even be changed later in response to new needs or new technology opportunities. System form is limited not by vendor specification, but only by the imagination of its users. Therefore, another benefit of the Beowulf approach is its property of what may be called *just-in-place* configuration.

Beowulf systems are scalable. A wide range of system sizes is possible from a small number of nodes connected by a single low cost hub to a system incorporating complex topologies of many hundreds of processors. And, these systems can be expanded over time as additional resources become available or extended requirements drive system size upward.

System software development is a slow, tedious, and bug ridden process. Because of the relatively small market, vendors may not be able to maintain, let alone extend, the parallel system software of their high end MPPs. Software environments for new MPPs have been a source of continuous difficulty for the HPC community. In contrast, Beowulf leverages the heavy software development investment made by the academic and research computer science community. Linux and MPI are just a couple of examples of successful complex software projects that have been carried out in this context. In fact, there is now a trend of commercial vendors at least partially embracing these same software components.

Beowulf uses the same semantics and syntax for message passing that commercial MPPs use so that they provide the same user application programmer interface for that programming model. Programmers familiar with such machines as the IBM SP or the Intel Paragon are able to work directly with Beowulf without a significant learning curve. Beowulfs have been used as development platforms for software destined to be run on commercial MPPs as it is much cheaper to use a Beowulf while the software developer is given complete control over the low cost machine during the buggy period of code development.

It may be surprising, but Beowulfs are highly robust, mature, and stable as well as accessible to users. After a brief burn-in period, Beowulfs have remained continuously operational for more than half a year without rebooting.

2.4   A Critical Technology Convergence

The fundamental concepts underlying Beowulf-class computers come from multiple sources and in some cases have a long heritage. If so, then why are Beowulfs only now receiving such wide attention and why has there been a recent explosion in their implementation and application? The reason is that the evolution of certain trends both technically and in the marketplace have only recently combined with sufficient compelling force to advance the Beowulf model with respect to alternative approaches. Only in the last few years have the hardware and software technologies achieved sufficient capabilities, while market forces have opened the opportunity for cost effective Beowulf systems.

One important factor is the high performance computing market and the commercial response to it. Unfortunately, while many other areas of the computing industry are experiencing a period of rapid growth, high performance computing is static—if not shrinking. Most companies with an exclusive focus on the high end have either gone out of business or been subsumed by other larger companies. Few

U.S. manufacturers now offer high end computers. And the price/performance of the systems that are available is much worse than that of mass-market PC products. Therefore, we have entered a period where support for high performance computing by industry has been drastically reduced.

Until recently there was a wide disparity between the performance of the microprocessors employed in mass-market PCs and those used in the far more expensive scientific and graphics workstations. But in recent years, there has been such a dramatic convergence in the capabilities of the two classes of microprocessor that today that gap has been closed. The performance of PCs challenges that of workstation micros and arguably the highest performance microprocessor in existence has been packaged in a PC configuration.

Historically, a second dramatic distinction between high end workstations and mass-market PCs has been the quality and sophistication of their software environments. Low-end operating systems for PCs such as CP/M and MS-DOS proved sufficient as a basis for supporting shrink-wrap consumer software such as video games, word processors, and spreadsheet programs. But, as operating systems, they fell far short of systems like Unix and VMS, the industrial-grade, virtual memory, multitasking operating systems used on minicomputers and scientific workstations. However, with the porting of FreeBSD to PCs and the development of Linux which was also targeted for PCs, the software distinction has been eliminated and Linux is rapidly becoming the most widely deployed Unix implementation in the world. With the emergence of Linux, Beowulf-class systems became possible.

Critical to the achievement of Beowulf-class systems and in particular the realizability of their exceptional price/performance was the development of low cost, moderate bandwidth local area networks LANs. After many years of evolution and refinement, Ethernet controllers and routers became sufficiently cost effective that they could be used with PCs without dominating overall system price. The software that enables Linux to manage these devices was actually written by the Beowulf project at the NASA Goddard Space Flight Center, and is now part of almost every networked Linux system, Beowulf or otherwise.

Progress in system software and APIs, as noted previously, also has contributed significantly to Beowulf development. The combination of these trends all in the last few years has made it possible to consider exploiting M^2COTS PC technology for serious parallel applications. All that remained was for the approach to be attempted and evaluated. The original Beowulf Project initiated such studies in 1993.

2.5   The Beowulf System Node

As in all clustered systems, the fundamental building block is casually referred to as a "node" which is a stand alone computing system with complete hardware and operating system support to fully manage the execution of a user program and interact with other nodes over a network. Nodes of a cluster can be as small as a desktop system costing on the order of a thousand dollars or a mighty multiprocessor SMP costing millions of dollars. For a Beowulf cluster system, the node is usually a personal computer derived from the commercial mass market exhibiting an excellent price/performance ratio. This does not necessary imply the absolute lowest price system but rather the optimal balance of capability and cost, for the problem at hand.

A Beowulf hardware node incorporates a number of subsystems, each providing the Beowulf system integrator with multiple choices. These provide processing capability, information storage, and external I/O. System area networking will be described as a separate topic.

Processor

There are three principal families of microprocessors that are incorporated into personal computers and sold at low cost to the general public. The Intel x86 family is employed primarily in PCs with Microsoft MS-DOS, Windows, and NT operating systems; the IBM/Motorola PowerPC family is employed primarily in the Apple Macintosh computers to run the MacOS operating system; and the DEC Alpha family is available in PC style packaging and most often runs NT or Digital Unix. The Linux operating system has been ported to all three processor families (and several others). Intel processors are most widely used for Beowulf-class computing but Alphas have found a niche where floating point intensive computations are involved. All three families incorporate advanced memory management including caches, virtual memory and address translation. The choices facing the Beowulf designer includes:

- processor family,
- clock rate of processor
- cache size associated with processor

Motherboard

Motherboards are far more than a convenient surface onto which the chips are glued. They contain complex logic in their own right and can have significant effect on the performance, flexibility, and utility of a computer system. The motherboard chip set determines the relationship between the processor and the remaining system. Even for PCs, it is possible to have two to four processors on a single motherboard, sharing memory and peripheral devices. These are employed in true symmetric multiprocessor mode (SMP) permitting cache coherence across processors for shared memory operations. Motherboards determine the maximum amount of memory that can be incorporated by the node. The motherboard includes the interface ports to memory, controllers, and external peripheral devices. Motherboards today generally support both the older ISA bus and the newer PCI bus for high performance devices. The PCI bus itself is undergoing a transition, with higher speeds and wider data paths becoming available.

Memory

Performance and utility of a system is as much dependent on the memory subsystem as the processor. Memory technology is divided into SRAM (static random access memory) and DRAM (dynamic random access memory). SRAM is fast but of modest density while DRAM is relatively slower but of significantly higher density. SRAMs are used primarily for cache and is not usually purchased directly by the Beowulf integrator, although they are part of the processor choice. Main memory is made up of a number of DRAM parts packaged in SIMMs and DIMMs. Today, the choice space for main memory involves speed, capacity, burst mode, and on chip error correction. Memories are easily installed on processor motherboards and may be upgraded at any time.

Hard Disk

The only non-volatile storage on the system (other than some EPROM for motherboard/bios parameters) is secondary storage provided by hard disk drives. Nothing is cheaper than a spinning bit. Recent years have seen plummeting prices and soaring disk capacities. While commercial grade systems use SCSI disks and protocols, consumer grade systems use the lower cost EIDE standard which is somewhat slower but has superior ratios of capacity and throughput to price. Today, new systems routinely incorporate 4 to 20 GByte disks in PC based Beowulf nodes and may use more than one disk. Not only do disks provide non-volatile storage, they also provide the means of extending the apparent memory capacity either automatically through virtual memory demand paging mechanisms or explicitly through programmer control of the file system.

Floppy Drive

A portable 1.4 MByte storage device with form factor of 3.5" was once the dominant means of transferring code between systems. Now it is still used to some degree, but with the advent of the inexpensive CD-ROM and the availability of the Internet, it is losing preeminence as the favorite transfer medium. Floppy drives cost less than $20 and are crucial for initial system installation and crash recovery. One should be installed on every node.

Support Devices

Some additional devices are included on one or more nodes to facilitate certain types of servicing or monitoring operations. Among those are the following:

External Local Area Network Beowulfs always exist within an infrastructure that provides broad user support and access. Connection to this environment is provided through one or more network interface cards (NICs) attached to the local area network. One or more of the nodes in a Beowulf system have such cards and IP addresses that allow external access. The type of NIC is chosen to be compatible with the LAN environment.

CD-ROM Drive CD-ROM is an optical storage medium, 5.25 inches in diameter capable of storing about 650 MBytes. Drives cost well under $100 and can spin at up to 24 times the speed of the equivalent drives used to play music CDs. CD-ROMs have become the principal medium for the distribution of large software packages. For example, Linux is available from multiple sources on CD-ROM. One drive should be sufficient for an entire Beowulf system.

Monitor/Keyboard While not necessary, most Beowulfs have a direct user interface. One of the nodes is used as a host or user node with monitor, keyboard, and mouse interfaces. This node is employed primarily for system administration, diagnostics, and statistics presentation. It may also used as a high bandwidth graphical port for data visualization.

2.6   The Beowulf Network

Second only to the node itself, the internal system area network is the most important subsystem of a Beowulf cluster both in terms of achieving sustained performance and contributing to cost. Beowulfs often (but not always) employ the Ethernet and TCP/IP protocols developed and marketed for local area networks.

Early Beowulfs used 10 Mbps Ethernets but the majority today are integrated with 100 Mbps or Fast Ethernet. Greater bandwidth has been achieved both with Myrinet and Gigabit Ethernet at rates approaching 1 Gbps but these are expensive options, costing up to half the total price of a system. In contrast, a Fast Ethernet card costs under $50, and ports cost about $100 each on aggressively priced switches.

The network is medium through which processors communicate. Networks have evolved considerably from the passive multi-drop coaxial Ethernet cables that once connected small numbers of computers. Coax was replaced by active hubs that could connect up to 16 nodes relatively cheaply, but that still broadcast all traffic to all nodes. Switches are more complex, containing logic that identifies the destination of each data packet, and routes the packet to the appropriate port. Thus, each node connected to a switch has the entire bandwidth (100 Mbps) available for its own communication. Switches became cost effective in 1996 and by 1998, switches with 48 ports, each capable of 100 Mbps full duplex (i.e., in both directions at once) were easily affordable. Gigabit Ethernet switches up to twelve ports are available, but still costly. Other products at increased cost per port can support even larger networks. Using a combination of switches and processor nodes for storing, forwarding and routing, much larger configurations can be achieved on the order of a thousand nodes with total latency increase of less than a factor of three.

2.7   Linux

The operating system is the software environment that grants access to the processor and memory, provides services to the application programs, presents an interface to the end user, and manages the external interfaces to devices and the external environment. The most popular operating systems on PCs are sold by Microsoft, but several others exist including Linux, OpenBSD, FreeBSD and several commercial Unix variants. Beowulfs use an open source Unix-like operating system, i.e., a software system where all source code is freely available and can be studied and improved by the community. Linux, in particular, is the most popular operating system for Beowulfs.

Linux is a monolithic, multitasking, virtual memory, demand paged, POSIX compliant operating system. It is available at no cost over the Internet or at small cost on CD-ROMs. Linux comes with complete source code and is a powerful research tool for computer science. It was for this reason that Linux was selected, even at its earliest stage of evolution, as the basis for the Beowulf project. Linux supports the complete GNU programming environment including gcc and g++, g77, gdb, gprof, and emacs as well as compiler-compiler tools such as lex, yacc, and bison. It provides the X Windows user interface and window managers. It supports remote access, copying, procedure calls and communication stacks with sockets. Linux provides a complete file system and NFS for distributed files.

Linux is a powerful, flexible, and extensible environment that is as sophisticated and robust as any operating system widely available. It had been difficult to bring it up on a PC node. However, over the last couple of years, this process has been made much easier through a series of tools and distributions. One can even buy hardware with Linux pre-installed. Nonetheless, as with any powerful tool, some effort is required to get full capability and performance.

2.8   Message Passing for Interprocessor Communication

In order to effectively use a Beowulf, an application must contain parallelism. That is, it must be possible to make progress simultaneously on many fronts, so that many processors can pool their efforts and reach a solution more quickly. Ideally, applications would be structured so that as additional processing elements are added, the overall execution time would decrease proportionally. In order to write applications that have this property, a model of parallel computation must be adopted by the programmer. The most widely used model is referred to as message passing, or formerly, communicating sequential processes.

In the message passing model, a process executes on each node of the system. It performs operations primarily on data local to its node, i.e., stored within its memory or sometimes its secondary storage. Frequently, for the process to continue, it requires data from other parts of the computation being performed by other processors. Messages are transmitted containing the required information. Both data passing and synchronization among concurrent processes is accomplished in this manner. Information is not shared between processes or processors except by explicit interaction through messages.

Several message passing interfaces for concurrent programs have been developed. Of these, PVM and MPI are the most widely used. MPI is the product of a broad effort to provide a standardized programming interface and derived much from the earlier PVM. All commercial MPPs support the MPI programming model, providing a set of libraries to enable a common programming framework. The basic set of functions incorporated by MPI provide for an unprecedented degree of portability across platforms. Although it contains over one hundred functions,

MPI programs can be written using only six basic primitives. While not restricted to MPI, Beowulf programmers often rely heavily upon this set of tools.

2.9 Beowulf System Management

Merely assembling a collection of PCs is not sufficient to create a usable parallel cluster. General system design questions need to be addressed before assembling the cluster, some of which include:

- how the system is to be connected to external networks,
- how IP addresses are assigned to the individual nodes,
- how the file system is to be configured, and
- what security measures are required.

Once a system is operational, practical means for managing accounts is required. Is a directory system such as NIS appropriate, or should password files be distributed to each of the nodes? Similarly, the allocation and placement of software must be determined. You also have to consider where you want to install system software. Is it sufficient to make all software available via a network file system, or should some of it be installed locally on each node? How is all the software synchronized across nodes? Depending on how the system is to be used, access may have to be limited to parts of the system at different times so that certain users may run their applications undisturbed. Management of system resources is not a simple business.

Most Beowulf systems incorporate between 8 and 32 nodes and dedicate themselves to servicing a small group of users. These systems do not require as much administration as larger systems. Hardware and software problems are less frequent, and the machines are not generally pushed to their limits by users. Nonetheless, file system setup, software installation, and node configuration are vital tasks.

2.10 The Beowulf Challenge

Beowulf-class computing is a rapidly evolving domain of parallel computing with many installations and accomplishments but with much remaining to be done. Furthermore, Beowulfs present a very different business model to the user than conventional commercial offerings. Hardware and software upgrades are managed by the user or local system administrator, not by a representative from the vendor. Maintenance often consists of nothing more than replacing a broken component, possibly invoking a manufacturer's warranty in the process. Extensions to system configurations, either internal to the processing nodes, or expansion of the overall system structure, are performed locally. Although this may sound intimidating, it is no more complex than running and maintaining a Linux based PC workstation, standard practice for many students these days. Linux distributions are found on the shelves of many retailers as are a plethora of books on all aspects of Linux.

Beowulfs are well suited to single application users. A system in the hands of a single user is an effective platform for running a given application. However, there is much more to general parallel computing than the single user, stand-alone environment. Software technology to manage Beowulf resources in the presence of many simultaneous users and multiple programs is still in its adolescence. Research and advanced development is still required to make these systems truly general purpose in the most demanding user contexts, although much has been achieved and partial solutions to these problems already exist.

Beowulfs also exhibit the same attributes of other clustered systems in their differentiated effectiveness in processing the wide array of algorithm types. Not all applications run well on clustered systems because of the relatively long latencies and moderate interprocessor bandwidths of their system area networks. Beowulfs are no exception. Generally speaking, the more tightly coupled the system, the broader the range of useful applications it can perform. For clustered systems including Beowulfs, applications programmers must design their algorithms to be latency tolerant; that is, perform well even in the presence of long latency communications. As it happens, many important classes of applications and algorithms fall into this category. Research in this area over the last few years has demonstrated how wide this domain can be when advanced methodologies are applied. Having said this, Beowulf computers are not suitable for every application, even every parallel application, and understanding the limitations of these systems is important for their successful and productive application.

Beowulf scalability is still a topic of systems research. Systems of a couple of hundred processors have been effectively installed and employed. But we simply don't know how far Beowulfs can be scaled within the constraints of mass market hardware and available software technology. With the latest microprocessor technology, peak performance of greater than one trillion operations per second are within reach. That is equivalent to today's fastest computers, period.

The Beowulf challenge, then, has several elements. These are to

1. apply current Beowulf technology to suitable real world applications;
2. expand the range of appropriate applications through the development of advanced latency-tolerant algorithms;
3. devise new tools for the effective management of Beowulf clusters, especially for multi-user, multitasking working environments; and
4. develop low cost, effective scaling techniques for expanding the performance capabilities of Beowulf-class systems.

Beowulf users have proven to be much more than a collection of individuals; they have become a community, sharing results and methods. As with Linux itself, a distributed collective of dedicated developers has created a rapidly evolving set of tools that are shared by all Beowulf user groups. The Beowulf Challenge is to foster this community driven enterprise with a new generation of high end scalable computing.

3 Node Hardware

Beowulf is a network of nodes, with each node a low-cost personal computer. Its power and simplicity is derived from exploiting the capabilities of the mass-market systems that provide both the processing and the communication. This chapter explores all of the hardware elements related to computation and storage. Communication hardware options will be considered in detail in Chapter 5.

Few technologies in human civilization have experienced such a rate of growth as that of the digital computer and its culmination in the PC. Its low-cost, ubiquity, and sometimes trivial application often obscure its complexity and precision as one of the most sophisticated products derived from science and engineering. In a single human lifetime over the fifty year history of computer development, performance and memory capacity have grown by a factor of almost a million. Where once computers were reserved for the special environments of carefully structured machine rooms, now they are found in almost every office and home. A personal computer today outperforms the world's greatest supercomputers of two decades ago at less than one ten-thousandth the cost. It is the product of this extraordinary legacy that Beowulf harnesses to open new vistas in computation.

Hardware technology changes almost unbelievably rapidly. The specific processors, chip sets, and three-letter acronyms (TLAs) we define today will be obsolete in a very few years. The prices quoted will be out-of-date before this book reaches your bookstore's shelves. On the other hand, the organizational design of a PC and the functions of its primary components will last a good deal longer. The relative strengths and weaknesses of components (e.g., disk storage is slower, larger, cheaper and more persistent than main memory) should remain valid for nearly as long.

This chapter concentrates on the practical issues related to the selection and assembly of the components of a Beowulf node. You can assemble the nodes of the Beowulf yourself, or you can let someone else (a system integrator) do it. In either case, you'll have to make some decisions about the components. Many system integrators cater to a know-nothing market, offering a few basic types of systems, e.g., "Office" and "Home" models with a slightly different mix of hardware and software components. These machines would work in a Beowulf, but with only a little additional research, one can purchase far more appropriate systems for less money. Beowulf systems (at least those we know of) have little need for audio systems, speakers, joysticks, printers, frame grabbers, etc., many of which are included in the standard "Home" or "Office" models. High performance video is unnecessary except for specialized applications where video output is the primary function of the system. Purchasing just the components you need, in the quantity you need can be a tremendous advantage. Fortunately, customizing your system this way does not mean that you have to assemble the system yourself. Many system integrators, both large and small, will assemble custom systems for little or no price premium. In fact, every system they assemble is from component parts, so a custom system is no more difficult for them than a standard one.

There is an enormous diversity of choice both in type and quantity of components. There is more than one microprocessor family to consider and within each family multiple versions. There is flexibility in both the amount and type of main memory. Disk drives, too, offer a range of interface, speed, capacity, and number. Choices concerning ancillary elements such as floppy disk drives and CD-ROM drives have to be considered. Moreover, the choice of the motherboard and its chip set provide yet another dimension to PC node implementation. This chapter examines each of these issues individually and considers their interrelationships. A step-by-step procedure for the assembly of a processor node is provided to guide the initiate and protect the overconfident.

Finally, we reiterate that we make no attempt to offer a complete or exhaustive survey. There are far more products available than can be explicitly presented in any single book, and new products are being offered all the time. However, in spite of the impossibility of exhaustive coverage, the information provided here should contain most of what is required to implement a Beowulf node. Final details can be acquired from documentation provided by the parts vendors.

3.1   Overview of a Beowulf Node

The Beowulf node is responsible for all activities and capabilities associated with executing an application program and supporting a sophisticated software environment. These fall into four general categories:

1. Instruction Execution,
2. High speed temporary information storage,
3. High capacity persistent information storage,
4. Communication with the external environment, including other nodes.

The node is responsible for performing a set of designated instructions specified by the application program code or system software. The lowest level binary encoding of the instructions and the actions they perform are dictated by the microprocessor Instruction Set Architecture (ISA). Both the instructions and the data upon which they act are stored in and loaded from the node's random access memory (RAM). The speed of a processor is often measured in MHz, indicating that its clock ticks so many million times per second. Unfortunately, it is not possible to load or store data into memory at anywhere near the rate necessary to feed a modern microprocessor (450 MHz and higher rates are now common). Thus, the processor often waits for memory, and the overall rate at which programs run is usually governed as much by the memory system as the processor's clock speed.

Microprocessor designers employ numerous ingenious techniques to deal with the problem of slow memories and fast processors. Usually, a memory hierarchy is incorporated which includes one or more layers of very fast, but very small and very expensive, cache memories which hold copies of the contents of the slower, but much larger, main memory. The order of instruction execution and the access patterns to memory can have a profound effect on the performance impact of the small high speed caches. In addition to holding the application data set, memory must support the operating system and provide sufficient space to keep the most frequently used functions and system management tables and buffers co-resident for best performance.

Except for very carefully designed applications, it is crucial for a program's entire data set to reside in RAM. The alternative is to use disk storage either explicitly (out-of-core calculations), or implicitly (virtual memory swapping), but this usually entails a severe performance penalty. Thus, the size of a node's memory is an important parameter in system design. It determines the size of problem that can practically be run on the node. Engineering and scientific applications often obey a rule of thumb that says for every floating point operation per second (flops) one byte of RAM is necessary. This is a gross approximation at best, and actual requirements can vary by many orders of magnitude, but it provides some guidance, e.g., a 450 MHz processor capable of sustaining 200 Mflops should be equipped with approximately 200 MBytes of RAM.

Information stored in RAM is not permanent. When a program finishes execution, the RAM that was assigned to it is recovered by the operating system and reassigned to other programs. The data is not preserved. Thus, if one wishes to permanently store the results of a calculation, or even the program itself, a persistent storage device is needed. Hard disk devices which store data on a rotating magnetic medium are the most common storage device in Beowulf nodes. Data stored on hard disk are persistent even under power failures which makes hard disk the preferred location for the operating system and other utilities that are required to restart a machine from scratch. A widely held guideline is that the local disk capacity be at least ten times the main memory capacity. With the low cost of hard disk, a single drive can provide this capacity at a small fraction of the overall system cost. An alternative is to provide permanent storage capability off-node, providing access via the system area network to remote storage resources, e.g., an NFS server on one of the nodes. This may be a practical solution for small Beowulf systems, but as the system grows, it is easy to overwhelm a single server.

The results of computational activities performed on a Beowulf node must be presented to the node's external environment during and after a computation. This requires communication with peripheral devices like video monitors, printers and external networks. Furthermore, users need access to the system to start jobs and to monitor and control jobs in progress. System managers may need console access, the ability to install software distributions on CD-ROM or other media, or backup data to tape or other archival storage. The requirements are served by the I/O subsystem of the node. On today's PCs, these devices usually share the PCI bus, with some low-performance devices using the older ISA bus.

In a Beowulf system it is typical that only one or two nodes have extensive I/O capabilities beyond communication on the system area network. All external interaction is then funneled through these *worldly* nodes. The specific I/O requirements vary greatly from installation to installation, so a precise specification of the peripherals attached to a worldly node is impossible. We can, however, make firm recommendations about the I/O requirements of internal or *compute* nodes. The majority of nodes in a Beowulf system lack the personality of a worldly node. They have one major I/O requirement, which is to communicate with one another. The hardware and software involved in interprocessor communication is the subject of Chapter 5. For now, we will simply observe that the processor communicates with the network through the network interface controller (NIC) attached to a high-speed bus.

3.1.1 Principal Specifications

In selecting the proper node configuration for a new Beowulf, the choices can appear overwhelming. Fortunately, there is a small number of critical parameters that largely characterize a particular Beowulf node. These parameters usually relate to a few peak capabilities or capacities and are only roughly predictive of the performance of any given application or workload. Nonetheless, they are widely used and provide a reasonable calibration of the price/performance tradeoff space.

Processor clock rate The frequency (MHz) of the primary signal within the processor that determines the rate at which instructions are issued.

Peak floating point performance The combination of the clock rate and the number of floating point operations that can be issued and/or retired per instruction (Mflops).

Cache size The storage capacity (KBytes) of the high speed buffer memory between the main memory and the processor.

Main memory capacity The storage capacity (MBytes) of the primary system node memory in which resides the global data set of the applications as well as myriad other supporting program, buffering, and argument data.

Disk capacity The storage capacity (GBytes) of the permanent secondary storage internal to the processing node.

SAN network port peak bandwidth The bandwidth (Mbps) of the network control card and system area network communication channel medium.

System bisection bandwidth The bandwidth (Gbps) of the choke point in the system area network.

Other parameters that are sometimes of interest are the number of processors included in symmetric multiprocessing configurations, memory latency and bandwidth, measured performance of various benchmarks, and seek and access times to disks.

3.1.2 Basic Elements

The general Beowulf node is a complex organization of multiple subsystems that support the requirements for computation, communication and storage discussed above. Figure 3.1 shows a block diagram of a node architecture representative of the general structures found in today's PCs adapted to the purpose of Beowulf-class computing.

Microprocessor All of the logic required to perform instruction execution, memory management and address translation, integer and floating point operations, and cache management. Processor clock speeds can be as low as 100 MHz found on previous generation Intel Pentium processors to as high as 533 MHz of the DEC Alpha 21264 with the 400 MHz Pentium II representing near the sweet spot in price/performance.

Cache Provides the illusion of a much higher-speed memory than is actually available by keeping recently used data in a small but fast buffer. Multiple layers of cache may be employed; 16 KBytes of Level 1 (L1) and 512 KBytes of Level 2 (L2) cache are common. The effect of cache can be dramatic, but not all programs will benefit. Memory systems are so complex that often the only reliable

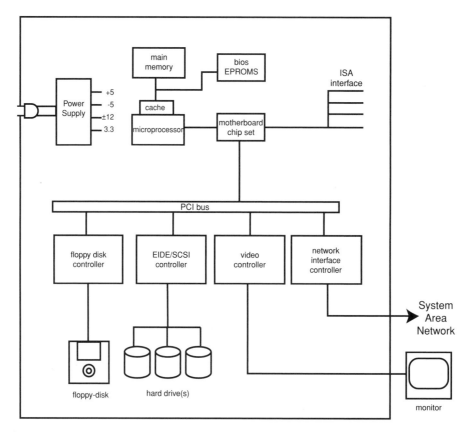

Figure 3.1
Block diagram of a typical Beowulf node. Some additional components, e.g., keyboard, mouse, additional network interfaces, CD-ROM drive, will be necessary on nodes responsible for I/O services.

way to determine the effectiveness of cache for a given application is to test the application on machines with different amounts of cache.

Main memory High density storage with rapid read/write access. Typical access times of 70 nanoseconds can be found with SIMM or DIMM memory modules with memory capacities between 32 MBytes and 256 MBytes.

EIDE/SCSI disk controller A sophisticated unit that manages the operation of the hard disk and CD-ROM drives, buffers data blocks, and controls the transfer of data directly to or from main memory.

Hard drive Persistent storage, even after processor power cycling, and backing store to the main memory for problems requiring data sets larger than the main memory can hold. Disk capacities range from 1 GByte to more than 32, but the most common and cost effective sizes today are between 4 and 20 GBytes. Hard disks conform to either the EIDE or SCSI interface standards. Access times of a few milliseconds are usual for these electro-mechanical rotating magnetic storage devices.

Floppy disk controller A very low-cost and low capacity storage medium of nominally 1.4 MBytes capacity (double size are available). Floppies are used primarily at boot time to install a minimal system capable of bootstrapping itself into a full configuration. Access times are long and the small capacity makes them unsuitable for other data storage roles. Nevertheless, their historical role as a boot medium makes them a valuable part of every Beowulf node.

Motherboard chip set A sophisticated special purpose controller that manages and coordinates the interactions of the various components of the PC through PCI, ISA, and other interfaces. It plays an important role in memory management, especially for symmetric multiprocessors (SMPs) where cache coherence is maintained through snooping cache protocols.

BIOS ROM memory The minimum set of functional binary routines needed to perform rudimentary functionality of the motherboard and its interfaces include bootstrap and diagnostic functions. Modern systems including writable BIOS EEPROMs that can have their contents directly upgraded from newer versions of the BIOS programs with replacement on the actual chips.

PCI bus The universal industry standard for high speed controllers. The common PCI bus operates a 32 bit data path at 33 MHz. The new PCI standard will support 64 bit data paths at 66 MHz.

ISA interface The Extended Industry Standard Architecture (EISA) is an old standard that was introduced with the Intel 80386 processor and is backwards compatible with the even older ISA standard. Although performance is not great, the longevity and stability of the standard means there are thousands of peripheral devices capable of using it. If PCI slots become scarce (four can easily be taken by a SCSI card, two network cards and a video card on an interactive node) it may be appropriate to add additional devices (modems, terminal concentrators, sound cards, etc.) to the EISA bus.

Video controller The video card converts digital signals from the processor into analog signals suitable for driving a video display. Modern high end video cards contain powerful on-board processors and often have many megabytes of memory and sophisticated programmable interfaces. Such a card might be appropriate for an I/O, or interactive node intended to drive a high resolution monitor for data visualization and interactive display. Other Beowulf nodes, however, have little need for video output. In fact, if it were not for the fact that most BIOS software will not boot without a video card, they would be unnecessary on the majority of Beowulf nodes. Video cards are available with either PCI or EISA connections.

Network interface controller This provides communication access to the node's external environment. One or more such interfaces couples the node to the Beowulf's system area network. A second network interface card (not shown) on a worldly node can provide the link between the entire Beowulf machine and the local area network that connects it to other resources in the user's environment such as file servers, printers, terminals, and the Internet.

Power supply Not part of the logical system but the power supply is an important component to the overall operation. It provides regulated output voltages of 5 volts, -5 volts, 12 volts, and -12 volts to support system operation. Power supplies are rated in Watts and have a general range of between 200 and 400 Watts per node.

3.2   Processors

The microprocessor is the critical computational component of the PC-based node and Beowulf-class systems. In the five year period since the first Beowulf was completed in early 1994, central processing unit (CPU) clock speed has increased by a factor of 8. More impressive is the single-node floating point performance sustained on scientific and engineering problems which has improved by a factor of 40 or more during the same period. A single PC today outperforms the entire 16-processor first generation Beowulf back of 1994.

With the proliferation of Linux ports to a wide array of processors, Beowulf-like clusters are being assembled with almost every conceivable processor type. But primary attention has been given to Intel processors and their binary compatible siblings from AMD and Cyrix. Recently, the DEC Alpha family of processors has also been effectively applied in this arena.

This section presents a brief description of the most likely candidates of micro-processors for future Beowulf-class systems. The choice is constrained by three factors: performance, cost, and software compatibility. Raw performance is important to building effective medium and high end parallel systems. To build an effective parallel computer, one should start with the best uniprocessor. Of course, this tendency must be tempered by cost. The overall price/performance ratio for your favorite application is probably the most important consideration. The highest performance processor at any point in time rarely has the best price/performance ratio. Usually it is the processor one generation or one-half generation behind the cutting edge that is available with the most attractive ratio of price to performance. Recently, however, the DEC Alpha has delivered both best performance and best price/performance for many applications. The third factor of software compatibility is an important practical consideration. If a stable software environment is not available for a particular processor family, even if it is a technical pace setter, it is probably inappropriate for Beowulf. Fortunately, Linux is now available on every viable microprocessor family, and this should continue to be the case into the foreseeable future. Some key features of current processors are summarized in Table 3.1.

3.2.1   Intel Pentium II

The Intel Pentium II processor family continues the legacy of the x86 family of processors that to some define the term PC. Having software compatibility with its previous generations, the Pentium II provides an easy and cost effective way to achieve significant performance at moderate price. The original target for the Linux operating system was the Intel 80386, and over the last five years this partnership of hardware and software technologies has matured into a formidable combination that rivals any Unix based workstation. The Pentium II combines the high performance core architecture of the previous generation Pentium Pro with the MMX enhancement for multimedia applications first implemented on the Pentium MMX processors. With Intel's new 0.25 micron fabrication technology, the Pentium II exceeds its predecessors by more than doubling its processor clock to 450 MHz.

The Pentium II family includes processors with clock speeds from 233 MHz to 450 MHz. Faster models should be coupled with newer motherboards incorporating bus speeds of 100 MHz. The Pentium II processor employs a radically different physical connector than the earlier Pentium processor Socket 7 and Pentium Pro Socket 8 PGA based zero insertion force (ZIF) sockets. Instead, a new Single Edge Contact (SEC) cartridge module integrates processor, separate data and instruction L1 caches, a unified L2 cache, the system bus interface, and a separate internal bus to the L2 cache. Each of the non-blocking L1 caches are 16 KBytes with a unified non-blocking L2 cache of 512 KBytes, 1 MByte or 2 MBytes. One floating point operation may be retired per clock cycle. It is to be expected that clock rates at and beyond 500 MHz will be realized in the near future and that dual processor systems will be available at reasonable cost providing systems of 1 Gflops peak performance.

3.2.2   DEC Alpha

The DEC Alpha21164 and 21164PC microprocessors retain the performance lead in floating point operation. The 0.35 micron fabrication technology devices operate at a clock rate of up to 533 MHz and are capable of issuing four operations per cycle, two of which may be floating point. This gives the Alpha an unprecedented peak performance of over 1 Gflops. It was this capability that led Cray Research Inc. to adopt the DEC Alpha as the processing core of its T3D and T3E Massively Parallel Processors.

The Alpha uses a Reduced Instruction Set Computer (RISC) architecture distinguishing it from Intel's Pentium processors. RISC designs, which have dominated the workstation market of the last decade, eschew complex instructions and addressing modes, resulting in simpler processors running at higher clock rates, but executing somewhat more instructions to complete the same task. As a result, the Alpha is significantly smaller than the 7+ million transistor Pentium II. The 21164PC has separate 8 KByte L1 caches for data and instructions. The L2 cache is on the motherboard, the AlphaPC 164SX. The 21164 processor is compatible with the AlphaPC 164LX motherboard and includes a larger L1 data cache of 16 KBytes and a unified, 3-way set associative L2 cache of 96 KBytes. The Alpha, unlike the Pentium II, is a true 64 bit architecture.

3.2.3   AMD K6

AMD has provided cost effective and performance competitive microprocessors that are binary compatible with the x86 instruction set. Designed for a 100 MHz system bus using the Super 7 socket, it includes unique instructions for 3D graphics computing.

3.2.4   Future Processors

The next two years will be very interesting for Beowulf-class systems as new microprocessors with very high performance become available. Clock rates climbing to 1 GHz and instruction level parallelism increasing the number of execution units

Chip	Vendor	Speed (MHz)	L1 Cache Size I/D
Pentium Pro	Intel	200	8K/8K
Pentium II	Intel	266	16K/16K
Pentium II	Intel	333	16K/16K
Pentium II	Intel	400	16K/16K
K6-2	AMD	400	32K/32K
Alpha 21164PC-03	DEC	533	8K/16K
Alpha 21164-P6	DEC	433	8K/8K
Alpha 21164-P8	DEC	533	8K/8K

Table 3.1
Key features of selected processors, early 1999.

promise peak performance in the low multi-Gigaflops region by 2001. Here are some of the expected high performance processors.

Merced   Intel is undertaking its first 64 bit architecture design with a new instruction set, new cache design, and new floating point processor design. With clock rates approaching 1 GHz and multi-way floating point instruction issue, Merced should be able to provide between 1 and 2 Gflops peak performance. This processor is already a success from a marketing standpoint with more than one major vendor signing up to integrate it into their product line.

K7   AMD has announced an aggressive new processor, the K7, that is x86 binary compatible while benefitting from the DEC Alpha's high speed bus technology running at 200 MHz. Operating at excess of 500 MHz clock speed, the K7 will include separate 64 KByte L1 data and instruction caches and an L2 cache of 512 KBytes going up to 2 MBytes. The K7 will include three independent out-of-order floating point pipelines. As this technology matures and is migrated to a 0.18 micron line it could achieve a peak performance of 2 Gflops.

Alpha 21264   The next generation of the DEC Alpha architecture is targeting an internal clock speed of 1 GHz by year 2000. Their system bus technology will operate at 333 MHz. Advanced architecture strategies are being included to increase its multiple execution pipeline efficiency including out of order execution. Even with its initial clock speed of 525 MHz which was slightly less than the intended 575 MHz, its performance should be excellent on compute intensive problems. There are also plans for a follow-on, the 21364 that will be produced in 0.18 micron and run at clock rates exceeding 1 GHz.

3.3   Motherboard

The motherboard is a printed circuit board that contains most of the active electronic components of the PC node and their interconnection. The motherboard
provides the logical and physical infrastructure for integrating the subsystems of
the Beowulf PC node and determines the set of components that may be used. The
motherboard defines the functionality of the node, the range of performance that
can be exploited, the maximum capacities of its storage, and the number of subsystems that can be interconnected. With the exception of the microprocessor itself,
the selection of the motherboard is the most important decision in determining
the qualities of the PC node to be used as the building block of the Beowulf-class
system. It is certainly the single most obvious piece of the Beowulf-node other than
the case or packaging in which it is enclosed.

While the motherboard may not be the most interesting aspect of a computer, it
is, in fact, a critical component. Assembling a Beowulf node primarily involves the
insertion of modules into their respective interface sockets, plugging power and signal cables into their ports, and placing configuration jumpers across the designated
posts. The troubleshooting of non-functioning systems begins with verification of
these same elements associated with the motherboard.

The purpose of the motherboard is to integrate all of the electronics of the node
in a robust and configurable package. Sockets and connectors on the motherboard
include the following:

- Microprocessor(s)
- Memory
- Peripheral controllers on the PCI bus
- Peripheral controllers on the EISA bus
- Floppy disk cables
- EIDE cables for hard disk and CD-ROM
- Power
- Front panel LEDs, speakers, switches, etc.
- External I/O for mouse, keyboard, joystick, serial line, etc.

Other chips on the motherboard provide:

- The system bus that links the processor(s) to memory
- The interface between the peripheral buses and the system bus
- Programmable read-only memory (PROM) containing the BIOS software

3.3.1   A Typical Beowulf Motherboard

It would be infeasible to specifically represent even a large (let alone exhaustive) list of available motherboards. Fortunately, this is unnecessary due to important similarities found among motherboards. For illustrative purposes, we present the general functional features of a current generation motherboard, the Intel SE440BX. Although some differences will exist with this and the boards that you may use, their overall capability will be mostly the same.

Form Factor This motherboard conforms to the ATX Slot 1 form factor of 12 x 7.75 inches.

Microprocessor A single Pentium II processor with an integrated 512K Byte L2 cache is incorporated through an SEC connector with host bus speeds of 66 MHz and 100 MHz supported.

Main Memory Up to 384 MBytes of synchronous DRAM is supported through three 168-pin dual inline memory module sockets with error checking and correction.

Chip Set The Intel 82440BX includes the 82443BX and 82371EB chips to manage general motherboard operation including a 100 MHz 64 bit wide system bus, an accelerated graphics port, PCI bus control, a PCI-to-ISA bus bridge, DMA controller, two fast IDE interfaces for disks and devices, the Universal Serial Bus (USB) interface, a real-time clock, and power management.

I/O The SMC FDC37C777 is an advanced I/O controller supporting conventional serial RS-232 and parallel I/O ports. Two USB ports are supported.

Expansion Slots Three PCI interface slots and one ISA interface slot is provided along with an additional interface slot that can be used either as an ISA or PCI interface.

3.3.2   Selection Considerations

The motherboard restricts as well as enables functionality. In selecting a motherboard as the basis for a Beowulf node, the requirements for its use should be considered. These include:

- processor family
- processor clock speed
- number of processors

- memory capacity
- memory type
- disk interface
- required interface slots

Currently the choice of processor is likely to be the Intel Pentium II or the DEC Alpha 21164. In the near future, the AMD K7, the DEC Alpha 21264, or the Intel Merced may be the likely candidates. In most cases, a different motherboard is required for each choice. Clock speeds for processors of interest range from 350 MHz to over 500 MHz and the selected motherboard must support the desired speed. Motherboards containing multiple processors in symmetric multiprocessor (SMP) configurations are available, adding to the diversity of choices. Nodes for compute intensive problems often require large memory capacity with high bandwidth. Motherboards have a limited number of memory slots, and memory modules have a maximum size. Together, these will determine the memory capacity of your system. Memory bandwidth is a product of the width and speed of the system memory bus. The Intel SE440BX motherboard discussed below has a 64 bit wide, 100 MHz memory bus. In practice, it can deliver about 600 MBytes per second from memory to processors. The Alpha PC164SX and PC164LX motherboards have 128 bit wide, 100 MHz buses. A PCI bus for peripherals is almost universal, but motherboards supporting double speed (66 MHz) PCI and PCI-2 are becoming available.

While there is more than one choice of the type of memory including conventional DRAM, EDO RAM, and SDRAM, SDRAM currently provides the highest bandwidth and motherboards should be selected that support it. The two disk interfaces in common use are EIDE and SCSI. Both are good with the former somewhat cheaper and the latter slightly faster under certain conditions. Most motherboards come with EIDE interfaces built-in and some include a SCSI interface as well, which can be convenient and cost-effective if you choose to use SCSI. On the other hand, separate SCSI controllers may offer more flexibility and options. Motherboards have a fixed number of PCI and ISA slots, and it is important to select one with enough slots to meet your needs. This is rarely a consideration in Beowulf compute nodes, but can become an issue in a system providing I/O services.

3.3.3 Layout of Major Components

Motherboards have evolved in physical shape and layout as hardware integration has improved, clock speeds increased, and resource requirements changed, but the general size and shape, or the form factor, of the motherboard PC cards have been limited to just a few. The most prevalent are the AT (baby AT and full AT), ATX, and NLX style motherboards. The AT boards were used primarily for early Intel 80286, 80386, and 80486 processor families. While the first Beowulf built in early 1994 was based on the 80486, few new Beowulfs are built using AT boards. The NLX style motherboard is standardized and permits easy removal from its enclosure. The most prevalent style for boards used in Beowulf-class systems is the ATX form factor. These come in several variations usually referred to as "Socket 7," "Socket 8," and "Slot 1," referring to the receptacle where the microprocessor is attached. Pentium and Pentium MMX processors are ordinarily found on ATX Socket 7 motherboards while Pentium Pro microprocessors use Socket 8 ATX motherboards. Pentium II microprocessors, which are more likely to be found in future Beowulfs, employ Slot 1 ATX boards with the new SEC processor package and interface connector.

Motherboards differ in their layout of components. The large and small chips, the peripheral interface sockets, the external cable connectors, and jumpers provide the designer with ample opportunity for customization and optimization, resulting in a wide variety of parts, and layout. Nonetheless, most of the major functions and support elements are similar due to industrial standardization of interfaces and customer expectations. Figure 3.2 shows an approximate layout of the principal components of the Intel SE440BX described above. For purposes of description, we assume the board is oriented with the I/O ports pointing upwards.

The processor is the most important component on the motherboard. The Pentium II processor cartridge contains several chips including the microprocessor itself, L2 cache SRAM, and bus interface with an integrated passive heat sink. A 242 pin Slot 1 SEC (Single Edge Contact) connector near the top of the right side of the board and laid out horizontally provides the mechanical and electrical interface to the motherboard. Processors of different speed can be used with this board.

The main memory of the motherboard is located in three horizontal sockets below and parallel to the processor cartridge. These dual inline memory module (DIMM) sockets have 168 pins and will hold either 64-bit non-ECC or 72-bit ECC (Error Correcting Code) supported memory modules. A number of different memory capacity modules are supported including 8, 16, 32, 64, and 128 MBytes for a maximum capacity of 384 MBytes. (Note: some motherboards can support up to 1 GByte of main memory). Both 66 MHz and 100 MHz SDRAM speeds are supported.

Between the SEC and DIMM connectors is a square chip package containing the 82443BX PCI/AGP controller, one of the two elements making up the motherboard's 440BX chip set. This chip provides interface control for the processor and the main memory as well as for the PCI bus and accelerated graphics port.

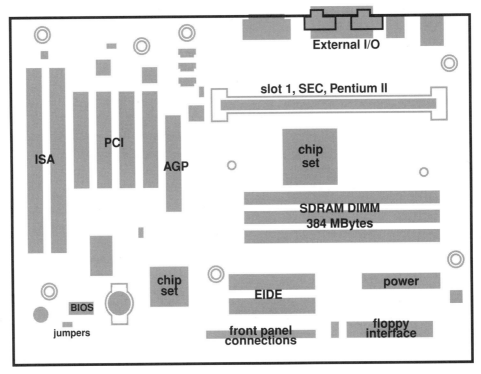

Figure 3.2
Layout of the Intel SE440BX motherboard for Pentium II processors. The detailed layout will vary considerably from product to product, but the same components will usually be found on other motherboards.

The Accelerated Graphics Port (AGP) connector is just to the left of the SEC slot. This connector supports high performance graphics/video controllers and can support transfers up to 500 MBytes per second. Beowulf compute nodes rarely employ this device, but it might be used in a system devoted to visualization.

The power supply connector sits just below and on the right side of the DIMM sockets. This 20 pin connector provides +3.3, +5, -5, +12, and -12 volt power sources from the external (usually built in to the tower package) power supply as well as ground connections, a *power good* signal, and a *remote on/off* control line.

Below and on the left side of the DIMM sockets are two independent bus mastering EIDE interfaces. Each interface can support two such devices, e.g., hard disk and CD-ROM drives. The floppy drive interface connector is along the bottom edge of the motherboard to the right and just below the IDE interface sockets.

Along the lower edge of the motherboard below the IDE sockets is a long thin sequence of pins that provide front panel connection to the motherboard. Inputs to this include the *reset* switch, the *sleep* switch, and the *power* switch. Outputs to the front panel include *power on* LED, *hard drive activity* LED, and for an off-board speaker.

Fan connectors are found along the right side of the board and at the lower left-hand corner of the processor SEC socket. Along the top edge of the motherboard on the right side is the mechanically integrated set of back panel external connectors. These include connectors for the keyboard and mouse, 2 USB ports, 2 RS-232 serial ports, a parallel printer port, a game port, and audio jacks.

The dominant feature of the left side of the motherboard is the series of vertically oriented sockets that accept the huge variety of expansion cards. Expansion cards sit perpendicular to the motherboard, and are oriented so they may be mechanically secured to the case for added stability. Frequently, these cards have external ports which are accessible through slots in the back of the case.

The two longest sockets are dedicated to the venerable ISA interface standard. These are provided primarily for backwards compatibility to older expansion cards. These slots are useful for low speed devices that do not require the capability of the high performance PCI bus.

The Peripheral Component Interconnect or PCI bus standard provides a 188 pin high speed connector in support of video systems, hard disk drives, network interface controllers, and other data intensive peripheral modules. The PCI bus is discussed in Section 3.7. Three PCI slots are grouped together, again vertically, just to the right of the ISA sockets. A fourth slot is provided that shares access with the rightmost ISA slot; either one but not both of these slots can be used at the same time.

The second of the chip set components, the Intel 82371EB part provides the bridge between the PCI bus and the ISA bus and IDE controllers.

At one time, motherboards were permeated with jumpers. These were single or dual lines of pins which could be electrically shorted by attaching a small jumper plug. Almost everything on the motherboard was configurable through a series of jumper placements. Dozens of such settings could be required. This process was often difficult to carry out and highly error prone.

With advanced plug-n-play technology and more sophisticated programmable configuration and BIOS software, almost all configuration settings can be performed through software during setup using the BIOS routines. In the lower left hand corner of the motherboard is a single 3-pin jumper that allows the system to be switched among three modes. The normal mode allows the BIOS to use the installed configuration information for booting the system. The configure mode brings up the maintenance menu for setting new configuration parameter values. The third mode requires a floppy disk to support a recovery procedure to acquire the BIOS configuration values.

3.4   Memory

The memory system of a personal computer stores the data upon which the processor operates. We would like a memory system to be fast, cheap and large, but available components can simultaneously deliver only two (any two) of the three. Modern memory systems use a hierarchy of components implemented with different technologies that together, under favorable conditions, achieve all three. When purchasing a computer system one must select the size and type of memory to be used. This section provides some background to help with that choice.

3.4.1   Memory Capacity

Along with processor speed, memory capacity has grown at a phenomenal rate, quadrupling in size approximately every three years. Integrated circuits of 64 Mbits are in use with memory modules using 256 Mbit parts becoming cost effective in the near future. Prices for Random Access Memory (RAM) have also continued to decline and now cost about one dollar per MByte; a little more for higher speed/capacity SDRAMs, a little less for older and smaller DRAM. A general principle is that faster processors require more memory. With increasingly sophisticated and demanding operating systems, user interfaces, and advanced applications such as multimedia there is demand for ever increasing memory capacity. As a result of both demand and availability, the size of memory in Beowulf-class systems has progressively expanded. Today, a typical Beowulf requires at least 128 MBytes of main memory and this can be expected to grow to 1 GByte within the next two to three years.

3.4.2   Memory Speed

In addition to the capacity of memory, speed of the memory can have a significant impact on the overall behavior and performance of a Beowulf node. Speed may be judged by the latency of memory access time and the throughput of data provided per unit time. While capacities have steadily increased, access times have progressed only slowly. However, new modes of interfacing memory technology to the processor managed system bus has significantly increased overall throughput of memory systems. This is due to the fact that the memory bandwidth internal to the memory chip is far greater than that delivered to the system bus at its pins. Significant advances in delivering these internal acquired bits to the system bus in rapid succession have been manifest in such memory types as Extended Data Output DRAM (EDO-DRAM) and Synchronous DRAM (SDRAM). Common access times are 70, 60, and 50 nanoseconds for main memory (DRAM). SDRAMs can deliver 8 bytes every 10 nanoseconds, making them the preferred component for newer high-speed buses. Further improvement to the apparent performance of the entire memory system as viewed by the processor comes from mixing small memories of fast technology with high capacity memory of slower technology.

3.4.3   Memory Types

Semiconductor memory revolutionized the cost and capacity of memory systems, breaking the 20 year dominance of magnetic core technology in the mid 1970s. Semiconductor memory is available in two fundamental types. Static random access memory or SRAM is high speed but moderate density while dynamic random access memory or DRAM provides high density storage but operates more slowly. Each plays an important role in the memory system of the Beowulf node.

SRAM   SRAM is implemented from bit cells fabricated as multi-transistor flipflop circuits. These active circuits can switch state and be accessed quickly. They are not as high density as are DRAMs and consume substantially more power. They are reserved for those parts of the system principally requiring high speed and are employed regularly in L1 and L2 caches. Current generation processors usually include SRAMs directly on the processor chip. L2 caches may be installed on the motherboard of the system or included as part of the processor module.

Earlier SRAM was asynchronous or ASRAM and provided access times of between 12 and 20 nanoseconds. Recent motherboards operating up to 66 MHz used synchronous burst SRAM or SBSRAM providing access times between 8.5 nanoseconds and 12 nanoseconds. The high speed processors being employed as Beowulf nodes use pipelined-burst SRAMs or PBSRAM with access times of 4.5 to 8 nanoseconds.

DRAM   DRAM is implemented from bit cells fabricated as a capacitor and a single by-pass transistor. The capacitor stores a charge passively. The associated switching transistor deposits the state of the capacitor's charge on the chip's internal memory bus when the cell is addressed. Unlike SRAM, reading a DRAM cell is destructive, so after a bit is accessed the charged state has to be restored by recharging the capacitor to its former condition. As a consequence, DRAM can have a shorter access time (the time taken to read a cell) than cycle time (the time until the same cell may be accessed again). Also, isolation of the cell's storage capacitor is imperfect and the charge leaks away requiring it to be refreshed (rewritten) every few milliseconds. Finally, because the capacitor is a passive, non-amplifying device, it takes longer to access a DRAM than an SRAM cell. However, the benefits are substantial. DRAM density can exceed ten times that of SRAM and its power consumption is much lower. Also, new techniques for moving data from the DRAM internal memory row buffers to the system bus have narrowed the gap in terms of memory bandwidth between DRAM and SRAM. As a result, main memory for all Beowulf nodes is provided by DRAM in any one of its many forms.

Of the many forms of DRAM, the two most likely encountered in Beowulf nodes are Extended Data Output DRAMs (EDO DRAM) and Synchronous DRAM (SDRAM). Both are intended to increase memory throughput. EDO DRAM provides a modified internal buffering scheme that maintains data at the output pins longer than conventional DRAM, allowing improved memory data transfer rates. While many current motherboards support EDO DRAM, the higher speed systems likely to be used as Beowulf nodes in the immediate future will employ SDRAM instead. SDRAM is a significant advance in memory interface design. It supports a pipeline burst mode that permits a second access cycle to begin before the previous one has completed. While one cycle is putting output data on the bus, the address for the next access cycle is simultaneously applied to the memory. Effective access speeds of 10 nanoseconds can be achieved with systems using 100 MHz systems bus.

3.4.4   Memory Hierarchy—L1 and L2 Caches

The modern memory system is a hierarchy of memory types. Figure 3.3 shows a typical memory hierarchy. Near the processor at the top of the memory system are the high speed Level 1 or L1 caches. Usually a separate cache is used for data and instructions for high bandwidth to load both data and instructions into the processor on the same cycle. The principle requirement is to deliver the data and instruction words needed for processing on every processor cycle. These memories run fast and hot, are relatively expensive, and now often incorporated directly on the processor chip. For these reasons, they tend to be very small with a typical size of 16 KBytes. Because L1 caches are so small, and the main memory requires long access times, modern system architectures usually include a second level or L2 cache to hold both data and instructions. Access time to acquire a block of L2 data may take several processor cycles. A typical L2 cache size is 512 KBytes with future L2 caches planned to reach 2 MBytes within the next one to two years.

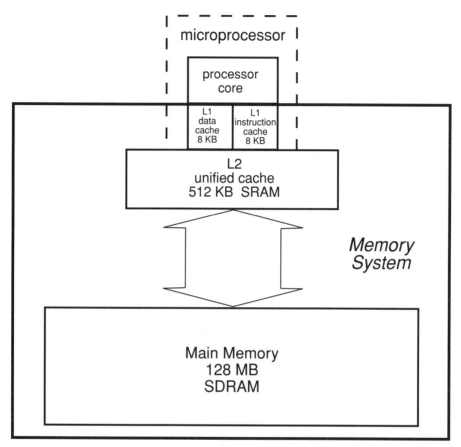

Figure 3.3
A node memory hierarchy with sizes typical of Beowulf nodes in 1998.

L2 cache is expensive, and manufacturers often offer otherwise identical processors with different amounts of L2 cache at very different prices. The performance impact of a larger L2 cache is difficult to predict, and varies tremendously from application to application as well as with the size of the application's data set. The only reliable way to determine whether a larger L2 cache is cost-effective is to run benchmarks that are as close as possible in size and operation to the actual code that will run in production.

Cache memory is usually implemented in SRAM or static RAM technology which is fast (2 to 10 nanoseconds) but relatively low density. Only when a datum required by the processor is not in cache does the processor directly access the main memory.

Main memory is implemented in one of the DRAM technologies. Beowulf nodes
will usually include between 128 MBytes and 512 MBytes of SDRAM memory.

3.4.5 Package Styles

The packaging of memory has evolved along with the personal computers in which
they were installed and has converged on a few industry-wide standards. Single
Inline Memory Modules (SIMM) and Dual Inline Memory Modules (DIMM) are
the primary means of packaging DRAMs and most modern motherboards use one
or more of these forms. Both are short but wide printed circuit cards with flat
thin memory chips mounted on one or both sides. The lower edge of the DIMM
or SIMM has a sequence of pins. On a SIMM, the adjacent pins on opposite sides
of the board are connected together to form a single joint pin. On a DIMM, these
pins are separate. The most common form factors are the 72 pin SIMM and the
168 pin DIMM.

3.5   BIOS

Even with effective industry wide standardization, hardware components will differ
in detail. In order to avoid the necessity of customizing a different operating system
for each new hardware system, a set of low level service routines are provided,
incorporated into read only memory (ROM) on the mother board. This basic
I/O system (BIOS) software is a logical interface to the hardware, giving a layer
of abstraction which facilitates and makes robust higher level support software.
Besides the system BIOS that is hardwired to the motherboard, additional BIOS
ROMs may be provided with specific hardware peripherals. These include the video
BIOS, the drive controller BIOS, the network interface controller BIOS, and the
SCSI drive controller BIOS. The BIOS contains a large number of small routines.
These are organized in three groups: Startup referred to as POST (for Power-On
Self-Test), Setup, and System Services.

The POST startup BIOS routines manage initialization activities including running diagnostics, setting up the motherboard chip set, organizing scratch pad memory for the BIOS Data Area or BDA, identifying optional equipment and their respective BIOS ROMs, and then bootstrapping the operating system. The CMOS
setup routine provides access to the system configuration information which is
stored in a small CMOS RAM. The system services routines are called through
interrupts directly from hardware on the motherboard, from the processor itself,
or from software. They allow access to low-level services provided by the system

including the CPU, memory, motherboard chip set, IDE, PCI, USB, boot drives, plug-n-play capability, and power control interfaces.

3.6 Secondary Storage

With the exception of the BIOS ROM, all information in memory is lost during power cycling except for that provided by a set of external (to the motherboard) devices that fall under the category of secondary storage. Of these, disk drives, floppy drives, and CD-ROM drives are most frequently found on Beowulf nodes. Disk and floppy drives are spinning magnetic media while CD-ROM drives (which are also a spinning media) use optical storage to hold approximately 650 MBytes of data. The newer DVD technology is likely to replace CD-ROM in the near future. Besides persistence of storage, secondary storage is characterized by very high capacity and low cost per bit. While DRAM may be purchased at about $1/MB, disk storage costs 2 or 3 cents per MByte and the price continues to fall. For the particular case of Beowulf, these three modes of secondary storage play very different roles.

CD-ROMs provide an easy means of installing large software systems but are used for little else. Even for this purpose, only one or two nodes in a system are likely to include a CD-ROM drive because installation of software on most of the nodes is performed over the system area network.

Floppy discs are fragile and slow and don't hold very much data (about 1.44 MByte). They would be useless, except that they were the primary means of persistent storage on early PCs, and PC designers have maintained backward compatibility that allows systems to boot from a program located on floppy disk. Occasionally, something goes terribly wrong with a node (either due to human or system error), and it is necessary to restore the system from scratch. A floppy drive and an appropriate "boot floppy" can make this a quick, painless and trouble-free procedure. Although other means of recovery are possible, the small price of about $15 per node for a floppy drive is well worth the investment.

The hard drive serves three primary purposes. It maintains copies of system wide programs and data so that these do not have to be repeatedly acquired over the network. It provides a large buffer space to hold very large application data sets. And it provides storage space for demand paging as part of the virtual memory management system. When the user or system memory demands exceed the available primary memory, page blocks can be automatically migrated to hard disk, making room in memory for other information to be stored.

There are two dominant interface types between the hard disk drive and the motherboard: EIDE and SCSI. The earlier IDE interface evolved from the PC industry while SCSI was a product of the workstation and server industry. Today, both are available. In the past, SCSI performance and cost were both significantly greater than IDE. But the EIDE standard closed the performance gap a few years ago, while the price difference still exists. Perhaps equally important is that many motherboards now include EIDE interfaces as integral components so that no separate control card is required to be purchased or to take up a PCI socket. SCSI drive capacities can run a little higher than IDE drives which may be important for some installations. Several different SCSI standards exist, including Wide, UltraWide, SCSI-2 and SCSI-3. Systems are usually downwards compatible, but it is safest to match the drive's capabilities with that of your SCSI controller. Beowulf-class systems have been implemented with both types and your needs or preferences should dictate your choice. The authors have continued to rely on EIDE drives due to their lower cost.

The primary performance characteristic of a hard drive is its capacity. EIDE hard drives with 17 GByte capacities are available for under $300 and 1 GByte drives cost below $100. Also of interest is the rotation speed, measured in revolutions per minute (rpm), which governs how quickly data can be accessed. The fastest rotation speeds are found on SCSI drives, and are now around 10000 rpm.

3.7 PCI Bus

While the PC motherboard determines many of the attributes of the PC node, it also provides a means for user defined configuration through the Peripheral Component Interconnect or PCI bus. This interface is incorporated as part of virtually every modern motherboard providing a widely recognized standard for designing separate functional units. PCI is replacing the ISA and EISA buses as the principal means of adding peripherals to personal computers.

The PCI standard permits rapid data transfer of 132 MBytes per second peak using a 33 MHz clock and 32 bit data path. A 64 bit extension is defined enabling peak throughput of 264 MBytes per second when used. A further advance, sometimes referred to as PCI-2, will permit bus clock rates of 66 MHz for a peak transfer bandwidth of 528 MBytes per second.

The PCI bus permits direct interconnection between any pair of PCI devices, between a PCI device and the system memory, or between the system processor and the PCI devices. PCI supports multiple bus masters allowing any PCI device to take ownership of the bus, permitting among other things direct memory access transfers without processor intervention. Arbitration among the pending PCI masters for the next transfer action can be overlapped with the current PCI bus operation, thereby hiding the arbitration latency and ensuring high sustained bus throughput.

High throughput is enabled by a process called linear burst transfers. A block of data being sent from one device to another on the PCI bus is moved without having to send the address of each word of data. Instead, the length of the block is specified along with the initial address of the location where the block is to be moved. Each time a word is received, the accepting unit increments a local address register in preparation for the next word of the block. PCI bus transfers can be conducted concurrently with operation of the processor and its system bus to avoid processor delays caused by PCI operation.

Although bus loading limits the number of PCI sockets to three or four, each connected board can logically represent as many as eight separate PCI functions for a total of 32. Up to 256 PCI buses can be incorporated into one system, although one rarely sees more than two.

The PCI standard includes complete bit-level specification of configuration registers. This makes possible the automatic configuration of connected peripheral devices for plug-n-play reconfigurability and elimination of jumpers.

3.8   Examples of a Beowulf Node

The following are examples of two classes of nodes derived from experience with two Beowulf systems in use today. There are many other choices and the products of other vendors in many cases are as worthy of consideration as the ones listed here. But these two systems provide useful starting points as you derive your own parts list to build or purchase the next generation of Beowulfs.

There are a few points of interest concerning the two configurations presented. In both cases, Fast Ethernet is employed with 100 Mbps peak throughput. Networking is discussed in Chapter 5.

As discussed earlier, a CD-ROM is not included because it is assumed that system installation will be performed over the network. A floppy drive is included to facilitate initial installation and crash recovery. Finally, the BIOS requires a video card to boot, so a very inexpensive one is included on every system.

3.8.1   Intel Pentium II Based Node

The majority of Beowulfs over four generations of systems in the last five years have
employed microprocessors from Intel or, to a lesser extent, their clones from AMD
or Cyrix. This is because they have been among the least expensive systems to
build, the system architectures are open providing a wealth of component choices,
and the Linux operating system was first available on them. While not the fastest
processors in peak performance, their overall capability has been good and their
price/performance ratios excellent. The most recent microprocessors in this family
and their motherboards support clock speeds of 450 MHz.

The node described here represents the most recent additions to the Naegling
(Beowulf's sword) system at Caltech's Center for Advanced Computing Research.
This system contains a mix of Pentium Pro and Pentium II nodes and in the Fall
of 1997 was one of the first to demonstrate greater than 10 Gflops sustained performance. The Pentium Pro nodes operate at 200 MHz while the Pentium II nodes
run at a variety of clock speeds. This is a common feature of Beowulf systems that
grow by incremental expansion over a period of multiple technology generations.

Processor Intel Pentium II, 450 MHz, $650

Motherboard Intel SE440BX, $142

Memory Generic SDRAM, 100 MHz, 128 MBytes DIMM without ECC, quantity
3, $175 each

Hard Disk Western Digital "Caviar", AC38400, 8.4 GByte, 5400 rpm, 9.5 msec
seek, 33.3 MByte per second, EIDE interface, $186

Floppy Disk TEAC 1.44 MByte, $16

Network Interface Controller D Link, DFE-500, Fast Ethernet, 100 Mbps $30

Video Card Trident 9680, 1 MByte, PCI, $15

Package Generic tower case with power supply and cables, ATX form factor, $72

3.8.2   DEC Alpha Based Node

The second example is representative of a new direction in Beowulf technology.
Assembled at the Los Alamos National Laboratory, Avalon's nodes were assembled
by a system-integrator before being shipped to the laboratory for $1701 per node

which is why separate prices per component are not provided below. This 140-node system is based on the high speed DEC Alpha processor which has a peak performance of over 1 Gflops due to its clock rate of 533 MHz and its ability to issue two floating point operations each cycle. Avalon is the 113th fastest computer in the world based on the widely cited LINPACK benchmark,[1] and was awarded the Gordon Bell Prize for best price-performance ratio in 1998.

Processor DEC Alpha 21164A, 533 MHz

Motherboard DEC AlphaPC 164LX

Memory Generic SDRAM, 256 MBytes DIMM with ECC

Hard Disk Quantum Fireball ST3.2A, EIDE U-ATA, 3.1 GByte

Floppy Disk TEAC 1.44 MByte , $16

Network Interface Controller Kingston Fast Ethernet, 100 Mbps, with DEC "Tulip" chip set

Package Generic tower case with power supply, ATX form factor

3.9   Boxes, Shelves, Piles, and Racks

Our review of Beowulf hardware would be incomplete without some mention of the technology used to actually physically support (i.e., keep it off the floor) a Beowulf system. Packaging is an important engineering domain that can have significant influence on the cost and practical aspects of Beowulf implementation and operation. Packaging of Beowulfs has taken two paths: the minimalist "Lots of Boxes on Shelves", captured so well by the acronym of the NIH LOBOS system, and the "looks count" strategy as adopted by several projects including the Hive system at NASA Goddard Space Flight Center and the Japanese Real World Computing Initiative. The minimalist approach was driven by more than laziness. It is certainly the most economical approach, and is remarkably reliable as well. This is due to the same economies of scale that enable the other low-cost, high-reliability subsystems in Beowulf. In the minimalist approach, individual nodes are packaged in exactly the same "towers" that are found deskside in homes and offices. These towers incorporate power supplies, fan cooling, and cabling and cost less than a

---

[1] http://www.top500.org/top500.list.html

hundred dollars. Towers provide uniform configuration, standardized interface cabling, effective cooling, and a structurally robust component mounting framework but are flexible enough to support a variety of internal node configurations. Industrial grade shelving, usually of steel framework and particle board shelves is strong, readily available, easily assembled, and inexpensive. It is also flexible, extensible, and easily reconfigured. You can find it at your nearest home and garden center.

When assembling such a system, care should be taken to design tidy power distribution and networking wire runs. Extension cords and power strips work fine, but you should consider physically attaching them to the shelving with screws or wire-ties so that the system does not become an unmaintainable mess. Similar considerations apply to the Ethernet cables. Labelling cables so the ends can be identified without laboriously tracing the entire run can save hours of headache.

Different approaches are possible for video and keyboard cables. In our systems, most nodes do not have dedicated keyboard and video cables. Instead, we manually attach cables to nodes in the very rare circumstances when necessary maintenance cannot be carried out remotely. Linux's powerful networking capabilities makes it unnecessary to maintain constant console video and keyboard access to each and every node of the system.

Rack mounting is considerably more expensive but offers the possibility of much higher physical densities. New motherboards with rack mountable form factors that incorporate Fast Ethernet controller, SCSI controller and video controller offer the possibility of building Beowulf nodes that can be packaged very tightly because they don't require additional daughter cards. It is likely that these systems will be important in the future, as larger Beowulf systems are deployed and machine room space becomes a major consideration.

3.10   Node Assembly

We conclude this section with a checklist for building a Beowulf node. Building Beowulf nodes from component parts may not be the right choice for everyone. Some will feel more comfortable with systems purchased from a system integrator, or they simply won't have the manpower or space for in-house assembly. Nevertheless, one should not overlook the cost, which can be several hundred dollars per node and carefully weigh the luxury of having someone else wield the screwdriver vs. owning 25% more computer power. Keep in mind that cables often come loose in shipping, and there is no guarantee that the pre-assembled system will not require as much or more on-site trouble-shooting as the home-made system.

Although targeted at the reader who is building a Beowulf node from parts, this checklist will also be useful to those who purchase pre-assembled systems. Over the lifetime of the Beowulf system, technology advances will probably motivate upgrades in such things as memory capacity, disk storage, or improved networking. There is also the unavoidable problem of occasional maintenance. Yes, once in a while, something breaks. Usually it is a fan, a memory module, a power supply, or a disk drive, in that order of likelihood. More often than not it will occur in the first few weeks of operation. With hundreds of operational nodes in a large Beowulf, some parts replacement will be required. The checklist below will get you started if you decide to replace parts of a malfunctioning node.

To many, the list below will appear obvious, but, in fact, experience has shown that a comprehensive list of steps is not only convenient, but likely to simplify the task and aid in getting a system working the first time. Many sites have put together such procedures and we offer the one used at Caltech as a helpful example.

Before initiating the actual assembly, it helps to get organized. Five minutes of preparation can save half an hour during the process. If you're assembling a Beowulf, you will probably build more than one unit at one time, and the preparation phase is amortized over the number of units built.

- Collect and organize the small set of tools you will be using:
  - #2 Phillips head screwdriver
  - anti-static wrist strap
  - anti-static mat to place assembly
  - needle-nose pliers
  - 1/8th inch blade flat blade screwdriver
  - small high intensity flashlight

- Organize all parts to be assembled. If more than one unit is to be built, collect like parts together bin-style.

- Provide sufficient flat space for assembly including room for keyboard, mouse and monitor used for initial check-out.

- Work in a well lighted environment.

- Follow the same order of tasks in assembling all units; routine leads to reliability.

- Have a checklist, like this one, handy, even if used only as a reference.

- When first opening a case, collect screws and other small items in separate containers.

- Keep food and drink on another table to avoid the inevitable accident.

After you have done one or two systems, the process becomes much quicker. We find that we can assemble nodes in well under an hour once we become familiar with the idiosyncrasies of any particular configuration.

Many of the instructions below may not apply in every case. Included are directions for such sub-assemblies as monitors, keyboards, sound cards that rarely show up in the majority of Beowulf nodes. However, there is usually at least one such node that is more heavily equipped to support user interface, operations support, and external connections for the rest of the system.

In a number of cases, the specific action is highly dependent on the subsystems being included. Only the documentation for that unit can describe exactly what actions are to be performed. For example, every motherboard will have a different set and positioning of jumpers, although many of the modern boards are reducing or almost eliminating these. In these instances, all we can say is: "do the right thing," but we still indicate in general terms the class of action to take place.

3.10.1   Motherboard Pre-assembly

- Set every jumper on the motherboard properly.

- Look through your motherboard manual and verify every setting, since the default may not work for your CPU, memory, or cache configuration.

- Locate every jumper and connector: floppy, hard drive, PS/2, COM port, LPT port, sound connectors, speaker connector, hard disk LED, power LED, reset switch, keyboard lock switch, etc.

- Install the CPU

  - Pentiums, and Pentium Pros are keyed so that you will bend a pin unless you put it into the socket properly. Look at its gold pins: they will have an asymmetric pattern, and so will the socket. The Pentium II uses the SEC slot 1 connector which also has a key to prevent inserting the cartridge in backwards. Don't force.

  - Whatever the chip, match the notched corner of the CPU with the notched corner of the socket.

– When using a ZIF socket, lift the handle 90 degrees, insert the CPU, and then return the handle back to its locked position.

- Install the Memory

  – Main memory SIMM or DIMM

  Note pin 1 on the SIMM/DIMM and find the pin 1 mark on the motherboard. 72-pin SIMM/DIMM's are difficult to install wrong, but it is possible.

  Begin by placing the SIMM/DIMM at a 45 degree angle to the socket of bank 0, The SIMM will be angled toward the rest of the SIMM/DIMM sockets (and away from any SIMM/DIMM's previously installed), insert firmly into the socket, then rotate the SIMM/DIMM until it sits perpendicular to the motherboard, and the two clips on each edge have snapped around the little circuit board. There may or may not be a "snap," but you should verify the two clips are holding the SIMM/DIMM fast, and that it doesn't jiggle in the socket. Repeat this until you fill one, two, or more banks, remembering that a bank consists of two 72-pin SIMM/DIMM

  – Cache memory (if so equipped) Some older units may have L2 caches on the motherboard while newer processors include them within the processor module. Cache memory may be DIMM (dual in line memory module), or SIMM, in any case, install it now.

3.10.2   The Case

- Open the case and remove all the internal drive bays, locate all the connectors: speaker, hard disk LED, power LED, reset switch, keyboard lock switch, mother board power, peripheral power, etc.

- Now mount the motherboard in the case.

  – ATX style cases use only screws to mount the motherboard, and it is very straightforward.

- Plug in the keyboard to see if it fits.

- Plug in an adapter card and see if it fits.

- Start connecting the case cables to the motherboard now.

  – Pull out floppy cables, hard disk cables, PS/2 mouse cable, and find jumper wires for your case's front panel switches and lights. Line up pin 1's to the red side of cables.

— Be sure to find the speaker and install it. It usually is a 4-pin connector with two wires (one red, one black, which can be installed either way on the motherboard.

— If your case has holes for COM ports and LPT ports, you can punch these out and save a card slot by unscrewing the connectors that came on the slot-filler strip of metal, removing the connector, and mounting it directly on the case.

— Attach power cables to the motherboard.

  * ATX style cases have only one power connector which is keyed to only fit one way

  * The AT-style power connector comes in two pieces, and must be connected properly. THE BLACK WIRES MUST BE PLACED TOGETHER WHEN PLUGGING THEM INTO THE MOTHERBOARD.

  * Ensure that the CPU cooling fan is connected to the power supply, this is usually a 4 pin male connector that goes to one of the power supply connectors.

3.10.3   Minimal Peripherals

- Floppy disk drive

  — Mechanical

    * It may be necessary to re-install the floppy mounting bay, if it was taken out previously.

    * The floppy drive must protrude from the front of the case, take off one of the 3.5 inch plastic filler panels from the front of the case, then slide the floppy drive in from the front until the front of the drive is flush with the front of the case. Then, using two small screws that are supplied with the case, attach the floppy drives left side, then if the floppy drive bay is detachable, remove the bay with the floppy half installed, and with the drive bay out, install the screws for the right side.

    * If the drive bay is going to contain hard disks in addition to floppy drives, leave the drive bay out for now and go to the hard disk installation section before putting the drive bay back into the case.

  — Electrical

    * The floppy disk needs two connections: one to the power supply, and one to the motherboard or floppy controller. The power supply connector is shaped to prevent you from getting it backwards.

     * Some floppy power connectors are smaller than the standard connector, and most power supplies come with one of these plugs. These connectors can only be installed one way.

     * For data, a flat ribbon cable is needed. It is gray with 34 conductors and a red stripe to indicate pin 1. One end of the cable will usually have a twist in it. The twisted portion connects to a second floppy drive (drive B:). The end farthest from the twist connects to the motherboard or floppy controller.

- VGA card installation

  - If the motherboard has an integrated video adapter, go to step 3.

  - Plug the VGA card into the appropriate slot, depending on the type of card purchased (PCI slot for a PCI card, ISA slot for an ISA card.

  - Screw the top of the metal bracket that is attached to the adapter into the case using one of the screws supplied with the case.

- Monitor

  - Plug it into a wall power outlet.

  - Plug the video input plug, which is a 15-pin connector, into the back of your video card.

3.10.4 Booting the System

Setup is where you configure your motherboard's components, peripherals, and controllers. It is usually in ROM and can be run by pressing a certain key during POST. Check the CMOS settings using the setup program before booting for the first time. If you make changes, you will need to exit setup and save changes to CMOS for them to take effect. You will be able to change the date and time kept by the RTC (real time clock). Memory configuration like shadow RAM and read/write wait states can be changed from their defaults. IDE hard disks can be detected and configured. Boot sequence and floppy drives can be configured and swapped. PCI cards and even ISA cards can be configured, and PnP disabled (which should be done if running a non-Windows OS). ISA bus speed can be changed and ports can be enabled or disabled.

IDE disks are almost always configured as Auto detect or user-defined type. Use shadow video unless you have problems. Shadow the ROM of your NIC or SCSI card for better speed. For better speed and if you have EDO memory, you can usually use the most aggressive memory settings - just try it out before you stick with it to avoid corrupting data files.

- Minimum requirements for booting the system are:
  - A bootable floppy disk
  - Motherboard with CPU and memory installed
  - Video card on the motherboard
  - Floppy drive with one cable connected to it and power to it
  - Monitor plugged into the wall and the video card
  - Keyboard attached

- To boot the system proceed as follows:
  - Making sure that the power switch is off, attach a power cord from the case to the wall.
  - Turn on the monitor.
  - Turn on the power to the PC, and get ready to shut it off if you see or hear any problems.
  - Look for signs that all is working properly:
    * The speaker may make clicks or beeps.
    * The monitor should fire up and show something.
    * Make sure all of the memory counts.
    * The floppy drive light should come on one time during POST.

- Setup the system
  - Enter setup by hitting the appropriate key (delete, F1, F10, Esc, or whatever it is) and check the CMOS settings.
  - Change the CMOS settings and see if the computer will remember them.
  - Update the date and time.
  - View every setup screen and look at each of the settings.
  - Make sure the first boot device is set to be the floppy drive.
  - If you have EDO RAM, you may wish to optimize the memory settings now, or make any other changes you see fit.
  - Save your changes and reboot, rerun setup and make sure the updates were made.
  - After you have re-run setup, save any changes, make sure the bootable floppy is in the drive and let it try to boot from the floppy.

- If it does not boot, or there is some error message on the screen, or there is nothing on the screen, go to the troubleshooting section.

3.10.5   Installing the Other Components

If your PC can boot and run setup, you're almost done. Now you can begin to install all of the other components. You should begin to mount the drives in the case if you have not already done so.

- IDE Hard disk installation
  - Mechanical - This is similar to the floppy installation above, with the exception that the drive will not be visible from outside of the case.
  - Electrical
    * Most motherboard BIOS's today can read the IDE drive's specifications and automatically configure them. If it does not, you will have to get the drive's parameters (usually written on the drive) which include number of cylinders, number of heads, and number of sectors per track, and enter them in the drive parameter table in the CMOS setup.
    * A ribbon cable and power connector attach to each hard disk, the power cable has 4 wires in it and is keyed so it cannot be installed wrong.
    * Read the documentation that came with the hard disk to see how the jumpers are set, if you are installing one disk and no other IDE device, the jumpers can usually be removed. If you are installing more than one disk, decide which disk will be booted. The boot disk should go on the primary hard disk controller. Move jumper(s) on the hard disk to make it a MASTER or PRIMARY. Many newer hard disks will use pins labeled MA, SL, and CS - you will jumper the MA pins. The second hard disk or CD-ROM will be configured as a SLAVE or SECONDARY drive. You will jumper the SL pins on this device. Please use your drive's manual, or call the manufacturer's 800 number for proper jumper settings. If the CD-ROM drive will be alone on its own controller, follow the manufacturers directions, but it will usually be OK to jumper it as a slave. Once jumpered properly, the drives can be connected with the 18-inch 40-pin ribbon cables and powered up. Pin 1 usually goes next to the power connector.

- SCSI hard disk installation
  - Mechanical - see the floppy installation above, with the exception that the drive will not be visible from outside of the case.
  - Electrical
    * Unless the motherboard has the SCSI controller built in, the BIOS will not read a SCSI drive and the drive table should be setup with "not installed".

* A ribbon cable and power connector attach to each hard disk, the power
  cable has 4 wires in it and is keyed so it cannot be installed wrong. The
  other end of the ribbon cable plugs into the SCSI controller itself.
* Read the documentation that came with the hard disk to see how the
  jumpers are set, if you are installing one disk and no other SCSI devices, the
  jumpers can usually be removed so that it will be set to ID 0. Each SCSI
  device on the chain (ribbon cable) must have its own unique ID number,
  usually 0 through 7, with 7 being reserved for the controller itself.
* The last physical device on the cable has to be terminated, depending on
  the device, either with a jumper or some type of resistor networks that are
  plugged in. This is very important.

* NIC installation

  - Similar to the VGA card installation described previously. If there are any
    jumpers to be set, do it now and write the settings down. Read the installation
    manual that came with the card.

* Sound card installation

  - See NIC installation, above. If you are setting jumpers, make sure you don't
    set two cards to the same resource (IRQ, DMA, or port address) keep all
    settings distinct.

* At this point, you are ready to begin your Operating System installation, don't
  forget to connect the mouse, external speakers, and a network hookup, if you
  have these options installed.

3.10.6   Troubleshooting a PC that Won't Boot

* Connect at least the following four components to your PC each time you boot.

  - speaker

  - keyboard

  - floppy drive

  - monitor

* What should a normal boot look and sound like?

  - First, LED's will illuminate everywhere—the motherboard, the hard disks, the
    floppy drive, the case, the NIC, the printer, the CD-ROM, the speakers, the
    monitor, and the keyboard.

- The hard disks usually spin up, although some disks, especially SCSI's, may wait for a cue from the controller or may simply wait a fixed amount of time to begin spinning to prevent a large power surge during boot.

- The P/S and CPU fans will start to spin.

- The first thing displayed on the monitor usually will be either memory counting or a video card BIOS display.

- During the memory count, the PC speaker may click.

- When the memory is done counting, the floppy disk often screeches as its LED comes on (called floppy seek).

- The monitor may have messages from the BIOS, including BIOS version, number of CPU's, a password prompt, and non-fatal error messages.

- The last part of the power-on self-test (POST) is often a chart that lists the components found during POST, like CPU and speed, VGA card, serial ports, LPT ports, IDE hard disks, floppy disks, etc. If no system files are found, either on a bootable floppy or hard disk, you may get a message from the BIOS saying, "Insert Boot disk and press any key" or something similar. This is a non-fatal error, and you can put a bootable floppy in the drive and press a key.

- If the above happens, you will know that your motherboard is at least capable of running the ROM's POST. The POST has many potential problems, most of which are non-fatal errors, however any consistent error is a cause for concern. The fatal POST errors will normally generate no video, so you need to listen to the speaker and count beeps. The number of beeps and their length indicate codes for a technician to use in repairing the PC.

- At this point, the POST is done, and the boot begins.

• No video or bad video during boot

  - Check the monitor's power and video connection.

  - Try reseating the video card or putting it in a new socket.

  - Make sure the speaker is connected in case you are getting a fatal POST message, which could have nothing to do with video.

  - Swap out the video card and/or the monitor.

- Most notable and common POST messages are

  - HDD (or FDD) controller error. Usually, this is a cabling issue like a reversed connector.

  - Disk Drive 0 failure. You forgot power to the hard disk, or you've got the wrong drive set in CMOS (run Setup). Also make sure the disk is properly connected to the controller.

- Floppy troubleshooting

  - If the light stays on continuously after boot, you probably have the connector on backwards.

- Other things to check when having problems

  - Check the cables or try someone else's cables.

  - Recheck all the jumper settings on the motherboard.

  - Remove secondary cache, or disable it in Setup—this can fix a lot of problems.

  - Slow down the CPU—it may have been sold to you at the wrong speed.

  - Replace SIMM's with known working ones.

  - Replace the video card.

  - Remove unnecessary components like extra RAM, sound card, modem, mouse, SCSI card, extra hard disks, tape drives, NIC, or other controller card.

  - Remove all hard disks and try booting from floppy.

  - Remove the motherboard from the case and run it on a piece of cardboard—this will fix a problem caused by a motherboard grounded to the case.

4 The Linux Operating System

Linux shares much in common with a family of operating systems that are collectively known as Unix systems. The first version of Unix appeared in 1971, developed at Bell Labs by Ken Thompson and Dennis Ritchie. It eventually evolved into what is today known as Unix System V. AT&T was not allowed to sell operating systems in the 1970s because of antitrust laws, and therefore made the Unix source code freely available to many research institutions, especially university labs. The University of California at Berkeley made extensive modifications and enhancements to AT&T's Unix, including the socket network communication abstraction, and ultimately rewrote virtually all of the operating system, resulting in what is known as BSD Unix (Berkeley Software Distribution). In this chapter we will casually refer to System V and BSD when indicating the lineage associated with a particular feature of Linux.

As a result of the proliferation of Unix source code, many derivations of Unix have come into being, each with varying degrees of feature additions and modifications. Most of these derivations were developed by vendors such as Sun Microsystems and Hewlett Packard to power their workstations. But all of them share a basic set of system calls, application programming interfaces, and even source code originating from either the original AT&T or Berkeley distributions. Linux is sometimes called a Unix-like operating system because none of its kernel source code derives from either System V or BSD. However, Linux implements almost all the features of each, and largely conforms to the IEEE Portable Operating System Interface (POSIX) standard, which was devised to reconcile differences between System V and BSD.

If you have ever used a commercial Unix workstation running Sun Solaris, IBM AIX, SGI IRIX, HP-UX, or Digital Unix, you will be able to translate most of your experience to Linux. If your only experience has been with traditional PC operating systems, you will find many familiar elements, but will have to adjust to a different design philosophy. The core of the Unix user experience is the large set of modular programs that can be tied together through process pipes on the command line and concurrently executed to calculate some result. This has made Unix enormously popular among software developers, scientists, and engineers. In the past, some versions of Unix shipped with custom windowing systems, but today they all use the X Window system, originally developed at MIT, but now maintained by the The Open Group. Linux provides all of these familiar Unix features, in addition to its own set of enhancements and customizations.

4.1 History of Linux

The development of the Linux operating system is one of the most startling events in the history of computing and opened an entirely new model of how large, complex, and robust software systems could be created. Linus Torvalds was a student in Finland in 1991 when he became interested in task switching and virtual memory. Because of their low cost and ubiquitous nature, Torvalds initially used Intel 80386 microprocessor based PCs for his work. While binary upwardly compatible with its predecessor, the Intel 80286, the newer 386 differed dramatically in its support for advanced memory management including virtual address translation. This provided the necessary support for a serious operating system, and Torvalds developed an early version of his lightweight kernel to be compatible with Minix, a Unix clone developed for teaching operating systems concepts by Dr. Andrew Tanenbaum, a computer science professor at Vrije Universiteit in Amsterdam.

Torvalds' early version of Linux was primitive. While it had a virtual memory subsystem, it had few device drivers, and a primitive task scheduler. The virtual memory system had active memory mapping but did not include demand paging. There was no user interface, graphical or otherwise, just a text mode screen that ran a simple command shell. Nonetheless, Torvalds did one crucial thing. He made his early code, as limited as it was, available to the community via the Internet. He did this in October, 1991.

No one could have foreseen what would happen as a result of offering the seed of an operating system, freely to the world over a communications system that enabled the world to get to it, add to it, improve it, debug it, and use it. By early 1992, additional developers joined the team. These developers were distributed all over the world, many in the United States, and almost none had met each other in person.

There were many contributors to the early development of Linux and by the end of 1992, many enhancements had been incorporated including job control, demand paged virtual memory, basic networking subsystems and drivers. Linux was a usable operating system. With the release of this extended version, a core team began to make regular contributions. Eventually, release 1.0 was made available to the Internet community and represented a complete Unix-like operating system with the X Window system and the GNU programming environment. The source code was both free and publicly available.

Early versions of Linux were difficult to install. A series of distributions were developed to meet the needs of a growing community. At one time 30 floppy disks were required to install a complete Linux on a PC. Such early distributions provided

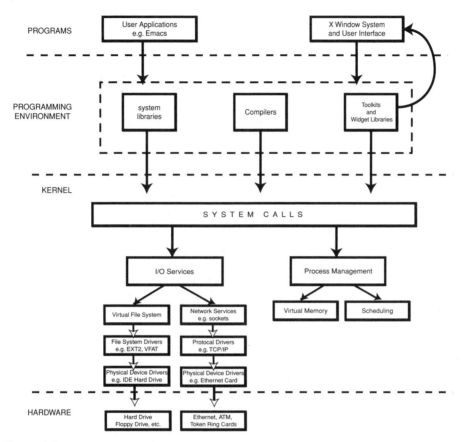

Figure 4.1
System component relationships in the Linux operating system.

over the Internet included Slackware and TAMU. With the availability of CD-ROM drives, distributions were made available on low cost CDs. Now, complete, easy-to-install commercial and non-commercial distributions of Linux are available at hundreds of web sites, FTP mirrors, by mail order, and even in shrink-wrapped packaging on the shelves of computer stores. Dozens of books are available to help the novice, and up-to-the-minute documentation is available at hundreds of web sites. A few of these resources are listed in Section 4.10.

4.2   Linux Kernels and Linux Distributions

Strictly speaking, Linux is just the *kernel* of an operating system, i.e., the master process that schedules user processes, controls devices and manages resources. In the early days, Linux was difficult to install and provided few of the tools and services that one would expect from a modern Unix-like operating system. Linux "distributions" provide the additional infrastructure that bridge the gap from a bare kernel to a fully functional operating system and user environment. Distributions provide two different and crucial services: simplified installation and a source for pre-packaged optional software components. Virtually all Linux distributions can be obtained either by downloading them from the Internet or by ordering a CD-ROM. You may wonder why you would want to pay for free software by ordering a CD. It costs money to put software on a CD, and organizations that do so need to recoup the costs involved. Several commercial Linux distributors provide technical support when you buy one of their CD-ROMs. Although support is also available separately under contract. Some vendors provide value-added features, and enhanced distributions that include commercial software such as accelerated X servers, Motif, and office productivity suites. Installation from CD-ROM is much easier than a network installation if you lack the infrastructure of a well-connected LAN and adequate temporary storage. Some of the more popular Linux distributions and their web sites are Red Hat Linux (www.redhat.com), Caldera Open-Linux (www.caldera.com), Slackware (www.slackware.org), Debian GNU/Linux (www.debian.org), S.u.S.E. Linux (www.suse.com), and Yggdrasil Plug and Play Linux(www.yggdrasil.com).

Installing a new operating system for the first time on a computer can be an intricate and highly technical procedure. Modern distributions have reduced what is essentially an extremely complex process into a series of question-and-answer screens, often with a convenient graphical user interface. Most users of computers buy operating systems pre-installed on their hard drives. The "magic" that goes into this installation procedure has been handled by the system integrator who sold the system. Today, it is possible to buy hardware systems with Linux pre-installed, but it is far more common to install Linux onto existing hardware that may already be running another operating system. Linux installation is discussed in Section 4.8.

The second major contribution made by distributions is the packaging of optional software packages. The relationships between these software packages, or applications, and the rest of the operating system environment are detailed in Figure 4.1. The popularity and success of Linux is due in large part to free software projects that are not directly affiliated with the Linux kernel development effort, but which have been incorporated into a fully functioning operating system and user environment. Chief among these is the GNU project, which has created a high-quality suite of POSIX compliant tools and utilities for program development, and general system support. Other software projects, such as the X Window System, the TeX document preparation system, the Apache web server, the Tcl/Tk and Perl scripting languages, sendmail, and others, combine to make Linux distributions fully functional environments. An increasing number of commercial software packages, such as the Java Development Kit, Adobe PDF viewers, and Netscape, are available free of charge for Linux. More recently, several high-profile commercial software firms have announced plans to support Linux versions of some of their products. Oracle, IBM, Informix, Sybase, Corel, and Computer Associates, among others are supporting their products on Linux. Some products are free of charge, while others have standard commercial licensing fees.

4.3 Linux Features

Linux is a full and complete Unix, developed with contributions from an international community. Linux, including every line of source code for the kernel and utilities, is available from many sources at little or no cost. There are no licensing fees to run Linux. It was originally restricted to the Intel x86 family of microprocessors, but has since been ported to many other architectures including the DEC Alpha, IBM PowerPC, Sun SPARC, Motorola 68k, and MIPS microprocessors. While other versions of Unix such as FreeBSD and Solaris have been successfully employed for Beowulf systems, the focus of this chapter is on Linux, its capabilities, interfaces, and installation.

Demand paging Linux provides complete support for virtual memory including transparent address translation and demand paging. Both the user virtual address space and the machine physical address space are organized into pages. These pages are contiguous blocks of memory, usually 4096 bytes in length. With some exceptions, a page of virtual memory may be mapped to any page of existing physical memory and the specific allocation is retained in a system directory table which is also stored in memory. The primary advantage of real virtual memory systems over more primitive systems that work directly in the physical space is that the virtual address space can be much larger than the actual number of pages provided by the physical installed memory of the system. This gives the user application an illusion of a very large amount of memory. This additional storage, if not in physical memory, has to exist somewhere, and the excess pages (those not in physical memory) are kept on a specifically designated and partitioned part of the system's hard disk. As Linux implements a demand paging strategy, only pages that are actually used are mapped into virtual memory. This allows for more efficient use of physical memory.

Virtual memory   The Linux operating system automatically manages the allocation and movement of pages between physical memory and disk. A virtual memory request (load or store operation) to a virtual/user address is translated by Linux with support from underlying the hardware. If the location is in cache, the data is taken from there. If in main memory, a piece of the allocated page is copied to cache. If, however, the page is not in main memory but on disk, then Linux moves it to main memory, having first cleared a place for it by migrating some other page to disk in its place and performing various housekeeping chores such as clearing TLB entries. A TLB is a piece of logic on the microprocessor called a Translation Lookaside Buffer which caches recent address mappings to speed address translation. All of this is transparent to the user application program, although some significant amount of time is required to obtain a page from disk (tens of milliseconds).

Multitasking   Linux is a true concurrent multitasking system. Multiple processes are active at any one time with a scheduler that recognizes priorities and a round-robin time-sharing mechanism between processes of the same priority. While many of these tasks are user applications, an important class of processes are so-called daemons which perform system services upon request. Network services, which provide the fabric of the Beowulf system, are often supported by daemon processes.

Multiple file systems   Linux provides a complete file handling system that will be discussed more fully in Section 4.4. Files are persistent objects that are used to archive data and pass state between successive program invocations. The file name space in Linux is used for other objects as well, for example, classes of I/O devices. These may be managed with precisely the same tools that were devised for file handling, thus bringing a uniform methodology to managing information handling functions. Linux can read and write over twenty different types of file systems, allowing it to operate on media originating from other operating systems, e.g., DOS floppy disks, or VFAT (Windows) disk partitions.

Networking support   Linux, like other modern Unix operating systems, is easily integrated with other systems via local area networks. It incorporates a robust networking layer that permits many forms of information exchange between Linux and machines running other operating systems over such networks. Linux allows user and system management to be initiated remotely. This important capability is crucial to the management of systems like Beowulf. System security and integrity can be preserved by a variety of means, up to and including use of sophisticated cryptographic protocols for authentication.

Linux includes a complete TCP/IP networking stack and features a selection of network device drivers exceeding that of many commercial operating systems. TCP/IP is a software interface to networking which can be implemented over a wide variety of physical devices and underlying protocols. Linux can be networked using a wide variety of Ethernet cards, ISDN, serial ports, parallel ports, infrared ports, modems, etc. A Beowulf system will usually connect its nodes using 100 Mbps switched Ethernet, but can utilize any TCP/IP capable medium.

Program development tools   The capabilities of Linux extend far beyond a layered approach to resource management. It incorporates a powerful program development environment based on the tools from the GNU project. In addition, several scripting languages including shells, Perl, Tcl/Tk and Python provide the glue that allows one to build complex behaviors from smaller, simpler modules.

Dynamically loadable, shared libraries   Many operating systems adopted dynamically loaded shared libraries to reduce memory consumption. Linux quickly implemented shared library support, especially because many early Linux systems ran with only 8 MB of RAM where every byte was precious. A Linux shared library is much like a Windows DLL. It is a set of code that gets loaded into memory once and is shared by multiple applications. Unlike some systems, Linux shared libraries posses a consistent version scheme, allowing multiple versions of libraries and applications to coexist.

Graphical user interface   The X Window System provides the (GUI) for Linux systems. The X Window system has been a standard feature of scientific and engineering workstations for over a decade, and forms the basis of the Linux GUI. The X Window system allows programs to perform graphical operations over the network. A variety of different "window managers" allow users to customize the look and feel of their desktop.

Robustness   Linux is an extremely reliable platform with systems routinely running for months or years under heavy interactive load without crashing. This robustness is as a product of hundreds of contributors, many years of development, and a very large user community intent on finding and eliminating bugs. Anyone can look at the source code, find bugs and submit patches to future releases.

4.4   File Systems

The file system is a major part of any operating system. It is a repository for programs and data and constitutes a large part of the "personality" of an operating system.

The term file system has two meanings in the Linux operating system. First there is the concept of a rooted directory hierarchy containing files and subdirectories. There is no notion of separate drive letters, only different disk partitions mounted as directories somewhere under the root directory structure. The second meaning of a file system refers to the specific formats for representing files and directories on a disk or in memory. For example, the format for storing files in MS-DOS differs from the format for storing files in MacOS. These constitute different file systems. Linux can work with over 20 of these file system formats, including MS-DOS, HPFS (OS/2), ISO9660 (CD-ROM), VFAT (Windows95), and the Linux native EXT2 file system. Any of these file systems can be mounted as directories within a Linux system's directory structure. Linux even includes a process file system, which resides in memory and allows access to system information through a file interface.

The earliest versions of Linux only supported the ability to read from and write to the Minix file system. In 1992 the first extended file system (EXT) was developed specifically for Linux. About a year later, an improved version of this file system, named EXT2, was written to overcome the performance deficiencies of EXT. Since then, EXT2 has served as the Linux native file system. EXT2 was designed to be extensible, so that future versions of the system could always be compatible with older versions. But EXT2 is not compatible with EXT. The most frequently used file systems are EXT2 for storing the main Linux system, a DOS or VFAT system for accessing Windows files, and ISO9660 to read CD-ROMs.

When EXT2 was written, an architectural change was made in the way the Linux kernel interacted with file systems. The code to handle specific file systems was separated from the operating system through a layer called the Virtual File System. That change has allowed Linux to easily incorporate new file systems. The VFS allows the operating system to use exactly the same code to mount, read, and write to file systems without worrying about the specific format of the file system.

Linux files possess the properties of both user and group ownership, in addition to permissions based on reading, writing, and execution permission. They also have long, case sensitive filenames. Not every file system supports these notions, in which case their files are assigned reasonable defaults. Files may be up to 2 GBytes long, a limitation imposed by the 31-bit signed integer passed to the `lseek` system

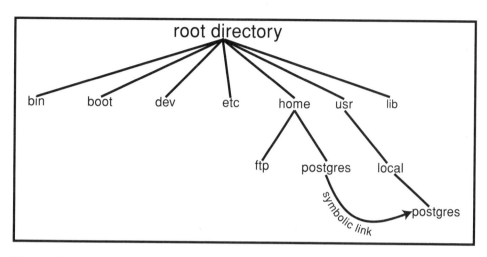

Figure 4.2
Hierarchical file system structure

call. The root file system is mounted at boot time, after which additional disk partitions and file systems can be mounted on the directory tree.

File systems are fundamentally tree structures, but EXT2, like most Unix file systems, allows the file system to form directed graphs, as shown in Figure 4.2. This is possible through the use of hard links and symbolic links. A hard link is a mechanism whereby a physical file may possess more than one logical name. When one filename is deleted, the file continues to exist under one of its other names. Only when the hard link count of the file reaches zero will it truly be deleted. This feature allows a file to exist in multiple parts of the directory structure without consuming additional space. The problem with hard links is that it is difficult to determine which logical filenames are really to the same physical file. A symbolic link resolves this problem by creating a new file that only points to an existing file. When a symbolic link is deleted, the file it points to remains unchanged. But when a symbolic link is read from or written to, the operation is performed on the original file. When the original file is deleted, it has no effect on the symbolic link, which is left pointing to a non-existent file.

Files are not record oriented and are instead treated as a stream of bytes, although these bytes are not necessarily located contiguously on disk. Unlike systems like MacOS, files are not typed and may contain either binary or text data. File types can be inferred through file extensions (as is done in Windows) or by interpreting so-called magic numbers at the beginning of files. However, file extensions are arbitrary parts of filenames and carry no semantic meaning to the file system. Any special meaning is merely an adopted convention, such as MIME, that may be of significance to applications such as editors and compilers.

The EXT2 file system is implemented to dynamically minimize fragmentation. With sufficient free disk space, files are written in contiguous blocks. As files are deleted, EXT2 is smart enough to defragment existing files that can benefit from the newly freed space. As a result, the file system almost never needs to be defragmented. On the other hand, once a file has been deleted, it is gone forever. but it is not always possible to undelete files. Other Unix file systems possess similar self-defragmenting properties, but if they become too fragmented, they require a complete backup and reinstallation to eliminate fragmentation.

The file system most often used by Linux systems to access remote files is NFS (Network File System), originally developed by Sun Microsystems, but Linux is also able to share files with Windows networks using the SMB protocol. NFS is a completely transparent distributed file system where the user never needs to know if a file is remote. There is no difference in the structure or filename format to access remote files. The autofs utility can be used to automatically mount local and remote file systems on demand when they are referenced, rather than maintaining persistent connections which can be costly in memory and other system resources.

As with other Unix implementations, Linux extends its filename space to devices and special interprocess communication mechanisms like FIFOs, providing a uniform interface to these different objects. For example, you can communicate through a serial port by opening a file such as /dev/cua0 and you can access the raw bytes on a floppy disk by reading /dev/fd0. Conventionally, all device files are stored in the /dev directory and usually represent system peripherals or virtual interfaces such as terminal sessions.

Devices are divided into two types, character and block devices. Character devices can be read from as a stream of bytes. For example, a serial line or tape drive can only be read as a sequential byte stream. Block devices can be accessed in a random order, and include hard disks and floppy drives. There is actually a third type of device file, called the FIFO (first in first out), but it does not correspond to a peripheral device. A FIFO is a virtual device to which bytes can be written. When the file is read, the bytes are returned in the order in which they were originally written. This mechanism is often used to simplify the programming of cooperating processes on a single machine, facilitating interprocess communication.

4.5 System Configuration

Although Unix systems are very reliable and well suited to running mission critical applications, they are also difficult to configure and administer. The same is true for Linux. Back when the first versions of Unix were being developed, there were no GUIs, and character screen terminals were something of a luxury. Memory was also scarce and very expensive, so simplicity in design was important. As a result, it was decided to store system configuration information in plain ASCII text files. This had the advantage that all system maintenance could be performed from a dumb terminal while running a text editor. A more elaborate system using special user-friendly programs to edit configuration data would have consumed more memory and disk space than could be afforded at the time. Besides, in the early days, there were only a few installations of Unix, so why bother?

That initial decision has left a long legacy of headaches that Linux and every other implementation of Unix has inherited. As more features were added to Unix, the number of configuration files increased, each using its own special format. Administering a system eventually required familiarity with well over 30 different configuration files, each with its own special format. Every piece of software that was developed, both servers and clients, also followed this trend, compounding the problem even further. Around the early 1990s, after the success of PC operating systems that used GUIs for many aspects of system configuration, many Unix vendors retrofitted their operating systems with friendly configuration programs that didn't require knowledge about how to manually edit each and every configuration file. But even though this facilitated system administration, these config programs did not cover all the bases and there still remained many situations where files needed to be manually edited.

The use of ASCII text files to configure Linux is both a blessing and a curse. The clear benefit is that it is easy to remotely administer a system—just start your favorite editor. The obvious downside is that it is easy to make mistakes when editing these files and it is extremely difficult to remember all the details of the file formats for different parts of the system. But despite all the preceding negativity, do not be discouraged. Many of the configuration files have manual pages that can be called up to answer questions about how to properly modify a file. More recently, the Linux community has made a concerted effort to make some of these tasks easier. Several Linux distributions include their own configuration tools, providing both text and GUI configuration modes. For example, Red Hat Linux provides a control panel (executed as /usr/bin/control-panel) from which user accounts, system time, printers, network setup, file system mounts, and other aspects of the system can be configured. A more powerful tool called linuxconf, now included with most Linux distributions, provides almost all of the configurability possible from editing files manually, but through a menu driven user interface. Linuxconf implements text mode and graphical interfaces in addition to a Web browser interface for easy remote configuration.

Despite the recent advancements in configuration utility programs, a passing familiarity with the essential configuration files is essential. You may not care to edit them by hand, but it is still helpful to know where they are and what they control. As with most other Unix implementations, almost all the important Linux configuration files are located in the /etc directory or its subdirectories. Among the most important configuration files with which you should become familiar are:

passwd, group   The passwd file stores user account, password, home directory, and shell information. The `group` file lists the user groups for the system. You should generally avoid editing either of these files yourself except in the most extreme emergencies. Mistakes can render it impossible to log in to the system. Instead, the `useradd`, `usermod`, `userdel`, `groupadd`, `groupmod`, and `groupdel` commands should be used to add, modify, and delete user accounts and groups.

inittab   is essential to properly booting a system. The first process to start when Linux boots is the master `init` process, which reads the `inittab` file to discover what processes it should start at boot time. The `init` process also implements the concept of run levels, which usually includes single and multiuser run modes and additional modes defined by the `inittab` file. See the discussion of the `rc/` directory below.

fstab   defines the file systems that can be mounted on the system. It includes local hard drive partitions, floppy and CD-ROM drives, and network file systems. The principal parameters for each file system include its type, where it should be mounted, and access permission (e.g., read-only or read/write).

inetd.conf   configures the behavior of the `inetd` server. Unix systems typically run an assortment of server programs, called daemons, to support tasks such as remote file transfer and remote login. Many of these daemons only occasionally have to do any work, and would otherwise spend most of the time idle, consuming precious memory resources. The `inetd` program was conceived to avoid simultaneously running many idle daemons. `inetd` will listen for connections on socket ports defined in `inetd.conf` and execute the corresponding daemons listed in the file to service the connection. That way one daemon runs all the time, invoking other daemons only as necessary. Heavily used daemons, such as web servers, should not be run from `inetd`.

shells stores the pathnames of command shells that can be used as interactive login shells.

exports informs the NFS mount daemon of which directories are being exported to which remote machines and under what restrictions.

hosts.deny, hosts.allow The explosion of computers interconnected via the Internet has made system security extremely important. Many commonly used daemons were initially developed with little or no regard to security. Rather than completely rewrite every daemon, a means of wrapping a daemon with an access control based security scheme was devised. This system is known as TCP-wrappers because it "wraps" an existing daemon with a screening program that tests for various security conditions before passing control to the daemon. These conditions are defined in the `hosts.deny` and `hosts.allow` files. TCP-wrappers utilizes a host-based authentication scheme, allowing or denying access to a daemon based on the IP address and hostname of a connecting machine. Therefore it is only a weak form of security and other measures including installing a firewall should be considered to protect your Linux network.

host.conf defines how hostname resolution is performed. When you refer to another machine by a hostname, it has to be translated to a numerical IP address. The `host.conf` file determines how the translation is performed.

hosts statically lists hostname to IP address mappings. Usually you will configure your `host.conf` file so that the name resolver will look in the `hosts` file first when resolving a hostname. Frequently accessed machines should be listed in the hosts file so that name lookups do not have to rely on the network. Beowulfs will almost always have all of their nodes listed in a `hosts` file.

rc.sysinit, rc/ At boot time, after the `init` process starts and reads the `inittab` file, shell scripts have to be executed to start up initial service daemons. Although which scripts are executed can be arbitrarily configured in inittab, the standard scripts are located in the `/etc/rc.d` directory. The first step `init` attempts is system initialization, at which time it will execute `rc.sysinit`, which will check and repair the file system prior to mounting it, and also do things like turn on user quotas and set the system clock. After this initialization step, init will enter a run level specified in `inittab`, at which point it will execute the `rc` script. The `rc` script starts and stops services depending on the new run level. Most of the services are started and stopped by scripts in the /etc/rc.d/init.d directory. Each of these scripts are written following a convention whereby a service is started when the script is invoked with an argument of "start" and stopped when invoked with an argument of "stop."

X11/XF86Config is found on any operating system that uses the XFree86 implementation of the X Window system. This file specifies details about the graphics hardware on the machine, allowing the X Window server to optimize for monitor refresh rates, graphics card memory, and acceleration features. Most of this information can be configured using the Xconfigurator utility program, but if you have special hardware, or need to perform unique customizations, you will likely have to learn how to edit this file.

lilo.conf is a Linux-specific file. It defines boot loader configuration parameters such as what partitions are bootable and what kernels to boot. You can maintain several different boot configurations, including the ability to boot multiple operating systems, by modifying this file. Configuration changes do not take effect immediately, and have to be committed by executing the LILO (LInux LOader) installer, /sbin/lilo.

4.6   Tools for Program Development

Beowulfs, like most other large-scale parallel computers today, are primarily development systems. Users tend to be programmers and applications designers. Thus, program development tools are particularly important to Beowulf users. Many of these tools come from the GNU project, initiated by Richard Stallman in the 1980s to create a completely free operating system. Linux has achieved many of the goals of the GNU project, and the GNU tools have been an integral part of Linux distributions from the earliest days. These tools are available on many other architectures as well, but we focus on their use in the Linux environment.

Together, these interoperable utilities provide the means of implementing even the largest software projects, managing its evolution, and verifying its correctness and dynamic behavior.

Emacs

Emacs is a powerful editor and environment for managing program development. Emacs can be used simply as a line-oriented text editor, but it also supports a staggering number of modes and features tailored to specific tasks. Modes exist for editing programming languages, with features like automatic indenting, rudimentary syntax checking, keyword highlighting, automatic compilation, and parsing of compiler-generated error messages. Other modes exist for editing text, sending and receiving mail, interacting with debuggers, shells and programming environments. Emacs' power comes from the extensibility of its built-in lisp-like extension language, and the thousands of programmers who have contributed to it over the years. For some, Emacs is not just an editor, it's a way of life.

Compilers and Languages

Most of the compilers and language support in Linux are derived from other projects - notably the GNU (GNU's Not Unix) effort undertaken by the free software foundation. Some of the many compiled languages that Linux supports include:

C, C++, and Objective C through the GNU C compiler and EGCS.

Fortran through g77 and f2c as well as a sizeable number of commercial compilers including HPF (High Performance Fortran) implementations,

Smalltalk through SmalltalkX,

Scheme and Lisp through UMB Scheme, Allegro Common Lisp, and other implementations including XLisp and Emacs Lisp among others,

Pascal and Modula-2/3 through the p2c Pascal translator, IPD Modula-2 and DEC Research Modula-3,

Prolog through SICStus and SWI Prolog,

BASIC though Chipmunk BASIC and ByWater BASIC,

Ada through the GNAT compiler, and

Java through a Linux port of Sun's Java Development Kit (JDK) as well as independent implementations such as the Kaffe virtual machine and the GNU Guavac compiler.

Some other compiled and interpreted languages supported by Linux include Eiffel, APL, FORTH, Simula, Sather, and ML as well as the scripting languages discussed below.

Despite the large number of languages supported by Linux, the mainstay of development work is the GNU C compiler, gcc. The GNU C compiler is required to compile the Linux kernel and most of the programs distributed with Linux. When maintenance of gcc by the Free Software Foundation lagged, a group of developers started the Experimental GNU Compiler System (EGCS) project to keep gcc up to date with the latest C and C++ standards. As a result, EGCS is now included with many Linux distributions as the standard C/C++ compiler. EGCS also has sought to better integrate the GNU Fortran compiler, g77, with the gcc code generation engine. Many scientific codes depend on the availability of good Fortran compilers, and several commercial Fortran compilers are available for Linux systems.

Libraries

The Linux C library closely adheres to industry-wide standards for Unix-like operating systems, including ANSI C, the IEEE POSIX 1003.1 standard, and the BSD suite of networking calls. Actual certification of standards compliance is a costly (in real money) and time consuming process. In some cases, commercial packagers of Linux distributions have sought and obtained certification (for example, Unifix's certification of POSIX.1 and FIPS 151-2 compliance), but most distributions have not been through a rigorous certification procedure. Nevertheless, Linux systems are extremely close to standards conforming, and it is very rare for programmers to experience problems when porting standards conforming software systems.

Make

Make determines which pieces of a large program need to be compiled or recompiled and issues the commands to create them. File dependencies are represented by a special syntax in configuration files usually called Makefile by convention. Virtually all Linux distributions ship with GNU Make and Berkeley Make. On most Unix systems, GNU Make is named gmake, but since the GNU development suite is the standard Linux compilation system, it is named make in Linux. Berkeley Make is included as pmake and is necessary because a certain portion of Linux software is borrowed from BSD Unix, which uses a different Makefile format. Make is not only used to manage software development projects, but can also be used to manage large documents produced with TeX or SGML, and is therefore an important utility with which to become familiar.

Scripting

Scripts are executable programs that do not require compilation and are interpreted directly from their ASCII text source code. Command shells such as sh and csh include a scripting syntax and can be used to construct simple system maintenance and utility programs. These so-called shell scripts use system commands as fundamental building blocks. Although analogous to DOS batch files, shell scripts also allow for conditional invocation of system utilities and looping and include the ability to execute a script from a script. Linux's shells include: the Bourne Shell (sh), Korn Shell (ksh), Bourne Again Shell (bash), C-Shell (csh,tcsh), and Z Shell (zsh).

Interpreted scripting languages such as Perl and Tcl, which are not user command shells, possess more powerful functionality, including advanced text processing, networking capabilities and the ability to interface with other programs and libraries, e.g., graphics libraries written in other languages. Scripting languages are used to quickly build programs that do not require the structure and performance of a compiled language, but still deliver a high level of functionality. Scripts written in Perl and Tcl generally require about 10% of the code necessary to write an equivalent program in C, and take less time to debug. This makes them very well suited to rapid development and prototyping. Available scripting languages include Expect, AWK, Perl, Tcl/Tk, Python.

Debugging/Performance Monitoring

The GNU Debugger, gdb, is a powerful source level debugger. It operates with a command line interface which some programmers find primitive. However, gdb can be combined with a graphical user interface (xxgdb), or the powerful Emacs editor (see above) to create a sophisticated environment that shows code in one window, program state in another, etc.

Gdb works best when programs have been specifically compiled to support source level debugging with the -g flag. In the past, (and on many commercial systems), compilation for debugging was incompatible with optimization, but it is possible to request optimization (-O) and debugging simultaneously from gcc. Gdb can even help you debug programs not specifically compiled with debug options, but some variable-name information will not be available.

After linking your program with the system debugging libraries, you can use gdb to start your program and step through it at various levels of granularity, generally a program statement or function-call at a time. You can also attach gdb to a stopped process (try `kill -STOP <pid>` first), or use it to analyze the final state of a program saved in a 'core' file. You will want to do this when your programs crash for unknown reasons or behave in unpredictable ways because of bugs. As a source level debugger, gdb allows you to interactively inquire about source level variables and data structures in a running and controllable program. You can specify source level conditional watch points and breakpoints, allowing you to control when and where your program starts and stops before manually inspecting program state. Debugging tends to be a black art and many programmers still resort to using extensive logging and print statements. This is especially true on Beowulf systems where there is still no convenient mechanism for controlling multiple gdb sessions.

Profiling of programs is well supported through profiling versions of standard libraries and gprof, the GNU profiler. You can use gprof to generate execution profiles of C and Fortran programs, determining how much time is spent in each procedure call. The strace tool allows you to record the reception of system signals and the execution of system calls in a program. Where gprof will help you determine information about code under your own control, strace will tell you things about what's happening inside the kernel.

Compiler Compilers

The compiler compiler is an oddly named beast, but is an essential tool in some circumstances. A compiler compiler does exactly what its name says. It is a program that produces compilers. It accepts grammar and token definitions as inputs and outputs the source code to a parser or compiler for the grammar. Virtually every scripting language available has been implemented using a compiler compiler to interpret the scripting syntax. Some compiler compiler tools for Linux are:

lex and flex Lex is a lexical analyzer that generates the token analysis procedures for Yacc programs. Flex is a faster and more versatile version of lex developed by the GNU project.

yacc, byacc and bison Yacc stands for Yet Another Compiler Compiler, and appeared in early versions of Unix. Byacc is the Berkeley version of yacc. Both can produce parsers for any language that can be represented as an LR(1) grammar. Bison is an upwardly compatible version of yacc produced by the GNU project. They are essential to compile a wide variety of programs.

PCCTS and ANTLR are not distributed with Linux, but are more powerful compiler compilers than Yacc or Bison and are growing in popularity. They produce LL(k) parsers, which represent a much larger set of languages than LR(1).

Version Control

Next to the compiler and editor, version control is the most essential element of a software development system. Version control allows you to track changes in a project over time, recover previous versions of a software system, and maintain separate branches of development. A version control system preserves the entire history of a software system or document collection. Although version control is most often associated with software development, it forms an important part of maintaining documentation, data, and anything utilizing words and numbers to represent information. It can even manage binary images and object code, although a proper database is often better suited to that task. The Concurrent Versions System (CVS) that is distributed with most versions of Linux was used to manage the development of the manuscript for this book. It allowed successive drafts of the book to be tagged and changes between versions to be preserved.

CVS, RCS, and SCCS are the principal version control systems available for Linux. RCS and SCCS are roughly equivalent, allowing you to lock a file, make changes to it, check in the changes, and unlock the file. RCS (Revision Control System) is produced and maintained by the GNU project while SCCS (Source Code Control System) is not free and dates back to the original AT&T Unix. But several free clones of SCCS exist, including a BSD Unix version. CVS is built on top of RCS, and allows multiple people to make changes to a file at the same time. It includes the ability to check out files over the network, resolve conflicting file changes, and user customization of configuration management through scripting. CVS is used by most major free software projects, including the Apache web server and Netscape's Mozilla. The authors used it to maintain at least nine separate up-to-date copies of this book on their laptop, office and home computers.

X Window System

No modern operating system is complete without a graphical user interface system. As with most implementations of Unix, Linux relies on the X Window System to provide graphics and windowing support. The X Window System was originally developed at MIT, but ownership was transferred to The Open Group in 1996. Unlike Windows or MacOS, the user interface policies of the windowing environment are not built into or dictated by the operating system. The X Window System runs as a separate server process, that processes requests from X programs to draw lines, display bitmaps, etc. A second program, called the window manager, performs the window mapping, movement, iconification, and other management tasks. The window manager also dictates the look and feel of the graphical operating environment.

Several commercial and free X servers are available for Linux, but most distributions use the XFree86 server, which is a freely redistributable port of X to the Intel x86 and other architectures. Numerous window managers are also available providing users with considerable choice in terms of the "look and feel" of their windowing environment. X window managers are extraordinarily customizable, and both appearance (menu styles, for example) and behavior (click-to-type vs. autofocus) are under user control. Some of the more popular window managers are listed:

twm is the original sample implementation of a window manager distributed with the X Window source code. Despite its simplicity, many users still rely on twm.

Motif refers to both a widget toolkit and a window manager designed by The Open Group. Coupled with CDE (Common Desktop Environment), Motif forms the standard windowing environment for most commercial versions of Unix. Commercial Linux ports of Motif and CDE exist and are widely used.

fvwm is a lightweight window manager based on twm, but provides features including loadable modules and virtual screens.

fvwm95 is a popular derivative of fvwm which very accurately mimics the Windows95 look and feel.

AfterStep is yet another popular derivative of fvwm that mimics the NeXTStep look and feel.

OpenLook is a free version of a window manger developed for Sun's now defunct OpenLook environment. It still enjoys a significant following.

Most window managers available for Linux are configurable independent of the display server and client programs. The window manager controls to which applications keystrokes are passed and the effects of mouse movement and clicking. Users can customize and program capabilities to a much greater extent than other systems. For example, most window managers allow you to set whether you must click on a window to give it focus, or if you must simply move your mouse over a window to give it focus. All window managers provide task activation facilities, either through menu driven mechanisms, task bars, or button panels. This high level of flexibility allows you to modify your work environment to suit your particular unique requirements.

The most notable and feature of the X Window System is its ability to display locally programs running on a physically distinct machine attached to the same network. Clients local to a display server optimize communication using shared memory, while remote clients use network protocols such as TCP to communicate with the X server. This remote display ability greatly facilitates the administration, maintenance, and use of Beowulf systems. It means that you only require a single display to interact with a cluster of processing nodes. The display node does not even have to be a part of the cluster, but can be the workstation sitting on your office desk.

4.7   Linux's Unique Features

There are a some features of Linux that are especially useful and sometimes unique when compared to other operating systems.

The /proc file system   Linux has a process file system, which serves as an interface to kernel data structures. It presents statistics, status information, and configuration data in a machine independent way accessible as a set of files. The /proc file system doesn't actually exist on your hard drive, but is made to appear that way for ease of use. By doing this, system information and devices can be manipulated by standard tools and remotely accessed through a network file system instead of using special tools specifically defined for that purpose. For example, system memory information can be obtained simply by reading the file /proc/meminfo.

Loadable kernel modules   Linux has always been highly customizable, but in the early years, customizations always required that you recompile the kernel. Though not overly difficult, compiling a kernel can be a tricky business that may present non-programmers a certain amount of difficulty. In addition, kernel compilation can be a lengthy process that is undesirable when all you want to do is add support for a sound card. These inconveniences gave way to the idea of loadable kernel modules, which are dynamically loaded extensions to a monolithic kernel. This approach yields many of the advantages of a microkernel without the performance impact. In a Beowulf system, loadable modules make system management a much easier task. It avoids the need to recompile a kernel, install it on every node of the system, and reboot every node. Instead, only the particular feature being added needs to be compiled as a module, and then installed on every node without rebooting a single machine.

Virtual consoles   A problem endemic to many operating systems is that they have only one user console. If the window system freezes, or some other error occurs, there is no way to recover without rebooting the machine. In addition, it is not possible to use the system effectively in text-only mode, if such a mode is even possible. Linux originally ran on PCs that sometimes had insufficient memory to run an X server. Also, many users simply had no need for a window system, and could work effectively from a text console. Therefore a virtual console system was added to Linux from the very early stages. The virtual console system allows you to simultaneously maintain separate login sessions. You can run an X server in one console, hit a function key combination and be presented with a text-only

console. This useful capability allows you to log in as root on a separate console
to fix problems or change system configuration while leaving your user workspace
unaffected.

Pluggable authentication modules   Linux also contains a highly configurable
authentication mechanism called PAM. PAM is an Internet standard for customizing programs that require authentication so that the authentication mechanism can
be changed without rewriting the program. For example, you normally log in to
a system by typing in an account name and password. With PAM it is possible
to substitute a face and speech recognition interface, or a fingerprint reader. That
is not to say that PAM actually provides these advanced authentication mechanisms. It only provides the interface by which these mechanisms can be connected
to programs requiring authentication. As biometrics research advances, Linux will
be able to easily incorporate these new authentication methods. Already, alternate
authentication systems, such as one-time passwords, have been deployed on Linux
using PAM.

Package management   A constant problem faced in the administration of operating systems is the installation, removal, and upgrading of software packages.
Several package management systems exist for Linux, but the one most widely
adopted is RPM, the Red Hat Package Manager. Even though it was developed by
Red Hat, it is not limited to Red Hat Linux systems, and several other distributions use the package format. RPM allows you to install a package and retain the
ability to completely remove it from your system. It also allows you to query a file
on your system to determine to which package it belongs. But most importantly,
RPM allows an entire Linux system to be upgraded without having to start from
scratch. RPM will resolve dependencies between multiple software packages and
cleanly upgrade existing packages to newer versions.

4.8   Installing an Initial System

While a cookbook-style installation of a Linux distribution is beyond the scope
of this book and is covered well in most distribution installation manuals, a few
cluster-specific notes are in order.

   Linux installation procedures rely on the fact that most PC class machines will
boot using the media in their floppy drive or CD-ROM drive as a source for the
initial program to be run by the processor. If a suitable floppy or CD-ROM is
installed, and the system is reset or power cycled, then the program on the floppy

or CD-ROM is run by the computer. (Actually, even this behavior is under software control. The BIOS system, usually stored in read-only memory on the motherboard actually determines the sequence of steps at boot time). Linux installations work by providing the user with a special "boot floppy" which actually directs the computer to run a minimal Linux system with just enough features to carry out the rest of the procedure. Often, this boot floppy requires a second or third "supplemental floppy" which may contain additional drivers and utilities.

Once the floppy-based Linux is running, the user answers a series of questions. For Red Hat distributions, one is required to select a language, select a keyboard type, and then select the media on which the remaining components of the distribution should be found. CD-ROM is common, and probably the most reliable. It is also possible to install using data that is stored on a remote NFS mountable file system, or a remote (possibly anonymous) FTP server. Network based installation offers instant gratification and low cost, but can be trickier to debug if something goes wrong.

4.8.1   Installation by CD or Network?

More often than not you will install Linux on a single machine from a CD-ROM. When you perform an installation on a network of machines or a Beowulf, it is often more appropriate to do a CD installation on the first machine, and install the rest of the machines across the network from the first, exporting the CD file system via NFS to the other machines. Cloning of nodes in this way is discussed in Section 6.3.

The simplest way to install Linux from a CD is to FTP installation floppy images from the Internet and the rawrite utility to write the images to floppy disks from DOS. After creating your boot floppies, the installation program will be able to access the files on the CD to install the operating system. Some distributions like Red Hat Linux, are distributed on bootable CDs. Newer computers that are able to boot from a CD-ROM will be able to start the installation process simply by booting from the CD.

Installation over the network is generally a slower process than CD installation. It requires network card, modem, parallel null modem cable, or other means of network connectivity. It usually does not make sense to attempt an installation over a low bandwidth network. Network installation is most suited for situations where you already have a Linux distribution on a computer on your LAN, and you want to install the distribution on other machines on the same LAN. Network installation requires you to know the IP addresses of the NFS, FTP, or SMB server which is exporting the distribution files to the destination machine. The destination machine must also have an IP address. You may also have to know the IP address of your name server if you only know the names of the machines serving as the source of the installation files. You will also have to create boot floppies with which you can initiate the installation process.

4.8.2   Installation Summary

As an aide to installing Linux on a single node, we provide the following "recipe" modeled after the Red Hat installation procedure. Most every Linux distribution can be installed in a similar way.

Boot the installation disk.   Insert boot floppy. Alternatively, if your machine can boot directly from CD-ROM, insert the CD-ROM and set your computer to boot from the CD. After booting, you will be presented with a "boot:" prompt and possibly some instructions. To get started quickly, just hit enter at this stage.

The kernel will boot, emitting probe information about the hardware it detects. From this point on, you will be guided through your installation by a series of menus.

Select language.   The first option you will have to select is a language. Most readers of this book will select English, although French, German, and a few others are supported.

Select the keyboard type.   The default US keyboard is usually selected, although different keyboard mappings are possible and indeed necessary for international keyboard configurations.

Partition your disk(s).   Before the installation can proceed, you will have to partition your disks. If your disk already has partitions, the installation program will detect them and allow you to delete them or add new ones. Unlike older Unix systems, PCs have a very logical partition scheme. Up to four primary partitions are permitted on each disk, and each primary partition may be subdivided into up to four partitions. Most installations will require only a few partitions, typically one or two file system partitions and a swap partition. Secondary partitions will only be needed for *multi-boot* installations, where multiple operating systems (e.g., Linux and Windows NT) exist on the same system. Casual Linux users may want to reserve hard disk partitions for other (possibly pre-existing) operating systems. For Beowulfs it is probably best to devote the entire disk to Linux.

You will always have to allocate a swap partition, even on large memory systems. By swapping out the initialization code Linux can run more efficiently. A general rule for choosing the size of your swap partition is to make it twice the size of your physical memory. but for systems with more than 64 Mbytes of physical memory, it is usually sufficient to have total swap space equal to your physical memory. The maximum usable size of a swap partition is only 127 Mbytes, so if you have a large memory system, and sufficient disk space, you may wish to create several swap partitions.

On a Beowulf, you will likely want to configure a worldly node that contains systems software, and also a large disk or disks for home directories. Home directories should be placed in a separate partition to facilitate backups, upgrades, and general maintenance. Internal nodes that do all of the parallel processing should have a large scratch partition. A scratch partition is an area that user programs can read and write large data files that will not permanently reside on the system. Experience has shown that all nodes should have about a 1 GByte partition for system space. About 200-500 Mbytes will be consumed with the initial installation depending on your exact choice of system software. Leaving extra space allows extra software to be added later.

Format your partitions. After partitioning your disk you will be asked to format the partitions. You will also have the option to check the disk for bad blocks. It is wise to check for bad blocks at this stage to avoid potential future problems.

Select installation method. For a network installation you may select NFS, FTP, or SMB depending on the type of network file service you are using. All of these methods require that a supplementary floppy be inserted. The supplementary floppy contains the necessary support programs for performing a network install. If you are not doing a network installation you will choose "Local CD-ROM." After this point you will be asked whether you are installing or upgrading the operating system. Select install because you are starting a fresh installation.

Select packages. The "base system" is the minimal set of software components needed to be to make a Linux system work. For a system to be useful, however, it needs extra software, such as compilers, editors, and productivity applications. Every distribution comes with a different, but largely overlapping, set of software. You will have to choose which software packages you want to install. Most installation programs also will provide you with information about the software packages in case you are not sure if you need a particular one. You can always install more software at a later time either from the packages accompanying your original distribution, or by downloading it from the Internet. If you download source code, you will have to compile it.

After selecting all the packages you want to install, you may indicate that you are done and start the installation. Sometimes you will not select a particular package that is necessary for another package to work. This is called a dependency, and you will be alerted to the problem and asked to decide whether or not to install the necessary package. Installation of the software can take some time depending on your chosen method. Network installations will generally take longer than CD-ROM installations unless you are on a fast network. You will receive visual feedback about the progress of the installation, including time elapsed and estimated time to completion.

Configure system. After all the software is installed, you have the option to enter some initial configuration information. You will almost definitely have to manually configure some settings after getting your system up and going, but you will want to set what you can at this stage. If the system will have a keyboard, mouse, and monitor, you will want to configure the mouse, indicating its type. Not every mouse understands the same protocols, so if you don't do this right, your mouse will not work. If you plan on using a graphical workspace, you will have to configure the X Window System. This usually consists of selecting your graphics card from a list. You may have some problems if your graphics card or the chip set used by your card is not listed. In this case, you should select one of the generic settings. Internal computation nodes do not need to be configured for a mouse or X Window support. All nodes, however, do require network configuration. You have to choose the name and IP address of each node. This should be decided before installation begins so you do not get stuck at this point. If you are not sure what to do, you should skip this stage, and configure the network manually at a later time.

Install LILO and reboot Before finishing up your installation you need to make it possible to boot your Linux system. First you need to choose a password for the root administrative account. This will allow you to log into the system to add new users and perform system maintenance activities. The last step is to install LILO, the Linux Loader. LILO is a small program residing on the first sector of your root partition or your master boot record that gets executed at boot time. It allows you to select what OS to boot if you have multiple operating systems installed, or what kernel to boot if you have multiple Linux kernels installed on the same partition. Beowulf systems should probably just install LILO on the master boot record, but single systems with multiple operating systems may have to install it on their root partition if they already have another boot loader installed. After you've installed LILO, the installer will reboot and start Linux.

Once Linux is installed on a single node, there are options for loading the rest of the system. You could follow the preceding procedure for all of the cluster nodes, but that would be time consuming and error prone if you have more than a very small number of nodes. Better ways to install Linux on the rest of your cluster are discussed in Chapter 6.

4.9 Keeping Up with Linux

At this stage you should have a basic understanding of what Linux is, what it can do, and how to set up a basic system. While we have tried to give more than just a cursory overview, it is impossible to capture all the details in a single chapter and we have glossed over some topics. You should keep in mind that installing Linux can be a time consuming process. Even though the installation process is made much easier today by menu-driven installation programs, you may well make mistakes the first few times and have to start over. After you've done this once or twice, future attempts will be far easier.

New releases Even though we have constantly referred to Linux as a static entity, it is really a moving target. Linux is constantly evolving as new work is always being done on the kernel. No central company or group controls the development of all the software that is typically run on Linux. Many independent programmers scattered across the world, working on their own and sometimes in groups, develop and maintain most of the software. The many people and organizations using the software submit bug reports when they run into problems, and most of the time the authors release a bug fix in a few days, or the bug finders submit their own patches. Since the source code to all of the software is freely available, users can fix problems quickly without necessarily having to rely on the author. Consequently, new versions of software are released on a monthly, and even weekly, basis. It is easy to feel overwhelmed by this rapid pace of change. We recommend that you only upgrade software as needed, otherwise you will be playing a constant game of catch up.

The free availability of Linux source code has made it possible to advance Beowulf research. Scientists and hackers alike have been able to modify and extend Linux source code to enhance network performance and add performance monitoring subsystems. Without this ability to customize the kernel, it would not have been possible to attain the performance demonstrated by the very first Beowulf, which used dual networks that logically appeared as one to increase network bandwidth. Those modifications, along with more recent software that is necessary to build a

Beowulf are now distributed on a CD-ROM from Red Hat Software, called Extreme Linux, which will be updated as Beowulf users add to, modify, and improve the software.

Documentation   Even though Linux software is constantly changing, it is remarkably easy to obtain information on how to use it. All software installed on a Linux system comes with a manual page, called a "man page" for short, that can be called up using the man command. This online documentation system has a long tradition dating from the early days of Unix. Man pages include information about system commands and software, system and library calls and programming interfaces. Linux has far more documentation than is contained in its man pages. On systems that use RPM, the `/usr/doc` directory contains supplementary documentation about the installed software packages. The Linux Documentation Project serves as the single most important external source of information about Linux. This project was started early on in an attempt to create an official set of Linux documentation, explaining how to do everything from installing the OS to compiling and configuring the kernel. The project has resulted in several books, including "The Linux Network Administrator's Guide," by Olaf Kirch. The most frequently used products of the project are the almost 200 HOWTO documents, explaining how to do both common and esoteric things with Linux. These HOWTOs generally give a brief overview of how to configure a piece of software or make a particular piece of hardware work with Linux. Every Linux distribution provides these HOW-TOs in either `/usr/doc/howto` or `/usr/doc/HOWTO`. They are available in ASCII text, HTML, TeX DVI, PostScript, PDF, and SGML.

Commercial software   You may have gotten the impression from this chapter that Linux only runs free software for which source code is available. While that is true for the vast majority of software used on Linux, many commercial software packages for Linux have been released, and their numbers are steadily growing. Commercial software vendors have started to recognize that Linux has a large user base and is an excellent platform for both server and client applications. Just a few of the firms providing Linux versions of some of their products are Netscape Communications, Adobe Systems, Computer Associates, Real Networks, Metro Link, Inprise, Informix, Sybase and Oracle.

Performance and reliability   Something we tend to take for granted about Linux is that it delivers performance equal to or better than that of major enterprise operating systems such as Solaris and Windows NT. That is actually a rather remarkable fact considering that Linux has been largely developed by people hacking code in their spare time. The efficiency of network drivers, process loading, context switching, and overall memory management all make Linux an attractive platform for computationally intensive tasks. These characteristics, along with the low cost, are largely the reasons why Linux is the predominant operating system used to build Beowulf clusters.

4.10   Suggested References

We have only touched on the most basic information necessary to become familiar with Linux. There are many excellent books and documents describing in much greater detail all that is necessary to install, use, and administer the Linux operating system. In order to help you get started, we have provided a list of references that either we have found useful or others we know have found useful in the course of setting up and using their Linux systems. By no means is this an exhaustive list. The absence of a Linux information source from this list should not be taken as an indication that it is lacking in quality.

4.10.1   Web Sites

Linux Documentation Project - http://sunsite.unc.edu/LDP/ The Linux Documentation Project organizes reliable documentation about Linux in several different online and printable formats.

Linux Information Headquarters - http://www.linuxhq.com/ The LinuxHQ web site is a resource for Linux kernel users and hackers, including the latest official and unofficial kernel patches.

Linux International - http://www.li.org/ Linux International is a non-profit organization that distributes news and information about Linux.

Linux Kernel Archives - http://www.kernel.org/ This is the official home of the Linux kernel source from which you can obtain the latest development and release versions of the Linux kernel.

Linux Online - http://www.linux.org/ Linux Online is a general resource on Linux containing links and information about vendors, distributions, applications, hardware, projects, and press releases.

Linux Journal - http://www.linuxjournal.com/ The Linux Journal is a magazine dedicated to covering the Linux operating system.

The XFree86 Project - http://www.xfree86.org/ The XFree86 Project develops and maintains a freely redistributable implementation of the X Window System that runs on Linux and many other Unix operating systems.

4.10.2 Books

Beginning Linux Programming by Neil Matthew and Richard Stones, Wrox Press, Inc. 1996.

Linux Application Development by Michael K. Johnson and Erik W. Troan, Addison-Wesley Publishing Company, 1998.

Linux in a Nutshell by Jessica Perry Hekman, O'Reilly & Associates, 1997.

Linux Network Administrator's Guide by Olaf Kirch, O'Reilly & Associates, 1995.

A Practical Guide to Linux by Mark G. Sobell, Addison-Wesley Publishing Company, 1997.

Red Hat Linux Unleashed by David Pitts, Sams Publishing, 1998.

Running Linux by Matt Welsh and Laur Kaufman, O'Reilly & Associates, 1996.

5 Network Hardware and Software

Networking converts a shelf full of PCs into a single system. Networking also allows a system to be accessed remotely, and to provide services to remote clients. The incredible growth of both the Internet and enterprise-specific intranets has resulted in the availability of high performance, low cost networking hardware which Beowulf systems use to create a single system from a collection of nodes. After we review networking hardware, with a particular emphasis on Fast Ethernet because of its superb price/performance ratio, we turn to the networking software options available to the Beowulf programmer, administrator and user. Networking software is usually described as a stack, made up of different protocol layers that interoperate with one another. We survey a few of the layers in the networking stack, focusing on those services and tools that are used extensively on Beowulf systems.

For Beowulf systems, the most demanding communication requirements are not with the external environment but with the other nodes on the system area network. In a Beowulf system, every Beowulf node may need to interact with every other node, independently or together, to move a wide range of data types between processors. Such data may be large blocks of contiguous information representing subpartitions of very large global data sets, small packets containing single values, or synchronization signals in support of collective operation. In the former case, a high bandwidth communication path may be required. In the latter case, low latency communication is required to expedite execution. Requirements in both cases are highly sensitive to the characteristics of the parallel program being executed. In any case, communications capability will determine the generality of the Beowulf-class system and the degree of difficulty in constructing efficient programs. The choice of network hardware and software dictate the nature of this capability.

5.1 Fast Ethernet

Beowulf was enabled by the availability of a low cost, moderate bandwidth networking technology. Ethernet, initially 10 Megabit per second (Mbps) and shortly thereafter 100 Mbps peak bandwidth, provided a cost effective means of interconnecting PCs to form an integrated cluster. Used primarily for commercial local area network (LAN) technology, Ethernet supplied the means of implementing a system area network (SAN) at about 25% the cost of the total system, even when employing low cost personal computers. While other networking was and continues to be available (and used in some Beowulfs), Ethernet has been a mainstay of many Beowulf implementations. With the very low cost of 100 Mbps Fast Ethernet and the rapid emergence of Gigabit Ethernet, it is likely to continue to play a critical role in Beowulf-class computing for some time to come. Ethernet, first developed at Xerox PARC in the early 1970s and standardized by the IEEE in the early 1980s, is the most widely used technology for local area networks. Ethernet continues to be an evolving technology. This section provides a brief overview of Ethernet technology and its operation.

Ethernet was originally developed as a packet-based, serial multi-drop network requiring no centralized control. All network access and arbitration control is performed by distributed mechanisms. Variable length message packets are made up of a sequence of bits including a header, data, and error detecting nodes. A fixed topology (no switched line routing) network passes packets from the source to destination through intermediate elements known as hubs or switches. The next step through the network is determined by addressing information in the packet header. The topology can be a shared multi-drop passive cable to which many Ethernet controllers are attached, a tree structure of hubs or switches, or some more complicated switching technology for high bandwidths and low latency under heavy loads.

5.1.1   Ethernet Arbitration

Distributed network control and access arbitration is accomplished by a technique referred to as the Carrier Sense Multiple Access with Collision Detect access protocol or CSMA/CD. Very simply, independent controllers on each Beowulf node monitor the activity of the SAN to determine when there is message traffic or when the network is available. A node that is ready to send a message packet waits for the network to be available and then initiates transmission sometime afterward. More than one node may attempt message transmission simultaneously. However, because of propagation delay time across the network, they would not see each other's packets until some short time thereafter and would be unable to avoid a conflict. The resulting collision of packets on the single shared network produces garbled data and none of the intended message traffic gets through to its destination correctly. Ethernet provides the means by which network nodes can detect the collision of packets and recover gracefully.

If two transmitting nodes detect a packet collision, each node continues to transmit briefly to ensure that all nodes see the collision and then they terminate the transmission. Each node will attempt to resend its message sometime later. The Ethernet protocol employs a random time generator algorithm that determines when the next attempt at transmission will occur. Every node that participated in the previous message packet collision is likely to attempt to retransmit at different

Preamble 1010.....1010	SYNCH 11	DESTINATION ADDRESS	SOURCE ADDRESS	TYPE	DATA	FRAME CHECK SEQUENCE
62 BITS	2 BITS	6 BYTES	6 BYTES	2 BYTES	16-1500 BYTES	4 BYTES

Figure 5.1
Ethernet Packet Format

times, thus avoiding a repetition of the same collision. Of course, other nodes could attempt to use the network medium and cause further collisions. The important aspect of the CSMA/CD approach is that there is no central controller managing network arbitration and only local knowledge is required at each node of the interconnect topology. As different entities are connected or disconnected from the network, at least at the lowest levels of network management, there need be no global update of network organization at each node. For other reasons, at a higher level, this may not be true.

5.1.2   Packet Format

The Ethernet message packet comprises a sequence of seven multi-bit fields, one of which is variable length. The fields include a combination of network control information and data payload. The structure of the Ethernet packet is shown in Figure 5.1 and is described below. The packet's variable length allows improved overall network performance across a wide range of payload requirements. Thus, a transfer of only a few words between nodes does not impose the full burden of the longest possible packet. However, even with this capability, sustained data transfer throughput is sensitive to packet length and can vary by more than an order of magnitude depending on payload size, even in the absence of network contention.

Preamble   Arrival of a message packet at a receiving node (whether or not the message is addressed for that node) is asynchronous. Prior to data assimilation, the node and the incident packet must first synchronize. The Preamble field is a 62 bit sequence of alternating 1s and 0s that allows the phase lock loop circuitry of the node receiver to lock on to the incoming signal and synchronize with the bit stream.

Synch   The Synch field is a 2 bit sequence of 1s (11) that breaks the sequence of alternating 1s and 0s provided by the Preamble and indicates where the remaining information in the packet begins. If the Preamble provides carrier-level synchronization, the Synch field provides bit field registration.

Destination Address The Destination Address field is 6 bytes (or 48 bits) in length and specifies the network designation of the network node intended to receive the packet. A message packet may be intended for an individual node or a group of nodes. If the first bit of the Destination Address field is 0, then the message is intended for a single receiving node. If the first bit is 1, then the message is multicast, intended for some or all network nodes. In the case of multicast communications, a group address is employed providing a logical association among some subset of all receiving nodes. Any node that is a member of a group specified by the message Destination Address field (with the first bit equal to 1) must accept the message. In the case of a multicast transmitted packet, a Destination Field of all 1s indicates that the packet is a broadcast message intended for all nodes on the network. Ethernet node receivers must be capable of receiving, detecting, and accepting broadcast messages.

In addition to distinguishing among single destination and multicast transmission, the Destination Address also determines whether the specified address is a globally or locally administered address. A globally administered address is one that is unique and provided by an industry wide assignment process. The address is built in to the network adaptor (interface card) by the manufacturer. A locally administered address is provided by the local systems administrator and can be changed by the organization managing the network. The second bit of the Destination Address field is a 0 if globally administered and a 1 if the address designation is locally administered. The sequence of bits of the Destination Address field is sent least significant bit first.

Source Address The Source Address is a 48 bit field that indicates the address of the transmitting node. The format of the Source Address is the same as that of the Destination Address. The Source Address is always the individual address and never a group address of the node sending a packet. Therefore the least significant bit is always 0. Likewise, the broadcast address is never used in this field.

Type The Type field is 16 bits in length and designates the message protocol type. This information is used at higher levels of message handling software and does not affect the actual exchange of data bits across the network. The most significant of the two bytes is sent first with the least significant bit of each byte of the Type field being sent first.

Data The message payload of the packet is included in the Data field. The Data field is variable length. It may have as few as 46 bytes and as many as 1500 bytes. Thus, a packet may be as small as 72 bytes or as long as 1526 bytes. The contents

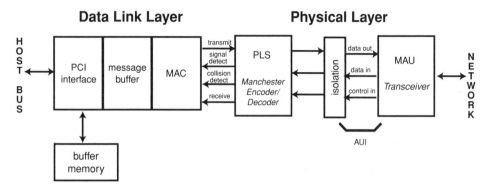

Figure 5.2
Ethernet NIC Architecture

of the data field are passed to higher level software and do no affect the network transfer control. Data is transferred least significant bit first.

Frame Check Sequence Error detection for message corruption in transmission is provided by computing a cyclic redundancy check (CRC) for the Destination Address, Source Address, Type, and Data fields. The four byte CRC value is provided as the last field of the message packet. It is computed by both the transmitting and receiving nodes and compared by the receiving node to determine that the integrity of the packet has been retained in transmission.

5.1.3 NIC Architecture

The Network Interface Controller (NIC) is a device that accepts message data from the host node processor and presents an encapsulated and encoded version of the data to the physical network medium for transmission. While there have been many different implementations of the Ethernet NIC hardware, with some enhancements, their basic architecture is the same. Figure 5.2 shows the block diagram of the typical Ethernet NIC architecture. The Data Link Layer of the architecture is responsible for constructing the message packet and controlling the logical network interface functions. The Physical Layer is responsible for encoding the message packet in a form that can actually be applied to the transmission medium.

Data Link Layer The Data Link Layer provides the logical interface between the host processor and the Physical Layer of the Ethernet. When a message is to be transmitted, the Data Link Layer accepts, temporarily stores, and encapsulates the message and controls the transmission process of the Physical Layer. When a message is being received, it accepts the packet from the Physical Layer, determines if the node is the correct destination, verifies bit integrity, unpacks the data into byte sequence, temporarily buffers the data, and passes it on to the processor. The Data Link Layer is made up of the Logical Link Control sublayer and the Media Access Control sublayer.

For most current generation Beowulf nodes, the Logical Link Control sublayer incorporates an interface to the PCI bus. This element of the Ethernet controller provides all logical control required to accept commands from the host processor and to provide direct memory access to the node main memory for rapid data transfers between memory and the network. Usually included is some form of FIFO buffering within the Data Link Layer to hold one or more incoming or outgoing messages in the node. The Logical Link Control sublayer presents variable length byte sequences to the Media Access Control sublayer and accepts data byte sequences from it. The exact form and operation of the Logical Link Control sublayer is not standardized and manufacturer differences are a source of headaches for device driver writers.

The Media Access Controller (MAC) is largely responsible for conducting the Ethernet protocol for both transmitted and received messages. Its two principle tasks are message encapsulation and packet collision handling. To transmit a message, the MAC accepts the byte sequence of the data to be sent, as well as the destination address, from the Logical Link Controller. It formats the message packet including the preamble, synch bits, destination address, its own address in the source address field, the protocol type provided by the logical link controller as well as the data field. It then computes the CRC value and appends it to the message packet. When receiving an Ethernet packet from the Physical Layer, the MAC strips away the preamble and synch bits and determines if the destination address is that of its host node. If not, the rest of the message is discarded and the receive process terminates. If the Destination Address field matches the local address, the MAC accepts the data, reformatting it into the correctly ordered byte sequence for the Logical Link Controller. The MAC computes the CRC and compares it to the value included in the message to verify transmission integrity.

The MAC is also responsible for handling the CSMA/CD low level media access arbitration protocol. The Physical Layer provides signals to the MAC indicating if there is packet transmission on the data link and if there is a collision among two or more packets on the link. When a signal is available, the MAC operates as above to determine if the message is for the host node, and if so, acquires the data. In the case of a collision, the MAC simply discards any partial incoming messages and waits for new packet data. When transmitting, the MAC is responsible for handling collision avoidance and resolution. As described above, the MAC waits for access to the data link and supplies the packet to the physical layer which begins transmission. If in the process of packet transmission the MAC receives a collision signal from the Physical Layer, after briefly continuing transmission (to overcome the network propagation delay) it terminates the message and begins its random roll-back sequence to determine a new time when it will again attempt to transmit the message.

Physical Layer   The Physical Layer (PHY) encodes the message packet provided by the Data Link Layer and converts it to electrical signals appropriate for the physical transmission medium. Upon receiving messages transmitted by other nodes, the Physical Layer acquires the electrical signals from the transmission medium, converts them to digital signals, and decodes them into the message's binary bit sequence. The PHY layer includes two major stages: the transceiver and the Physical Line Signaling (PLS) sublayer. The transceiver, also referred to as the Medium Attachment Unit (MAU) performs the electrical conversion from transmission media signals to logical signal levels.

The interface between the PLS sublayer of the Physical Layer and the MAC sublayer of the Data Link Layer exchanges data with bits represented as discrete voltage levels. This form of information representation is inadequate for Ethernet for two reasons. First, in a highly noisy (in the electrical sense) environment such as presented by a LAN, signal levels can be significantly attenuated and distorted. Second, in a single bit-serial communication protocol such as that employed by the Ethernet interconnect, both data and timing information need to be incorporated in the signal. For this reason, Manchester encoding is used to convey the information with the value of a bit specified by the sense (direction) of the signal transition rather than a specific range of values. With data fixed at the point of signal transition, the timing information is provided simultaneously.

The actual Ethernet signal is differential, that is, one line is high when the other is low and vice versa. The PLS sublayer converts the message packet provided by the MAC first into its Manchester encoded representation and then into differential form. The PLS layer performs the decoding task for incoming signals from the transceiver, converting Manchester sequences into regular bit strings. The PLS layer also provides the collision detect signal to the MAC.

5.1.4   Hubs and Switches

The Network Interface Controllers provide the connection between the processor node and the system area network. The effectiveness of the SAN and its scalability depend on the means by which the nodes are interconnected. These include passive multi-drop coaxial cable, active repeaters, and intelligent routing switches, as well as more complicated through-the-node store and forward techniques.

Repeaters and Hubs   An early advantage of Ethernet was that the medium of communication was a passive multi-drop coaxial cable. Over a limited distance and number of nodes, such a cable located all expensive logic and electronics in the NICs. As technology costs dropped and demands on network performance increased, alternative approaches could compete. Ironically, the coax cables that had helped keep costs down, became the dominant cost driver. Twisted-pair connections using inexpensive repeaters or hubs have now replaced coaxial cables in all but the oldest installations. Logically, hubs provide the same NIC interface. All nodes are visible from all other nodes and the CSMA/CD arbitration protocol is still employed. A repeater is an active unit that accepts signals from the distributed nodes on separate twisted pair wires, actively cleans up the signals, amplifies them to desired levels, and then redistributes them to all of the attached nodes.

Switches   The demand for higher sustained bandwidths and the need to include larger number of nodes on a single network spurred development of more sophisticated means of exchanging messages among nodes. Switches, like hubs or repeaters, accept packets on twisted-pair wires from the nodes. Unlike repeaters, these signals are not broadcast to all connected nodes. Instead, the destination address fields of the message packets are interpreted and the packet is sent only to the target node or nodes. This functionality is much more complicated than that of a simple repeater, requiring buffer space and logic not required by a hub. At the time of the earliest Beowulfs, the cost of switches was prohibitive. However, by the third generation of Beowulf systems (based on Intel Pentium Pro processors), the cost of switches was sufficiently low that they became standard Beowulf components.

Today, 16-way switches have dropped in price another factor of four or more, and they are the backbone of many moderate sized systems. Moderate cost switches with up to 48 connections are widely available. For greater connectivity, multiple switches can be interconnected. There is a catch, however. The network must be a tree; it may not contain any cycles.

A problem occurs with the tree topology. The bisection bandwidth of the root or top level switch becomes a communication bottleneck. All the traffic might have to go through this channel. A typical bandwidth for low cost, 16-way Fast Ethernet switches is between 1.2 Gbps and 1.6 Gbps. This is probably insufficient for a system with hundreds of nodes connected in a tree.

A new generation of switches provides much higher backplane bisection bandwidth and therefore the possibility of many more network ports. Switches with backplane bandwidths between 20 and 40 Gbps are available with moderate per port costs. The Caltech Naegling Beowulf employs a Lucent Technologies Cajun P550 switch to integrate up to 160 processors in a single system. This switch has a 45 Gbps backplane bisection bandwidth and 22 Gbps switched throughput. Several manufacturers including 3Com and Summit are competing in this market, and we expect prices to fall and performance to increase.

Auto-Negotiation   The use of smart active switches provides new opportunity for data transfer between Beowulf node NICs and the switch input ports. Auto-negotiation is a machine to machine language that allows the devices at the two ends of an interconnecting line to determine the best mode of operation. It permits full duplex operation in which a Beowulf node can both transmit and receive packets at the same time, doubling the effective bandwidth. Another feature of autonegotiation is that mixed mode systems can be created and legacy hardware can be integrated. Systems with 10 base-T, 100 base-T, and Gigabit Ethernet can be co-resident in the same system. Autonegotiation sometimes fails, and the symptom is very poor performance due to mismatched duplex assumptions. It is always possible to disable autonegotiation and manually set switches and NICs to a common configuration.

5.1.5   Gigabit Ethernet

The success of 100 base-T Fast Ethernet and the growing demands imposed on networks by high resolution image data, real-time data browsing, and Beowulf-class distributed applications has driven the industry to establish a new set of standards for Ethernet technology capable of 1 Gbps. Referred to as "Gigabit Ethernet," a backward compatible network infrastructure has been devised and early products are available from various vendors. A number of changes were required to Fast Ethernet including the physical layer and much of the data exchange protocols. However, to maintain compatibility with 100 base-T systems, means for mixed mode operation has been provided. Gigabit Ethernet is not cost effective for Beowulf-class computing yet. The early market for Gigabit Ethernet was expected to be for backbone service rather than direct terminal connections so the demand for NICs was assumed to be low and a large market has not yet emerged to amortize development costs. Both switches and NICs are substantially more expensive than 100 base-T systems.

Several factors will motivate the migration of next generation of Gigabit Ethernet into the role of SANs for Beowulf-class systems. While Fast Ethernet served well for 200 MHz Intel Pentium Pro processor based Beowulf nodes, Intel Pentium

II clock rates are more than double that and DEC Alpha processors operate at 533 MHz and higher. The PCI bus will soon support a data path twice as wide and twice the clock rate, permitting high bandwidth data transfers to peripheral devices including Gigabit NICs. A broader range of Beowulf applications can be effectively supported with higher bandwidth. The experience with Fast Ethernet demonstrated that a rapid and dramatic drop in price can be expected once the technology is adopted by the mass-market. The 1 Gbps technology is in place and experience by manufacturers is leading to rapid improvements and cost cutting. Some Beowulf installations have already experimented with Gigabit Ethernet and the Beowulf project has already delivered drivers to the Linux operating system for several Gigabit Ethernet cards.

5.2   Alternative Network Technologies

In spite of its popular use in existing Beowulfs, Ethernet-based networking is not the only technology choice for enabling inter-node communication. Other solutions exist that can deliver equal or better performance depending on the application. Fast Ethernet is a popular choice because of its ubiquity and consequent low price. A Fast Ethernet card costs only about 2% of the price of today's $1,000 Beowulf nodes. Only the network switches have a significant impact on the overall price of the system. With other networking technologies, each network interface card can cost as much as a 16-port Fast Ethernet switch. So you have to think carefully before committing to an alternative network. If the kinds of applications you intend to run require specific properties, such as low latency, which are not provided by Fast Ethernet, then it is likely worth the additional cost. For example, real-time image processing, parallel video streaming, and real-time transaction processing all require low latencies and do not work well with Fast Ethernet. We will briefly discuss the most common alternative networking technologies used by Beowulf systems. Not enough data has been collected on application performance in systems using these technologies for us to comment on when each should be used.

5.2.1   Asynchronous Transfer Mode

Asynchronous Transfer Mode (ATM) is a networking technology developed primarily by the telecommunications industry in order to consolidate both their data and voice networks. ATM is intended to support isochronous guaranteed-bandwidth data streams typical of communication channels, with the irregular traffic of typical computer applications supported only as a simple subset of the functionality.

Isochronous data is data that is sent at fixed intervals. A common example is digital voice data, where voice samples are taken at fixed intervals and delivered to the network. All ATM traffic is connection-oriented and uses small fixed-size switched cells 53 bytes long, 5 of which are headers and 48 are data. Cells have very limited addressing information and can only be passed along heavyweight pre-established connections.

ATM's long-distance communication bias is evident in its cost and design trade-offs. Despite its ability to be configured into large high-bandwidth networks, it is rarely used where cost-effective local communication is needed. In a SAN or LAN environment it is almost always more effective to over-provision with low-cost bandwidth (the Fast Ethernet approach) than to use expensive controlled bandwidth. In the WAN environment, where ATM should be an obvious choice, you are faced with the problems of converting from datagrams to a connection-oriented system.

A second issue limiting its acceptability in computer communication is its connection model. ATM networks are designed to be used only with virtual point-to-point connections, much like establishing a phone call. Every communication must be preceded by a costly "dial" phase. To minimize this overhead with typical IP traffic, the system is typically run in "IP over ATM" mode, where the ATM network provides only virtual point-to-point links. This ignores the expensive, complex parts of the switch, utilizing only the switching fabric.

5.2.2   FDDI

FDDI, Fiber Distributed Data interface, is a 100 Mbps packet network originally designed for fiber-optic links. It uses a token ring access protocol that allows slightly higher link bandwidth utilization, but results in a typically higher packet latency. Besides a larger packet size of 4500 bytes, it has few advantages over the much less expensive Fast Ethernet. FDDI gained popular use as a campus backbone network in the early '90s because it was the only technology that delivered 100 Mbps of bandwidth at the time. FDDI is sometimes used in Beowulf clusters because it can be tuned for high bandwidth or low delay around the token ring. Fast Ethernet sustained bandwidth now exceeds that of FDDI, so unless you require the low latency, it is probably a poor interconnect choice. It used to be that you would chose a token ring network when you wanted to prevent potential network starvation situations present in broadcast media, where a workstation might never gain access to the network. With high performance Fast Ethernet switches, starvation is no longer a problem.

5.2.3 Scalable Coherent Interface

The Scalable Coherent Interface (SCI) is an IEEE standard originally designed to provide an interconnect for cache-coherent shared memory systems. One of the first major deployments of SCI was on the Convex Exemplar SPP-1000 in 1994. SCI has not been able to gain ground in traditional networking markets, despite its ability to serve as a general purpose interconnect. The main reason Beowulf designers choose to use SCI is for its low latency of less than 10 microseconds. Current PC motherboard chip sets do not support the coherency mechanisms required to construct an SCI-based shared memory Beowulf. But if that functionality is ever added to commodity motherboards, we may see an increase in the popularity of SCI as researchers experiment with shared-memory Beowulf systems. Five years ago SCI delivered many clear advantages, but today commodity network technology has caught up, although SCI still delivers significantly lower latency.

5.2.4 Myrinet

Myrinet is a system area network designed by Myricom, Inc. On November 2, 1998, it was approved as American National Standard ANSI/VITA 26-1998. It is designed around simple low-latency blocking switches. The path through these switches is implemented with "header-stripping" source routing, where the sending node prepends the route through the network, and each switch remove the first byte of the message and uses it as the output port. Packets can be of arbitrary length.

The bandwidth of the adapter and switch is hidden from the application, and has regularly increased over time from the original 640 MB/s to the current 2.4 GB/s. A limitation of Myrinet is that the switches are incrementally blocking. If a destination port is busy in a multistage network, the packet is stalled and that stalled packet potentially blocks other packets traveling the network, even with unrelated source and destination nodes. This problem is mitigated by the network's high speed and the ability to construct topologies with rich interconnects. Blocking is minimized by higher density switches that reduce the number of a stages traversed by a typical message in a network of fixed size.

While Myrinet is the strongest provider of high-bandwidth SANs, it has the limitation of being provided by a single vendor. The price of the network adapters has remained high, typically exceeding the price of the entire computing node. Where Myrinet has a big advantage is customized protocols. It effectively provides a second processor that can do much of the protocol work and avoid interrupting the primary processor. The former advantage could be obtained for less money by adding a second primary processor, and the latter advantage is only significant with active messages, where the on-board processor can handle the message and generate a reply. Using customized protocols also encourages user-level access to the hardware. This can also be done with commodity hardware. Unfortunately, user-level access protocols have the disadvantage of precluding clusters from transparently scaling from standard TCP and Ethernet on small-scale machines to alternative hardware such as Myrinet on big clusters.

5.3 TCP/IP

Parallel computers have traditionally utilized special high performance interprocessor communication networks that use custom protocols to transmit data between processing elements. In contrast, Beowulf clusters rely on commodity networks whose original design goals did not include serving as the interconnect for a commodity supercomputer. The use of commodity networks implies the use of commodity protocols when you are trying to keep costs down. Thanks to the tremendous growth of the Internet during the last decade of the 20th century, TCP/IP has become the de facto standard network communication protocol. Network software vendors have been forced to abandon their proprietary networking protocols in favor of the once obscure but now ubiquitous Internet Protocol and Transmission Control Protocol. Beowulfs naturally default to communicating with these protocols.

The IP protocol is conceptually divided into different logical layers that combine to form a protocol stack. The IP stack commonly supports two services, TCP (Transmission Control Protocol) a reliable, ordered byte stream service and UDP (User Datagram Protocol) an unacknowledged datagram service.

The IP layer is a route-able datagram layer. Data to be transferred is fragmented into datagrams—individual packets of data. Packets are length-limited by the physical transport layer, and the IP layer contains the logic to fragment requests that are too large into multiple IP packets that are reassembled at the destination. Each datagram is individually route-able and contains a four byte IP address that specifies the destination host. This version of IP is called IPv4. A new version, called IPv6, will increase the address space available to IP applications. The four byte addresses used in IPv4 are too small for the total number of computers currently connected to the world's networks. This address depletion will be remedied by IPv6, which uses 16 bytes to represent host addresses.

Layered on top of IP is TCP, the most common IP service. TCP provides a reliable, sequenced byte stream service. While the underlying physical transport layer usually provides error checking, TCP provides its own final data integrity checking. Most multiple-hop physical transports provide only a best-effort delivery promise. TCP incorporates a positive-acknowledgement sliding-window retransmission mechanism that recovers from packet loss. It also tolerates latency while maintaining high performance in the normal case of no packet loss. TCP provides its own data stream packetization, avoiding fragmentation in the IP layer.

A second common service is UDP. UDP provides unsequenced, unreliable datagram transport. The advantages of UDP are that it has a relatively low latency because it incurs no start-up delay. Its primary disadvantage is that you typically have to provide retransmission services similar to those of TCP when you use UDP.

The drawbacks of TCP come from its ability to handle wide-area networks. New TCP streams utilize "slow start" to gradually detect the bandwidth limit of the network. Congestion is detected by recording dropped packets. Any corrupted or dropped packet immediately drops the offered load. The Nagel algorithm, used by TCP can cause problems for message passing libraries. In order to minimize "tinygrams" (short packets), Nagel's algorithm delays the sending of small messages until the acknowledgment for an initial small message is returned. You can avoid this behavior by either compiling the Linux kernel with an option not to use Nagel's algorithm, or by constructing your programs to use large messages.

5.3.1   IP Addresses

The destination of an Internet Protocol packet is specified by a 32 bit long IP address(or 128 bits for IPv6) that uniquely identifies the destination host. IP addresses are usually written in "dotted decimal notation," with the bytes of the address written as a decimal numbers separated by decimal points. The IP address range is divided into networks along an address bit boundary. The portion of the address that remains fixed within a network is called the network address and the remainder is the host address. The division between these two parts is specified by the netmask. A typical netmask is 255.255.255.0, which specifies a 24 bits of network address and eight bits of host addresses.

Three IP address ranges have been reserved for private networks:

- 10.0.0.0 - 10.255.255.255
- 172.16.0.0 - 172.31.255.255
- 192.168.0.0 - 192.168.255.255

These address ranges are permanently unassigned and will not be forwarded by Internet backbone routers or conflict with publicly accessible IP addresses. We will use IP addresses from the range 192.168.1.0 – 192.168.1.255 in the following examples.

In the past only a few netmasks were permitted. The netmasks were split on byte boundaries. These boundaries were given the names Class A (255.0.0.0 with about 16 million host addresses), Class B (255.255.0.0 with about 64 thousand host addresses)) and Class C (255.255.255.0 with 254 host addresses). Netmasks may now fall on any bit boundary, but are split on byte boundaries where possible. The Class names are still used when this occurs. We will use the Class C network 192.168.1.0.

Two addresses in the host address range are reserved: the addresses with all host bits 0 or 1. The host address with all bits set e.g., 192.168.1.255 is the network broadcast address. Packets sent to this address will be forwarded to every host on the network. The address with all bits unset is not a host address at all—it is the network address. Similarly when a larger network is divided into subnets the highest and lowest address ranges are best avoided. While the Class C network 192.168.0.0 is valid, starting at 192.168.1.0 is recommended. It is syntacticly possible to specify an invalid netmask—one with non-contiguous set bits. A "slash" notation is sometimes used to avoid this, e.g., 192.168.1.0/24 specifies our network of 192.168.1.0 with a netmask of 255.255.255.0.

5.3.2   Zero-copy Protocols

One way to improve network performance, especially for high performance networks, is to eliminate unnecessary copying of data between buffers in the kernel or between the kernel and user space. So-called zero-copy protocols give applications nearly direct access to the network hardware, which copies data directly to and from buffers in the application program.

Implementing true "zero-copy" TCP from user-level applications is difficult. On the transmit side the kernel must wire down the pages, so that they are not moved during the network operation, and set copy-on-write in the virtual memory system, so that there isn't a race condition with an application writing the data while it is being transferred. Transmit buffers are often quickly re-used, so the copy-on-write results in page copies rather than data buffer copies. If many small writes are done to socket, all of the data pages must be wired down until the ACK is received. After all of this kernel overhead not much work has been saved. Protocol layers must still construct the protocol headers and do the TCP checksums over the data to be transmitted.

When a frame arrives the kernel has to decide where to put it. While it is possible to only read the variable-length IP header and defer handling the data, if the user-level process isn't already waiting in a `read()` call with a large enough buffer, the system has to perform a copy. The kernel also still has to process the TCP checksum. while some of this work can be handled by a smart adapter, that just moves part of the protocol stack onto a co-processor, but does not eliminate. When the protocol stack must function with all types of network adapters, zero-copy becomes impossible because of details like byte alignment. The Ethernet header is 14 bytes, which always misaligns the IP header fields. Several research projects have developed methods for direct user-level-program access to the network because modifying the existing socket interface to use a zero-copy mechanism is very difficult. The most notable projects are the Virtual Interface Architecture (VIA) and U-Net, but neither is yet in widespread use.

5.4 Sockets

Sockets are the low-level interface between user-level programs and the operating system and hardware layers of a communication network. They provide a reasonably portable mechanism for two (or more) applications to communicate, and support a variety of addressing formats, semantics and underlying protocols. Sockets were introduced in the BSD 4.2 release of Unix, and are being formally codified by the POSIX 1003.1g Draft standard. Since its introduction, the sockets API has been widely adopted and is available on all modern Unix variants, including Linux. On Linux, the socket API is supported directly by the operating system. but research projects have proposed lower-level, so-called "zero-copy protocols" which would allow applications more direct access to the kernel. See Section 5.3.2 for more details.

The socket API is powerful but not particularly elegant. Many programmers avoid working with sockets directly, opting instead to hide the socket interface behind one or more additional layers of abstraction, e.g., remote procedure calls, or a library like MPI. Nevertheless, our survey of networking would not be complete without a brief introduction to sockets. Readers intending to program with sockets should consult both on-line, e.g., **man socket**, and printed documentation. The excellent book by Stevens[1] has many examples and thoroughly covers the finer points of sockets programming.

The basic idea behind the socket abstraction is that network communication resembles file I/O sufficiently closely that the same system calls can be used for both.

---

[1]W. Richard Stevens, Unix Network Programming, 2nd ed., Volume 1: Networking APIs: Sockets and XTI, Prentice Hall, 1997

Once a network connection is established between two processes, the transmission and receipt of data is performed with `read` and `write`, just as one sends data to a file, a tape or any other device. The socket API is primarily concerned with naming and locating communication end-points, i.e., sockets, and assigning them to file descriptors suitable for use by `read` and `write`.

A socket is created by invoking the `socket` system call with arguments specifying an address family, a socket type and a protocol. Theoretically, there are an enormous number of possible combinations, but in practice only two make up the vast majority of socket applications.

Unreliable, connectionless, datagram sockets The Internet address family, `AF_INET`, the stream socket type `SOCK_DGRAM` and the Unreliable Datagram Protocol `IPPROTO_UDP` allow one to create, connectionless, datagram sockets. These sockets allow for the transmission of a single message or datagram at a time. Neither the integrity nor the delivery of the data is guaranteed by the underlying protocol layers, so error correcting codes, sequencing and acknowledgment/retry are up to the application. A UDP socket is analogous to a conventional real-world, postal service mailbox. Many-to-one communication is the norm, i.e., one UDP socket (mailbox) can receive datagrams (letters) from multiple senders, and one-to-many communication is possible simply by addressing datagrams (letters) to different recipients. Bi-directional communication is possible if two parties regularly reply to one another's messages, but the correspondents must be aware that messages can occasionally be lost, damaged or delivered out of order. Return addresses are always available for UDP datagrams.

`SOCK_DGRAM` sockets are very lightweight, consuming only one file descriptor and demanding minimal processing in the lower levels of the protocol stack. They are small and fast, and are appropriate for tasks which can tolerate the lack of reliability and for which resource consumption may be an issue. One must carefully weigh the costs, however. If reliability is established at the application layer by means of acknowledgments, error correcting codes, etc., the speed and size advantage may disappear. Many implementations of NFS use UDP datagram sockets as the underlying transport mechanism.

Reliable, connection oriented, stream type sockets Sockets in the Internet address family, `AF_INET`, of type `SOCK_STREAM` generally use the Transmission Control Protocol `IPPROTO_TCP` and provide reliable, connection oriented virtual circuits. TCP provides a connection oriented channel like a conventional two-party telephone circuit. Once established, bi-directional communication flows between two end-points until one of them is closed. The channel is stream oriented, which means that individual messages are merged seamlessly into a continuous stream of data. The receiver gets no information about the individual `write` requests made by the sender. Data is returned to `read` requests in sequence, but without message boundary markers of any kind. Reads do not correspond to whole `writes` and it is very common for the OS to deliver only part of the data requested in a `read`, or to accept only part of the data requested by a `write`.

SOCK_STREAM sockets are very reliable. Failure usually means some kind of misconfiguration or that the remote server has crashed. Thus the burden on the programmer is greatly reduced. Occasionally, the lack of message boundaries means that the application must insert markers of some kind into the data stream, but this is far easier than overcoming the unreliability of `SOCK_DGRAM` sockets. The greatest shortcoming of `SOCK_STREAM` sockets is their resource consumption. Each open circuit requires its own file descriptor, of which there are only a finite number available, as well as kernel resources to maintain the state of the connection. Maintaining thousands of simultaneously active stream sockets would impose a significant burden on a system.

Server vs. client programming Frequently in network programs there is a clear distinction between servers and clients. Servers are programs that run more-or-less indefinitely, waiting for requests or connections that are initiated by clients. This distinction is not always so clear-cut, and the sockets API actually allows considerable flexibility in cases where the roles are blurred.

Client tasks Clients are usually much simpler than servers from a network programming perspective. The client has three basic tasks:

1. create a local socket with an otherwise unused address;
2. determine the address of the server;
3. establish a connection (TCP only); and
4. send and receive data.

Clients create sockets using the `socket` function discussed above. Since the client is usually content to let the operating system choose an unused address, there is no need to call `bind` (see below). Sending and receiving data is done with the conventional `read` and `write` system calls, or for SOCK_DGRAM sockets, the `sendto`, `sendmsg`, `recvfrom` and `recvmsg` functions may be more convenient. The only task of any complexity is identifying the address of the server. Once the server's address is known, the `connect` system call is used to establish a SOCK_STREAM channel.

Socket addresses   Addresses in the `AF_INET` family are represented by a `struct sockaddr_in`, found in the header file `<netinet/in.h>`. Internet family addresses consist of two numbers: an IP address and a port number. The IP address contains enough information to locate the host computer on the Internet using the Internet Protocol (IP). It is usually written in the familiar "dotted" notation, i.e., 131.215.145.137. In a program it is represented as a four-byte integer in network (i.e., big-endian) byte order. Obtaining the Internet address of a foreign server usually involves recourse to one or more library functions like `gethostbyname`, `inet_aton`, or the constants `INADDR_ANY`, `INADDR_LOOPBACK` defined in the the include file `<netinet/in.h>`.

The port number is a 16-bit integer that is unique for each socket end-point on a single Internet host. Servers usually "advertise" their services so that their port numbers are "well-known." There is a registry of officially recognized port numbers,[2] and the file `/etc/services` contains a partial listing of that registry which can be searched by the library utility `getservbyname`. However, for new, private or experimental services it is more common for servers and clients to simply agree on a port number in advance, e.g., by referring to a macro in a shared header file. Conventional wisdom is that such a port should be greater than 5000, less than 49152 and different from any registered port.

One final subtlety is that the `sin_port` and `sin_addr` fields in the `sockaddr_in` structure must be stored in network byte order. The functions `htonl`, `htons`, `ntohl` and `ntohs` can be used to convert long and short integers between host and network byte order. On big-endian machines (e.g., the IBM Power PC family of processors) these are no-ops, but on little-endian machines (e.g., the Intel x86 family of processors), they perform byte swapping.

Server tasks   Servers are more complicated than clients. There are a number of different design choices for servers with various tradeoffs between response time, scalability (how many clients can be supported), resource consumption, programming style and robustness. For example, one must decide between a multi-threaded server, a server that forks a new process for every connection, or a server that is invoked by the Internet daemon `inetd`. A few tasks are common to all these design choices:

1. create a local socket;
2. select a port number and make it known to clients;
3. bind the port number to the socket;

---

[2] `ftp://ftp.isi.in-notes/iana/assignments/port-numbers`

4. listen for connections (TCP only);

5. accept connections (TCP only); and

6. send and receive data.

Creating a local server socket is no different from creating a local client socket. Selecting a port number, and making it known to clients is discussed above. Once a port number is selected, the server must call `bind` to associate the address with the socket. The caller must specify a complete address, including both the port number and IP address in the `sockaddr_in` structure. Usually, the IP address is set to the constant `htonl(INADDR_ANY)`, which indicates that the socket should accept any connections (or datagrams for `SOCK_DGRAM` sockets) destined for any IP address associated with the host. (Recall that machines often have several IP addresses.) Other possibilities are `htonl(INADDR_LOOPBACK)`, or a value obtained from `gethostname`, `gethostbyname`, etc.

Communication with `recvfrom` and `sendto`   Once a `SOCK_DGRAM` socket is bound to an address, it is ready to send and receive datagrams. `Read` and `write` may be used to communicate with clients. The `recvfrom` call is particularly useful for servers because in addition to the contents of the datagram, it also supplies the caller with a return address, suitable for use in a subsequent call to `sendto`.

Listening for and accepting connections   `SOCK_STREAM` sockets, on the other hand, must take a few more steps before they are ready for use. First, they must call `listen` to inform the OS of their intention to accept connections. The `accept` system call allocates a new file descriptor which can be used with `read` and `write` to communicate with the foreign entity. In addition, `accept` supplies the caller with the address of the connecting entity.

Many of the design choices for server software architecture are concerned with the detailed behavior of `accept`. It can be made blocking or non-blocking, and upon acceptance of a connection, a new thread or process may or may not be created. Signals (including timer signals) may be used to force a premature return and `select` can be used to learn about status changes. The large number of possibilities tends to make servers much more complex than clients.

5.5   Higher Level Protocols

Sockets form the lowest layer of user-level network programming. If you go any lower, you enter the realm of driver-writing and operating system internals. Most Beowulf users don't write applications using sockets. Sockets are usually reserved for the systems programming arena, where basic client/server functions are implemented. Beowulf users depend on higher-level programming abstractions to develop applications. MPI (Message Passing Interface), discussed in Chapters 8 and 9, and PVM (Parallel Virtual Machine) are the workhorses of scientific computing on Beowulfs, providing not only platform-independent message passing semantics, but also frequently-used parallel programming constructs. These APIs are not familiar to the enterprise systems programmer first entering the world of parallel computing. Enterprise network applications are distributed systems in the truest sense of the term and are developed using higher level protocols that do not require meddling with sockets. Remote procedure calls and distributed object are the two most common programming interfaces applied in this vein; and they are equally suitable to parallel application development. If you come from a corporate computing or distributed applications development background, you will be happy to find that you can apply the same familiar software technologies to develop Beowulf applications.

5.5.1   Remote Procedure Calls

Programming with sockets is part of the client/server programming model, where all data exchange is explicitly performed with sends and receives. This model exposes the underlying transport mechanisms to the programmer and is sometimes compared to programming in assembly language. A remote procedure call (RPC) follows a different paradigm of distributed computation, removing the programmer from explicit message passing. The idea behind a remote procedure call is to make distributed programs look like sequential programs. A procedure is called inside a program, but rather than executing on the local machine, the local program suspends while the procedure executes on a remote machine. When the procedure returns, the local program wakes up, and receives any results that may have been produced by the procedure.

RPC was not designed for parallel programming so much as distributed programming. Parallel programming is a more tightly coupled concept where a single program (conceptually) works on a problem, concurrently executing on multiple processors. Distributed programming is a more loose notion where two or more programs may require services from one another, and therefore need to communicate, but they are not necessarily working on the same problem. Web browsers and web servers are examples of distributed programs. Nevertheless, RPC can be used effectively on Beowulf systems, especially for porting applications that are already designed to use it.

In principle, the remote procedure call is a simple idea that should eliminate all the complexity of explicit message passing. As always, there are some difficulties.

By invoking a remote procedure, you cause an action to be executed in a disjoint address space. This requires the caller to marshal procedure parameters, converting them to some platform independent representation to allow for a heterogeneous environment. When marshaling parameters, if the native data representation format differs significantly from the platform independent representation, buffer allocation and type conversion can be costly. In addition, procedures need to be exported through a naming service, so that they may be located and invoked. All of this additional overhead can adversely impact performance.

Two different RPC implementations are commonly found on Unix systems. The first is ONC RPC, originally known as Sun RPC, but later renamed ONC, for Open Network Computing. This is the RPC standard used by Linux and Beowulf systems. The second implementation is DCE RPC, which is the standard remote procedure call interface for The Open Group's Distributed Computing Environment. The two systems are incompatible and offer different features. The advantages of the DCE version are that it permits asynchronous procedure calls and provides a more efficient parameter conversion protocol, which bypasses network-encoding when two communicating machines share the same binary data representation format. ONC RPC only permits synchronous procedure calls and requires parameter conversion regardless of homogeneity. This makes it a less attractive candidate for writing distributed programs on Beowulf clusters, even though it is standard software.

Writing RPC programs is not without difficulty. Although they provide a conceptually familiar mechanism, the data encoding process introduces additional complexity for the programmer. Rather than simply call a procedure in your program, you must generate support code that performs data encoding and the actual network communication. ONC RPC provides a tool called `rpcgen` and a data representation format called XDR, for extended data representation, that automates this code generation. XDR provides a language specification to describe data, which you use to specify the types of parameters passed to a procedure. The `rpcgen` program then compiles your procedure definition, generating code that will encode and decode parameters. It also produces a header file that you include in your C program to reference the remote procedure. Using pregenerated procedures is rather painless because it is quite like calling normal library routines. Actually creating a remote procedure can be an involved process, requiring an understanding of XDR and `rpcgen`.

The synchronous nature of ONC RPC calls makes it unsuitable for writing general parallel programs. Synchronous calls effectively serialize your program because the calling node stops doing all work while the called node executes a procedure. Asynchronous RPC allows you to initiate independent actions on a remote node without waiting for them to complete. This maps better to parallel programming on a Beowulf, because you can tell processors to perform arbitrary work without blocking, and interprocessor coordination can be relegated to synchronous calls.

5.5.2   Distributed Objects: CORBA and Java RMI

As the software development advantages of object oriented programming languages became more popularly evident during the late '80s and early '90s, programmers saw that they could extend the concept of a remote procedure call to that of a remote object allowing remote method invocations. You could represent network services as objects distributed across a network and use method invocations to perform transactions, rather than esoteric socket-based protocols or unwieldy collections of remote procedure calls. Again, the idea was to simplify the programming model by making distributed programs appear like sequential programs—you should be able to reference objects and invoke their methods independent of their location on the network.

Distributed objects are mostly used to build corporate enterprise applications that require access to data spread out in different locations across the network. Sometimes this actually requires coordinating computation with machines in different parts of the world. A common use is to simplify the implementation of application specific network databases that can become difficult to implement using a client/server approach and SQL queries. It is much easier for a programmer to write something like the following than to pass an embedded SQL query to a vendor-specific client API.

```
EmployeeBenefits myBenefits;
EmployeeRetirementPlan myRetirement;
EmployeeID myID;
SSN mySSN;

mySSN = getSSN(); // Get my social security number from some input source
myID  = employeeIDs.getID(mySSN);           // Lookup my employee ID
myBenefits   = employeeBenefits.getBenefits(myID); // Lookup my benefits
myRetirement = myBenefits.getRetirementPlan();     // Lookup my retirement plan
```

Here the program may be accessing anywhere from one to three databases in different parts of the network, but the programmer doesn't have to be aware of that fact. In a client/server program, the programmer would have to specifically set up connections to network databases, issue queries in SQL or some other query language, and convert results into a usable form. With distributed objects, a programmer can access network resources in a transparent manner. To the programmer, employeeIDs is just another object to be used through its public methods. In reality, `employeeIDs` may represent a directory service on another machine. The `employeeBenefits` object may be a database located in yet another part of the network, and the result of the `getBenefits()` call may be a reference to an additional database. Alternatively, all of the objects may actually reside in one location as one database. The point is that the programmer doesn't have to know.

Several distributed object systems have been designed over the years, but the most promising ones for Beowulf application development are CORBA and Java RMI. Microsoft's DCOM is also a viable alternative for NT-based clusters. The Object Management Group (OMG), established in 1989, saw the need to establish a vendor independent standard for programming with distributed objects in heterogeneous systems. Their work has produced the Common Object Request Broker Architecture specification, or CORBA for short.

The foundation of CORBA programming is tied to the CORBA Interface Definition Language (IDL), with which object interfaces are defined. Even though programmers manipulate CORBA objects as native language structures, IDL defines them in a language and operating system independent manner. An IDL definition specifies the relationships between objects and their attributes. IDL definitions must be compiled with a preprocessor to generate native language code stubs with which objects are actually implemented.

The other half of the CORBA system is the Object Request Broker (ORB), of which the programmer does not have to be explicitly aware. An ORB is a server process that provides the plumbing for distributed object communication. It provides services for locating objects, translating remote method invocations into local invocations, and converting parameters to and from platform independent representations. As you can probably guess, going through an intervening daemon to perform object instantiation and method invocation sacrifices performance. However, ORBs have proven effective in providing the middleware necessary for heterogeneous distributed application development. There are many free CORBA implementations suitable for deployment on a Beowulf, as well as several commercial ones, but the fastest one and most preferred appears to be OmniORB, freely available from Olivetti & Oracle Research Laboratory.[3]

In 1995 Sun Microsystems introduced the Java programming language and runtime environment. Since then, it has gained enormous popularity and support in both industry and academia. Java's promise of platform independent "write once run everywhere" programming has made many programmers willing to put up with its growing pains and performance deficiencies. Java has been touted as an ideal

---

[3]The OmniORB home page is: `http://www.orl.co.uk/omniORB/omniORB.html`

Internet programming language, because of its platform independence, dynamic binding, mobile code properties, and built-in security model. However, to achieve all of this, Java requires significant runtime support.

Unlike programming languages like C and Pascal, Java is not compiled to assembly language native to the CPU's instruction set. Rather it is compiled to a platform independent byte-code that is interpreted by the Java Virtual Machine (JVM).[4] A JVM will often be implemented with a just-in-time compiler (JIT) that will compile the byte-code into native code on the fly at runtime to improve performance. Even with this enhancement, Java has yet to match the performance of C or C++. Nevertheless, there is a good deal of interest in using Java to program computing clusters.

Java has been used to write parallel programs from the very beginning since it has a built-in platform-independent thread API. This makes it much easier to write scalable multi-threaded applications on symmetric multiprocessors. The Java thread model only allows parallel programming in shared memory environments. Java threads cannot interact between disjoint address spaces, such as nodes in a Beowulf cluster. That is why Java includes its own distributed object API, called Remote Method Invocation (RMI).

Like CORBA, Java RMI allows the invocation of methods on remote objects. Unlike CORBA, RMI is a language intrinsic facility, built entirely in Java, and it does not require an interface definition language. RMI requires an additional server, called the Java Remote Object Registry. You can think of the RMI registry as a lightweight ORB. It allows objects to register themselves with names and for RMI programs to locate those objects. Java RMI programs are easy to write because once you obtain a reference to a named object, it operates exactly as though the object were local to your program. Beowulf users have already started using Java RMI to simulate molecular dynamics and future processor architectures. Using Java for these compute intensive tasks is ill-advised at this point in time because the performance of the Java runtimes available for Linux, and therefore most Beowulfs, at this stage trails that of other platforms. NT or Solaris based Beowulf systems will probably have more success using Java as of early 1999.

Using distributed objects for parallel programming on Beowulf is a natural way to write non-performance oriented applications where the emphasis is placed on ease of development and code maintainability. Distributed object technologies have been designed with heterogeneous networks in mind. Beowulf clusters are largely ho-

---

[4]For more information about the JVM, see the "Java Virtual Machine Specification" at http://java.sun.com/docs/

mogeneous in terms of the operating system, data representation, and executable program format. Therefore it is often the case that distributed object systems contain additional overheads that are not necessary on Beowulf clusters. In the future, we may see distributed objects tailor their implementations for high performance on Beowulf-like systems as the use of PC clusters becomes more common in corporate computing.

5.6   Distributed File Systems

Every node in a Beowulf cluster equipped with a hard drive has a local file system that processes running on other nodes may want to access. Even diskless internal nodes at least require access to the worldly node's file system so that they may boot and execute programs. The need for inter-node file system access requires Beowulf clusters to adopt one or more distributed file systems. Most distributed file systems possess the following set of characteristics that make them appear indistinguishable from the local file system.

Network Transparency Remote files can be accessed using the same operations or system calls that are used to access local files.

Location Transparency The name of a file is not bound to its network location. The location of the file server host is not an intrinsic part of the file path.

Location Independence When the physical location of a file changes, its name is not forced to change. The name of the file server host is not an intrinsic part of the file path.

5.6.1   NFS

Beowulf clusters almost always use the Network File System (NFS) protocol to provide distributed file system services. NFS started its steady climb in popularity in 1985, after Sun Microsystems published the protocol specification for adoption as an open standard. This version of the protocol, NFS version 2 (NFSv2), has been widely adopted by every major version of the Unix operating system. A later revision of the protocol, NFSv3, was published in 1993, and has been implemented by several vendors, but as of early 1999, it is not supported as standard Linux software. The standard Linux NFS software still conforms to the NFSv2 specification.

   NFS is structured as a client/server architecture, using RPC calls to communicate between clients and servers. The server exports files to clients which access the files as though they were local files. Unlike other protocols, an NFS server is stateless, meaning it doesn't save any information about a client between requests. This means that all client requests are considered independently and must therefore contain all the information necessary for execution. All NFS read and write requests must include file offsets, unlike local file reads and writes which proceed from where the last one left off. The stateless nature of the NFS server causes messages to be larger, potentially consuming network bandwidth. The advantage of statelessness is that the server is not affected when a client crashes. The best way to configure NFS on a Beowulf system is to minimize the number of mount points, set the read and write buffer sizes to the maximum allowable values (8192 bytes), and use the autofs daemon discussed later in this section. You can set the buffer sizes using the `rsize` and `wsize` options for the NFS file systems listed `/etc/fstab`. A typical `fstab` entry for mounting `/home` may look like the following:

```
b001:/home  /home nfs  rw,hard,intr,bg,rsize=8192,wsize=8192 0 0
```

The original Linux NFS implementation only allowed a single NFS server to run at a time. This presented severe scaling problems for Beowulf clusters, where many internal nodes would mount home directories and other file systems from the worldly node. A single NFS server would serialize all network file system accesses, creating a severe bottleneck for disk writes. Disk reads were not as adversely impacted because the clients would cache files locally. More recent versions of the Linux NFS implementation allowed multiple servers operating in read-only mode. While this was useful for certain LAN applications, where workstations might mount read-only `/usr/` partitions, it was not of such great benefit to Beowulf clusters, where internal nodes frequently require NFS for performing disk writes. The very latest versions of the Linux NFS code released in 1998, starting with version 2.2beta32, have added support for multiple servers in read/write mode. This new functionality has not yet been extensively tested, and the performance gains not fully quantified. However, it is expected that this addition will increase the scalability of NFS as used in Beowulf clusters.

5.6.2   AFS

The Andrew File System (AFS) was originally developed at Carnegie Mellon University as a joint venture with IBM in the mid-80s. Its purpose was to overcome the scaling problems of other network file systems such as NFS. AFS proved to be able to reduce CPU usage and network traffic while still delivering efficient file system access for larger numbers of clients. In 1989, development of AFS was transferred to Transarc Corporation, who evolved AFS into the Distributed File System

(DFS) included as part of the Distributed Computing Environment (DCE). AFS effectively became a proprietary technology before Linux was developed, so AFS never played much of a role in the design of Beowulf systems. Recently, however, AFS-based file systems have become available for Linux, and a new interest in this network file system has emerged in the Beowulf community. The inability of NFS to effectively scale to systems containing on the order of 100 processors has motivated this experimentation with more scalable file system architectures. However, improvements have been made in the Linux NFS code which may obviate the need to explore alternative network file systems.

5.6.3   Autofs: The Automounter

As you add more nodes to a Beowulf, the startup time of the system can increase dramatically because of contention for the NFS server on the worldly node that exports home directories to the rest of the system. NFS is implemented using ONC RPC, which only supports synchronous RPC calls. Therefore the NFS server becomes a single bottleneck through which the other systems must pass, one at a time. This phenomenon was a problem on local area networks until Sun Microsystems developed an automounting mechanism for NFS. The Linux version of this mechanism is the autofs service. Autofs only mounts NFS partitions when they are first accessed, rather than automatically at startup. If the NFS partition is not accessed for a configurable period of time (typically 5 minutes), autofs will unmount it. By using autofs, you can reduce system startup times as well as reduce overall system load.

5.7   Remote Command Execution

5.7.1   BSD R Commands

The BSD R commands are a set of programs that first appeared in 4.2BSD to execute commands and copy files on remote machines. The major commands are:

rsh The remote shell allows you to execute shell commands on remote nodes and also initiate interactive login sessions. Interactive login sessions are initiated by invoking `rlogin`.

rlogin The remote login command allows you to start a terminal session by logging in to a remote node.

rcp Allows the copying of files from one node to the other.

The `rsh` command is the standard way of executing commands and starting parallel applications on other nodes. A lot of system software, including the PVM and MPI libraries, relies heavily on `rsh` for remote command execution. `rsh` requires that an `rsh` server (`/usr/sbin/in.rshd` on most Linux systems) run on the remote node. The `rsh` program connects to the server, which then checks that the client's originating port is a privileged port before taking any further action. On Unix systems, only processes with root privileges may open privileged ports between 1 and 1024. The `rsh` check is a historical artifact dating from the days when you could be reasonably sure a connection originating from a privileged port could be trusted on that basis alone. After performing the check, the server compares the client's host address against a file called `/etc/hosts.equiv` which contains a list of trusted hosts. Connections originating from trusted hosts do not require a password to be granted system access. If the host is not in `/etc/hosts.equiv`, the server checks the home directory of the user with the same user id as the user originating the connection for a file called `.rhosts`. The `.rhosts` file can contain a list of hosts from which a user can connect without entering a password. It is like `hosts.equiv`, but checked on a user basis rather than a global basis. If the host is not found in `.rhosts`, then the user is challenged for a password in order to execute the remote command. The `rsh` command is extremely useful for performing system administration tasks, and launching parallel applications. However, it only allows the execution of a command on one other node. Many times you will want to execute a command on multiple nodes at a time. Typically, Beowulf users will write shell scripts that spawn multiple copies of `rsh` to do this work. We present one such script, called `prsh` in Section 6.4.4.

5.7.2   SSH—The Secure Shell

The secure shell, SSH, is a set of security conscious drop-in replacements for the BSD `rsh`, `rlogin`, and `rcp` commands. The SSH counterparts are `ssh`, `slogin`, and `scp`. The main problem with the BSD R commands is that they transmit passwords across the network in plain text, which makes it extremely easy to steal passwords. In addition, the use of `.rhosts` files tends be a weak point in system security. Yet another problem is that the R commands have to be installed as suid root because they must open privileged ports on the client node. The R commands are more than adequate to use in an ostensibly secure environment, such as the internal nodes of a guarded Beowulf system (see Section 6.1.3), which are normally configured with their own private network. However, nodes exposed to the external world should only be allowed access via a secure mechanism such as SSH.

SSH is a commercial product developed by SSH Communications Security, Ltd., which offers both Win32 and Unix versions. The Unix version is available as open source software and can be downloaded from `http://www.ssh.fi/` with precompiled binaries available at many sites. SSH encrypts all network communication, including passwords, and uses a public key based authentication system to verify host and user identities. Many Beowulf systems install SSH as standard system software, a practice we strongly recommend. Eventually, the use of `rsh` will have to be discarded because of its reliance on a fundamentally insecure authentication model. `Rsh` also makes poor use of the limited number of privileged ports between 512 and 1024, using two of them for every connection that maintains a standard error stream. Thus, the worldly node of a Beowulf with 32 internal nodes and 4 users executing commands on all nodes would have its allowable `rsh` connections maxed out. Even if the additional security is unnecessary, SSH should be used to keep from running out of privileged ports.

6 Managing Ensembles

If building a Beowulf only involved assembling nodes, installing software on each one, and connecting the nodes to each other with a network, this book would end right here. But as you may have guessed, there is more to building a Beowulf than just those things. Once you have assembled a Beowulf, you have to keep it running, maintain software, add and remove user accounts, organize the file system layout, and perform countless other tasks that fall under the heading of system management. Some of these management tasks are very similar to those of traditional LAN administration, about which entire books have been written. But the rules have not yet been fully established for Beowulf system administration. It is still something of a black art, requiring not only familiarity with traditional LAN management concepts, but also some parallel programming skills and a creative ability to adapt workstation and LAN software to the Beowulf environment. This chapter attempts to describe some of the more common approaches applied by practitioners of this evolving craft as well as present some alternative procedures that have not yet become common practice.

Even though both corporate LANs and Beowulf systems are composed of collections of networked PCs, they differ significantly in terms of their installation, use, maintenance, and overall management. A LAN is usually formed from a loosely coupled heterogeneous collection of computers that share disk and printing resources, in addition to some network services, such as web and database servers. A Beowulf cluster is a more tightly coupled collection of computers where the majority of components are identically configured and collectively operate as a single machine.

6.1 System Access Models

Before assigning IP addresses to Beowulf nodes, designing the network topology, and booting the machine, you need to decide how the system will be accessed. System access literally refers to how a user can log in to a system and use the machine. Allowable system access modes relate directly to how you configure your system both logically and physically. There are three principal schemes for permitting user access to Beowulf machines, the first of which is seldom used.

6.1.1 The Stand-alone System

The most basic way of configuring a Beowulf is to set it up as a stand-alone system unattached to any external networks. This design requires a user to be in the same room as the Beowulf, sitting at its front-end keyboard and monitor to write and execute programs. The only times this is usually done are when first assembling the system and also when upgrading or debugging the system. Certain high-security environments may require that a system be configured in this manner, but the utility of the system becomes limited when the system cannot be accessed over an external network. Institutions which decide to configure a Beowulf in this manner should include multiple front-end nodes, so that multiple users may simultaneously use the machine. When a system is configured in this manner, it is not necessary to pay any special attention to the IP addresses used. Any valid set of network addresses will do, but it is advisable to use the reserved address ranges mentioned in Chapter 5.

6.1.2   The Universally Accessible Machine

At the opposite end of the spectrum from the stand-alone configuration lies the universally accessible machine. In this configuration, each system node draws its IP address from the pool of addresses assigned to an organization. This allows internal nodes to be directly accessible by outside connection requests. In other words, every node is accessible from the entire Internet. The primary negative aspect of this configuration is that it greatly increases management tasks associated with security. It also unnecessarily consumes a large quantity of IP addresses that could otherwise be used by your organization's local area network. If your local area network already sits behind a firewall and uses a reserved address range, then this may be an appropriate configuration, allowing access to any node from any machine on your LAN. Also, some applications such as web and database load balancing servers, may require exposing all nodes to the external network. However, you will have to take care in arranging your network switches and associated connections so as to prevent LAN traffic congestion from interfering with Beowulf system traffic. In addition, if you choose to add multiple network interfaces to each node, you should probably not attach them to the external network.

6.1.3   The Guarded Beowulf

Somewhere in between the first two configurations stands the guarded Beowulf, which is probably the most commonly used configuration. The guarded Beowulf assigns reserved IP addresses to all of its internal nodes, even when using multiple networks. To communicate with the outside world, a single front-end, called a "worldly node," is given an extra network interface with an IP address from the organization's local area network. Sometimes more than one worldly node is provided. But in all cases, to access the rest of the system, a user must first log in to a worldly node. The benefit of this approach is that you don't consume precious organizational IP addresses and you constrain system access to a limited number of controllable access points, facilitating overall system management and security policy implementation. The disadvantage is that it is not possible for internal nodes to access the external network. But that can be remedied by using IP masquerading which will be discussed later. For increased security, it is often desirable to place the worldly nodes behind a firewall. In the rest of this chapter, we will use the Guarded Beowulf as the canonical example system unless explicitly stated otherwise.

6.2 Assigning Names

Beowulf system components need to communicate with each other, and for inter-component communication to be possible, each component, or node, requires a unique name. For the purposes of this chapter, node naming refers to both the assignment of IP addresses and hostnames. Naming workstations on a LAN can often be quite arbitrary, except that sometimes segmentation of the network restricts the IP addresses available to a set of workstations located on a particular segment. Naming Beowulf nodes requires a bit more thought and care.

Beowulf clusters communicate internally over one or more private system area networks. One (or perhaps more, for redundancy and performance) of the nodes has an additional network connection to the outside. These nodes are referred to as worldly nodes to distinguish them from internal nodes, which are connected only to the private cluster network. Because the internal nodes are not directly connected to the outside, they can use the reserved IP addresses discussed in Chapter 5. Specifically, most clusters assign their worldly node to address 192.168.1.1, and assign internal nodes sequentially to addresses in the range 192.168.1.2 to 192.168.1.253. The worldly node will always have a second network interface, possessing a routeable IP address that provides connectivity to the organizational LAN.

From long experience, we have found that internal hostnames should be trivial. Most Beowulf clusters have assigned very simple internal hostnames of the format <cluster-letter><node-number>. For instance the first Beowulf named its nodes using simply the letter b as a prefix, but made the mistake of calling its first node b0. While it is natural for those steeped in the long-standing computer science tradition of starting indices at zero, it is better to map the numbers contained in hostnames directly to the last octet of the node IP address. For example, 198.168.1.1 becomes node b1, 198.168.1.2 becomes b2, etc. As you can see, there can be no b0 node, because 198.168.1.0 is a network number, and not a host address.

Directly mapping the numbers starting from 1 facilitates the writing of custom system utilities, diagnostic tools, and other short programs usually implemented as shell scripts. If you plan on having more than 9 nodes in your system, it might be desirable to name all of your nodes using 2 digits. For example, b1 becomes b01 and b2 becomes b02. Similarly, for systems with more than 99 nodes, b1 should become b001 and b10 should become b010.

When physically administrating a cluster, it is often necessary to know the MAC addresses of the network cards in nodes, as well as their names and IP addresses. The simplest reason is that when something goes wrong with a node you have to walk into the machine room and diagnose the problem, often simply rebooting the culprit node. For this reason, it is recommended that you label each node with its hostname, IP address, and the MAC addresses of the network interface cards. If you use a consistent IP address to hostname mapping, you can get by with just labeling the nodes with their names and MAC addresses. MAC addresses go in the bootptab (see Section 6.3.3), so you will want to record them when you install the NICs into their cases. If you forgot to do this, the ifconfig command will report the MAC address of configured controllers. For small systems labelling of nodes is largely superfluous, but for larger numbers of nodes, this simple measure could save you many hours.

6.2.1   Dynamically Assigned Addresses

So far we have discussed naming nodes with statically assigned addresses. Every time a node is booted, it obtains its hostname and IP address from its local configuration files. It is not always necessary to configure your system this way. If all of your internal nodes have identical software images, there is no reason why they necessarily require fixed IP addresses and hostnames. It is possible to configure a system so that every time an internal node boots, it receives an IP address from a pool of available addresses. Worldly nodes need to continue using fixed IP addresses because they provide resources to internal nodes that must be accessed through a known host address. The advantage of using dynamically assigned addresses is that internal nodes become completely interchangeable, facilitating certain system maintenance procedures. If you decide to convert your universally accessible machine to a guarded Beowulf, all you have to do is change the IP addresses in the DHCP or BOOTP server's configuration files, rather than update config files on every single node. The downside of dynamic addressing is that unless you take proper precautions it can become difficult to determine what physical box in the machine room corresponds to a specific name. This is where the suggested labeling of nodes with MAC addresses described above comes in handy. If you know the

MAC address of a misbehaving node, you can find it by visually scanning the labels. All in all, it is easier if the mapping between MAC addresses, hostnames and IP addresses changes as infrequently as possible.

6.3   Cloning Nodes

After choosing a configuration scheme, the next step in turning your mass of machines into a Beowulf is to install an operating system and standard software on all of the nodes. This can be a daunting task for even a small system containing only 8 nodes. After reading Chapter 4, you should be familiar with how to install Linux on a single machine. In practice, you do not want to go through that entire procedure dozens of times. Fortunately, you can install one internal node, and clone the remaining nodes.

The internal nodes of a Beowulf cluster are almost always identically configured. The hardware can be slightly different, incorporating different generation processors, disks, and network interface cards. But the file system layout, kernel version, and installed software are the same. Only the worldly node exhibits differences, as it generally serves as the repository of user home directories and centralized software installations exported via NFS.

In general, you will install the operating system and extra support software on the worldly node first. Then you will configure a single internal node, and clone the rest from it. This way you only have to configure two systems. Aside from saving time up front, cloning also facilitates major system upgrades. You may decide to completely change the software configuration of your internal nodes, requiring an update to all of the nodes. By cloning internal nodes, you only have to go through the reconfiguration process for one machine. In addition, cloning makes it easier to recover from certain unexpected events like disk failures or accidental file system corruption. All you have to do is install a new disk (in the case of a disk failure) and reclone the node.

At the moment, there are no standard software distributions for node cloning. Most Beowulf sites either write their own software, or borrow it from colleagues, but most of the software follows the basic procedure we are about to describe. Node cloning relies on the BOOTP protocol discussed in the previous section to provide a node with an IP address and a root file system for the duration of the cloning procedure. In brief, the following steps are involved:

1. Manually configure a single internal node.
2. Create tar files for each partition.

3. Set up a clone root directory on the worldly node.
4. Configure bootp on the worldly node.
5. Install a special init script in the clone root directory on the worldly node.
6. Create a boot disk with an NFSROOT kernel.

The basic premise behind the cloning procedure is for the new node to mount a root file system over NFS, which contains the cloning support programs, configuration files, and partition archives. When the Linux kernel finishes loading, it looks for a program called `/sbin/init`, which executes system initialization scripts and puts the system into multiuser mode. The cloning procedure replaces the standard `/sbin/init` with a program that partitions the hard drives, untars partition archives, and executes any custom cloning configuration scripts before rebooting the newly cloned system.

6.3.1   Creating Tar Images

To get ready for cloning you have to configure an initial internal node. How you configure it will depend on how you intend to use your Beowulf. But you will more than likely install the basic operating system and network clients like the NFS automounter. Whether or not you install a full set of compilers and message passing libraries is up to you, but in general, development tools are not duplicated across internal nodes and normally reside on the worldly node.

After configuring the internal node, you need to make an archive of each disk partition, omitting `/proc`, which is not a physical disk partition. Some cloning software may provide a front-end that asks you some questions and automatically archives each partition for you. But most of the time you will have to take care of it yourself. The normal procedure is to change your current working directory to the partition mount point and using the tar command like:

```
tar zlcf /worldly/nfsroot/partition-name.tgz .
```

The `l` option tells the `tar` command to only archive files in directories stored on the local partition, avoiding files in directories that serve as mount points for other partitions. A potential pitfall of this archiving method is that you may not have enough room on the local disk to store the partitions. Rather than create them locally, you should store the tar file on an NFS partition on the worldly node. Ultimately, you will have to transfer the files to the worldly node, so you might as well do it all in one step.

6.3.2   Setting up a Clone Root Partition

Now you need to create a root directory for cloning on the worldly node. This should be exported via NFS to the internal node network. The directory should contain the following subdirectories: `bin, dev, etc, lib, mnt, proc, sbin, tmp`. The `proc` and `mnt` directories must be empty, as they will be used as mount points during the cloning process. The `dev` directory must contain all the standard Linux device files. Device files are special, and cannot be copied normally. The easiest way to create this directory is by letting tar do the work for you by executing the following command as root:

```
tar -C / -c -f - dev | tar xf -
```

This will create a `dev` directory containing all the device files found on your system. All the remaining directories can be copied normally, except for `tmp` and `etc` which should be empty. You should have no need for a `usr` directory tree. It is possible to trim down the files to the bare minimum necessary for cloning, but it isn't necessary. You will need to add an `fstab` file to `etc` containing only the following line, so that the `/proc` file system may be mounted properly:

```
none    /proc    proc    default    0 0
```

You also may need to include a `hosts` file.

   Once you have your NFS root file system in place, move the partition archives to the root file system. Depending on the specific cloning software you are using, you may have to create a special directory to store these files. If you are writing your own cloning scripts, place the archives in a sensible location for your scripts. Then replace the NFS root `sbin/init` executable with your cloning init script. This script will be invoked by the clone node's kernel to launch the cloning process. Tasks performed by the script include drive partitioning, archive extraction, and configuration file tweaking. Some configuration files have to be tweaked if your nodes aren't set up to configure themselves through DHCP or BOOTP. The primary configuration files are ones dependent on the node IP address, such as `/etc/sysconfig/network` and `/etc/sysconfig/network-scripts/ifcfg-eth0` on Red Hat based systems. At this point you can add the NFS root directory to the list of exported file systems, making sure to export it only to your internal node network.

6.3.3   Setting up BOOTP

Next you have to decide what IP addresses the cloned nodes will use during the cloning process. These should probably be the same ones they will use after the cloning process, unless you are using DHCP to provide dynamic addresses. Once you select the IP addresses, you can create a `bootptab` file and enable the `bootpd` daemon on the worldly node. The `bootptab` file must include a root path entry for the NFS exported root directory. You specify this with the `rp` option, as in the example below.

BOOTP[1] was originally devised to allow the booting of diskless clients over a network. To provide this service, the BOOTP daemon makes available the name of a directory on the server containing a boot kernel, the name of the kernel file, and the name of a root directory structure exported via NFS that the diskless client can mount. As a more fundamental service, BOOTP provides a mapping between a hardware address and an IP address. A BOOTP client needs to fetch an IP address before making use of any additional information so that it may speak to NFS or other servers referenced by the configuration information.

The diskless client boot sequence involves obtaining an IP address, establishing a TFTP connection to the boot server and fetching a kernel, loading the kernel, and mounting an NFS exported directory as a root file system. Since a diskless client has no installed software, so you may wonder how it can even initiate this boot sequence. It may have some ROM-based facility for operating without a hard disk, or in the absence of EPROM NICs, a node may have some custom program it runs from a floppy disk or small hard drive. This may be a simple boot loader that duplicates a boot PROM, or an operating system kernel without any file system.

In most Beowulf clusters, a node almost always has an entirely local copy of the operating system and file system, and runs a BOOTP client only to retrieve its identity. The BOOTP software distributed with Linux is well-documented, so we won't describe it in length. To activate the BOOTP daemon, you should only have to create an `/etc/bootptab` configuration file, uncomment the line in `/etc/inetd.conf` (see Chapter 4) that invokes `bootpd`, and restart the `inetd` server on the BOOTP server, i.e., the worldly node. The `bootptab` file tells `bootpd` how to map hardware addresses to IP addresses and hostnames. It will look something like the example shown in Program 6.1

The `.default` entry is a macro defining a set of options common to all of the entries. Each entry includes these default options by including `tc=.default`. The other entries are simply hostnames followed by IP addresses and hardware addresses. Even though BOOTP can be used to boot diskless nodes, we only use it to assign IP addresses.

---

[1]"Bootstrap Protocol (BOOTP)," Internet Engineering Task Force RFC 951, `http://info.internet.isi.edu/in-notes/rfc/files/rfc951.txt`

```
.default:\
        :sm=255.255.255.0:\
        :ht=ether:\
        :gw=192.168.1.1:\
        :rp=/export/nfsroot/:
b002:ip=192.168.1.2:ha=0080c8638a2c:tc=.default
b003:ip=192.168.1.3:ha=0080c86359d9:tc=.default
b004:ip=192.168.1.4:ha=0080c86795c8:tc=.default
```

Program 6.1: Sample bootptab for a system with three nodes, b002, b003 and b004.

After making it to this final point, everything should be in place on the server to start the clone process. All that remains is to create a boot floppy that will launch the cloning process on the client.

6.3.4   Building a Boot Clone Floppy

Building a boot disk is yet another instance of Beowulf administration that requires familiarity with compiling the Linux kernel. This is because the boot disk does not actually perform the node cloning, but bootstraps the cloning procedure by talking to a bootp server to get an IP address and mount a root file system over the network. The default kernel you may have installed more than likely does not have this capability built-in. It is necessary to build a kernel with these abilities, commonly called an NFSROOT kernel because it mounts a root file system over NFS. The CACR Beowulf cloning software[2] contains a pre-built NFSROOT kernel, but it cannot be guaranteed to work with your system. The problem is that not all network drivers can be compiled into the kernel, and some even conflict with each other. Therefore, it is possible that the network drivers required by your system are not contained in our pre-built kernel.

If you are not already familiar with how to compile the Linux kernel, you can learn more about it from one of the suggested references listed in Section 4.10 or you can jump right into it after reading the instructions in the README file distributed with the kernel source, usually in **/usr/src/linux**. When you compile the kernel for a clone floppy, you must make sure that NFS root file system support is enabled.

In addition, include the network drivers for the interface cards you are using. Once compiled, the kernel will be stored in a file called **zImage** or **bzImage** depending on what compression option you use. If you use this unaltered kernel to create a

---

[2]The   CACR   Beowulf   node   cloning   software   can   be   downloaded   from http://www.cacr.caltech.edu/beowulf/.

boot floppy, it will still try to mount a local partition as the root file system. There is some black magic involved to make it boot using the NFS directory obtained via the BOOTP. The root device used by a kernel is stored in the kernel image and can be altered with the `rdev` program, usually located in `/usr/sbin`. You want the root device to be the NFS file system, but no device file exists for this purpose, so you have to create one. You can do this with the following command:

```
mknod /dev/nfsroot b 0 255
```

This creates a dummy block device with special major and minor device numbers that have special meaning to the Linux kernel. This interprets the device as an NFS root file system when set as a root device with:

```
rdev zImage /dev/nfsroot
```

Now that the kernel's root device is set to be mounted via NFS, you can write the kernel to a floppy with the `dd` command:

```
dd if=zImage of=/dev/fd0 bs=512
```

After creating your first clone disk, you should test it on a node and make sure everything works. After this test, you can duplicate the floppy and clone all of your nodes at once. This is a little inconvenient for systems with more than 16 nodes. Instead, you could make 16 floppies, and clone your nodes 16 at a time. Yet another option, if you have network interface cards with PROMs, is to not create a boot floppy. Instead, you can put the kernel in a directory accessible by TFTP and use BOOTP to boot the nodes with a cloning kernel. After your system is up and running, you don't have to mess with clone floppies if you don't want to. You can clone nodes that already have an active operating system, by installing a clone kernel and rebooting. This can even be done by logging into the machine remotely.

6.4   Basic System Administration

Simply getting a cluster up and running can be a challenging endeavor. Once you've done it for the first time, it won't seem so difficult anymore. For your first cluster, it will probably be a lot easier to skip the cloning process. You can go ahead and install identical software from scratch on all of your nodes, including your worldly node. After you get a feel for how you are using the system, you can fine tune it by removing nonessential software from internal nodes and setting up a node cloning system.

6.4.1   Booting and Shutting Down

Perhaps the most inelegant feature of a Beowulf cluster is how you turn it on and turn it off. There is no master switch you can flip to turn on the entire system. Unless you assemble some hardware to power up the system with one flick of the hand (and some people have), you will have to walk by each node and press a button. This isn't so bad for smaller systems, but can become time consuming for larger clusters. Unfortunately, there isn't an inexpensive way to get around this. Shutting down the system is very similar. First you need to shutdown the operating system on each node, and then power down each node. Shutting down the OS on each node isn't too hard. You can do this with the `prsh` command described in Chapter 5. Just tell it to execute the following shutdown command, or some variation thereof on each node:

```
/sbin/shutdown -h now
```

If your Beowulf nodes are equipped with ATX power supplies, you can avoid walking over to the machine room and turning each node off by hand. Rather, you can pass the -p option to `shutdown`, which will power off the nodes for you after the shutdown completes. Rarely will you ever have to completely shutdown and turn off a Beowulf cluster. Once you have turned the machine on, you will likely never turn it off, except for the few nodes that eventually suffer hardware failures or software bugs. It is not uncommon for Beowulfs to go several months without a forced reboot. Some systems are used to run applications that take several weeks to complete, so you should make sure that any such applications either have completed or have been checkpointed before rebooting the system.

6.4.2   The Node File System

The Linux operating system follows a convention called the Linux File system Hierarchy Standard.[3] Beowulf nodes by default follow the same convention with one or two twists. The main consideration in deciding how to set up node file systems isn't so much how to organize the directory structure, but rather how to partition the disks and what mount points to use for each partition. The primary partitions usually correspond to the following directories:

---

[3]The Linux FHS was formerly known as the Linux File System Standard (FSSTND). The latest version of the Linux FHS as well as the older FSSTND, are published at: http://www.pathname.com/fhs/

/ The root partition, containing system configuration and log files.

/boot An optional partition for storing kernel images. /boot is often just a regular directory in the root partition.

/home A partition containing all user directories.

/opt An optional partition for additional software.

/usr A partition containing all standard system software.

/scratch A partition used as scratch space for large temporary data files. For nodes with a very large disk or multiple disks it is common to have several scratch partitions, named scratch1, scratch2, and so on.

Invariably, you will want to locate user directories in /home on the worldly node and export /home to the internal nodes. If you have many users, you will probably need multiple disks and partitions to store all the home directories. Users who do not want to work out of their home directories on each node (perhaps they have certain parallel I/O needs) should store data on the internal node scratch partitions. Sometimes Beowulf systems are configured so that every node has access to every other node's file system. This technique, called "crossmounting," crossmounting can be very useful, as it allows internode resource access through a global namespace—the file system. If you decide to do this, you should use the autofs utility, discussed in Chapter 5, to mount the file systems on demand. Autofs will mount network file systems only when accessed, and will unmount them if they are not accessed for some period of time. This helps reduce node resource usage as well as overall network load.

If you are short on internal node disk space, you may want to have all of your internal nodes mount their /usr partitions from the worldly node. Most Linux distributions, including Red Hat, follow the Linux FHS guideline that no host dependent software be installed in /usr directory structure. Therefore, the contents of /usr can be safely shared across all nodes. The critical problem with this approach is not so much that it creates a single point of failure (the NFS server), but rather that it pollutes the network with extra traffic every time programs are loaded or configuration files are read from /usr. One method for dealing with this is to create a second physical network for system software related traffic, which will mostly result from NFS and rsh. Then reserve the first network only for user applications. Another way is to segment your Beowulf into multiple packs of nodes, where each pack contains a specially designated node that contains a local /usr partition that it exports to the rest of the pack. However, this means all of your internal nodes will no longer be identically configured. The most common arrangement is for every node to have a full local copy of /usr, especially now that hard drive storage capacities are so large and the prices so low. A typical /usr partition will consume about 5% of a 10 GB hard drive.

6.4.3 Account Management

User account management is generally handled in one of two ways. The first is to assign an account to a user on the worldly node, and then copy the /etc/passwd file to every node. The second is to configure your internal nodes to use NIS or NIS+ for user authentication. This requires you to only configure accounts on the worldly node, which should be the home of the NIS server. Each method has advantages and disadvantages which we will mention shortly. In both cases, setting up the account on the worldly node works the same way. You can either use the useradd command, which supersedes the older adduser command (this may be a symbolic link to useradd on some systems), or one of the emerging Linux system administration tools such as linuxconf. These commands will create a home directory for the new user containing system default config files and will create an entry in /etc/passwd storing the user's encrypted password, home directory location, and shell.

After creating an account for a new user on the worldly node, you have to provide some means for the internal nodes to access the user data for authentication. The most commonly implemented method is to simply copy the /etc/passwd file to all the internal nodes, usually using one of rdist, rcp, or prsh. You will also have to replicate /etc/group which will have also changed with the addition of the new user. More often than not, several people will have account granting privileges on your system, so you have to make sure to avoid attempting simultaneous updates. This should not be a problem as long as you do not develop a habit of manually editing the password and group files. User accounts should be removed with either userdel or deluser and groups should be removed with groupdel. But you will also have to update the password and group files on the internal nodes the way you did when you added the user.

The alternative method of managing user accounts is to use a directory service, such as NIS, to store user account information. This makes system administration a lot easier, since you only have to worry about one point of control for account management. As discussed in Chapter 5, NIS stores all directory data in a central server, which is contacted by clients to perform authentication. This has the side-effect of generating extra network traffic every time you log in to a Beowulf node. The node must contact the server to verify you are a valid user and also check your

password before allowing you to log in. The ultimate effect is to greatly slow down
parallel application launching. For this reason, many Beowulf sites forego NIS for
distributing account information.

6.4.4   PRSH—Parallel Remote Shell

Throughout the course of managing a Beowulf cluster, you will encounter an endless
number of tasks that will require you to execute a command on multiple nodes at a
time. It is possible to use rsh as the basis for a parallel remote command execution
facility. One of the authors has done just that by writing the **prsh** command.
The motivation for such a command is that you often have to kill a process on
some set of nodes, list files on a set of nodes, and generally execute any arbitrary
command on a set of nodes. Rather than create a pkill, pls, and p version of every
command, you only need a **prsh**, which will execute any command on any number
of nodes. For convenience it is possible to wrap this command with shell scripts
named pkill, pls, etc., that will execute the appropriate command on many nodes.
Alternatively, you could create symbolic links to the command and modify **prsh** to
execute a given command on multiple nodes based on the name under which **prsh**
is invoked. It is likely that future versions of **prsh** will include these features.[4] We
list the **prsh** man page so that you can get a better idea of how to use it.

NAME
prsh — An asynchronous, parallel rsh

SYNOPSIS
prsh [–debug] [–rsh-cmd word] [–ssh] [–prepend] [–timeout sec] [–nokill] [–
status] [–login-shell] [–help] [hostname ...] -- command [args]

DESCRIPTION
Prsh is a parallel asynchronous interface to *rsh*(1). It runs a *command* on a set
of remote *hostnames* listed on the command line. All remote commands execute
concurrently, and their standard output and standard error are delivered to **prsh**'s
stdout and stderr, respectively. The stdin of all remote commands is closed, c.f.
the **-n** argument to *rsh*(1).

   Prsh is particularly useful in a system area network, e.g., a Beowulf, where users
and system administrators frequently need to execute commands remotely on large
numbers of processors.

---

[4]You can download **prsh** source code from http://www.cacr.caltech.edu/beowulf/. prsh is
a Perl5 script and requires that Perl5 be installed on your system.

OPTIONS

Options control timeouts, status reports, output flushing, etc. Options may be entered with one -hyphen or two –hyphens and they may be abbreviated as long as they are unambiguous.

Detailed information about the options may be found in the online manual page.

EXAMPLES

- Set the default list of remote processors to the contents of a file

  export PRSH_HOSTS=‘cat /var/run/bnodes-up‘

- Ensure that we have a directory on every node's /scratch:

  ```
  prsh -- mkdir --parent /scratch/johns/tmp
  ```

- Kill the program `amok` (perhaps an MPI or PVM process) that is running out of control.

  ```
  prsh -- killall amok
  ```

- Ask every remote processor to touch a unique file in your home directory. This is a fairly severe test that network services, including NFS and rsh are intact between the remote nodes and the host node. Nodes that respond with OK are probably completely operational. Type this command on a single line.

  ```
  prsh --prepend -ssh --status -- touch $HOME/.checknodes/\‘uname
  --nodename\‘
  ```

ENVIRONMENT

Any switches in the `PRSH_OPTIONS` environment variable will be used before the command line arguments. The environment variable `PRSH_HOSTS` is used as a list of hostnames only if no hostnames are explicitly provided on the command line.

SEE ALSO

rsh(1), *ssh*(1)

6.5   Defending the Pack: Security Strategies

After the number of computers connected to the Internet exploded in the mid '90s, it became impossible to attach a computer to a network without paying some attention to preventive security measures. The situation is no different with Beowulf clusters, and is even more important, because making a Beowulf accessible via the

Internet is like setting up one or more new departmental LANs. We have already made some minor references to security, but will discuss it now in more detail.

Linux workstations and Beowulf clusters are not inherently more insecure than other computers. Any computer attached to a network has the potential to be broken into. Even if you take measures to restrict access to a computer as tightly as possible, software running on it may have exploitable bugs that can grant unauthorized access to the system. The only way to maintain a secure network is to keep abreast of the latest CERT advisories[5] and take some basic preventative measures. Several Beowulf systems have been victimized by crackers[6] cracker in ways that could have been prevented by paying a little bit of attention to security issues.

6.5.1 System Configuration

How you defend your Beowulf from attack will depend on what system access model you choose. The universally accessible machine is the most vulnerable, while the stand-alone machine is the most secure, as it is not attached to an external network. But few Beowulfs are stand-alone machines. The guarded Beowulf is the most practical configuration to defend, because its only entry points are its worldly nodes. It is possible to focus on implementing security measures for only the worldly nodes, and allow the internal nodes to completely trust each other. Even though it is possible for an intruder to gain access to the internal nodes once a worldly node is compromised, it is not necessary to completely secure the internal nodes. They can easily be recreated through cloning and generally do not store any sensitive persistent data. Despite the security advantages presented by the guarded Beowulf access model, other needs may demand the implementation of a universally accessible machine. For such a configuration, you have to secure each individual node, since each one constitutes an external access point.

6.5.2 IP Masquerading

Network Address Translation,[7] commonly referred to as NAT, is a technique devised for reusing IP addresses as a stopgap measure to slow the depletion of the IPv4 address space. NAT permits IP address reuse by allowing multiple networks to use

---

[5]CERT is the Computer Emergency Response Team, run by Carnegie Mellon's Software Engineering Institute. CERT posts regular bulletins reporting the latest Internet security vulnerabilities at http://www.cert.org/.

[6]Cracker is the accepted term among computer programmers for a rogue hacker who tries to gain unauthorized access to computer systems. The term hacker is restricted to those computer programmers not seduced by the Dark Side of the Force.

[7]"The IP Network Address Translator (NAT)," Internet Engineering Task Force RFC 1631, http://info.internet.isi.edu/in-notes/rfc/files/rfc1631.txt

the same addresses, but having them communicate between each other through a pair of non-shared IP address. IP masquerading is a type of NAT performed by the worldly node of a Beowulf cluster that makes external network connections appear to originate from the single worldly node. This feature allows the internal nodes to originate network connections to external Internet hosts, but provides security by not having a mechanism for an external host to set up a connection to an internal node.

The nice thing about IP masquerading is that it doesn't involve too many steps to set up. Only the node performing the masquerading requires any amount of reconfiguration. The internal nodes simply require their default route to be set to the internal network address of the worldly node, usually 192.168.1.1. You can do this with the route command as follows:

```
route add default gw 192.168.1.1
```

However, most Linux distributions perform gateway assignment at boot time based on a configuration file. Red Hat Linux stores gateway configuration information in the file /etc/sysconfig/network, which contains two variables, GATEWAY and GATEWAYDEV. These should be set to the IP address of the worldly node and the primary internal network interface name of the internal node. A typical network configuration file for an internal node might look something like the following:

```
NETWORKING=yes
FORWARD_IPV4=false
HOSTNAME=b001
DOMAINNAME=beowulf.org
GATEWAY=192.168.1.1
GATEWAYDEV=eth0
```

Configuring the worldly node to perform the IP masquerading requires a little more work, but nothing particularly difficult. The first requirement is to compile your kernel with support for network firewalls, IP forwarding/gatewaying, and IP masquerading. There are also some additional options you may want to include, but these are the essential ones. More information about the particulars of each option can be found in the Linux kernel source tree in the masquerading.txt documentation file and also in the IP Masquerade HOWTO[8].

After installing a kernel capable of IP masquerading, you need to enable IP forwarding. You can do this on Red Hat Linux systems by setting the FORWARD_IPV4

---

[8]The IP Masquerade HOWTO can be found on most Linux distributions in the /usr/doc/HOWTO/mini directory. Alternatively, it can be found online at any of the Linux Documentation Project mirrors, including http://sunsite.unc.edu/LDP/. Additional IP masquerading information is also stored at The Linux IP Masquerade Resource, http://ipmasq.cjb.net/.

variable to `true` in `/etc/sysconfig/network`. IP forwarding is merely the process by which a host will forward to its destination a packet it receives for which it is not itself the destination. This allows internal node packets to be forwarded to external hosts. The last step is to configure IP masquerading rules. You don't want your worldly node to forward packets coming from just anywhere, so you have to tell it specifically what packets to forward. At the time of this writing, you can do this by using the `ipfwadm` utility with 2.0.x Linux kernels. However, the procedure may change when the 2.2 Linux kernel is released.

The program `ipfwadm`, which is shorthand for IP Firewall Administration, configures firewall packet filtering and forwarding rules. It can specify rules based on the source and destination of a packet, the network interfaces on which a packet is received or transmitted, the network protocol used, destination and source ports, and quite a bit of other information. For the purposes of setting up a worldly node, you can use `ipfwadm` to tell the kernel to only masquerade for packets originating from an internal node. Use a command like the following:

```
ipfwadm -F -p deny
ipfwadm -F -a masq -S 192.168.1.0/24 -D 0.0.0.0/0
```

The first command sets the default forwarding policy to *deny*. This is a safety measure to make sure your worldly node doesn't forward packets not originating from internal nodes. The second command asks the kernel to only masquerade for packets originating from within the internal network (192.168.1.0) and destined for any location. Typically, these commands are placed at the end of `/etc/rc.d/rc.local`, so that they will be executed at boot time, but you can also create a script suitable for use in the `/etc/rc.d/init.d` startup system. The meanings of the various `ipfwadm` options can be garnered from the `ipfwadm` man page, but a quick summary is in order for the options necessary to configure a worldly node:

-F alters IP forwarding rules.

-a policy appends rules to the end of the selected policy list.

-p policy sets the default policy.

-S address/mask indicates that a rule applies only to packets originating from the given source address range.

-D address/mask indicates that a rule applies only to packets destined for an address in the indicated range.

6.5.3 Restricting Host Access

The primary way crackers force access to a machine is by exploiting known bugs
in commonly run server software. Many servers permit universal access without
authentication, making it easy for a cracker to exploit those bugs. It is possible to
restrict these attacks by limiting the hosts that can access your servers. You can
do this with the TCP wrappers package, which is distributed as standard Linux
software. The TCP wrappers package requires that a daemon be able to treat its
standard input and output as a socket connection. By requiring this, the TCP
wrappers daemon, `tcpd`, can accept connections for another daemon, check for au-
thorization, and then invoke the other daemon, turning the socket file descriptor
into the daemon's standard input and output. The `tcpd` daemon is normally invoked by `inetd` and listed in `/etc/inetd.conf` in front of each daemon. This is
because all daemons that support `inetd` launching are TCP wrappers compatible.
The TCP wrappers package uses the `/etc/hosts.deny` and `/etc/hosts.allow`
files (see Chapter 4) to decide whether or not to allow a server connection to proceed. You will usually want all Beowulf nodes to trust each other and only restrict
outside access to the system. Unless you are providing public services from your
cluster, such as web and database access, you will probably only want to deny
access to all services except login facilities.

Rather than protecting every single one of your daemons with TCP wrappers,
you can shield your entire system behind a firewall, where you can regulate network
access at both the packet and protocol levels. This is becoming an increasingly
necessary measure as security attacks become more common. Even though an
IP masquerading worldly node already has the necessary support to be used as a
firewall, you should not configure it as a firewall. Instead, you should place the
worldly node directly behind a firewall. Firewalls come in many shapes and sizes,
including dedicated hardware running custom ROMs. But the easiest way to set up
a firewall, is to use the Linux operating system and a spare PC equipped with two
network interface cards. The Linux Documentation Project[9] provides information
on how to do this in its Firewall HOWTO document. The benefit of securing your
Beowulf behind a firewall is that you can implement security policies at a single
administrative point and restrict access of arbitrary network packets rather than
on a connection attempt basis.

---

[9]The Linux Documentation Project pages are mirrored at several different web sites, but the
master page is located at: `http://metalab.unc.edu/LDP/`

6.5.4   SSH: Secure Shell Revisited

No matter how careful you are about restricting access to services through TCP Wrappers and firewalls, the bottom line is that you don't know how many networks and hosts are being traversed when a user logs into your Beowulf cluster. The easiest way to break into a system is to steal someone's password. You have little control over the quality of passwords your users choose, but you can exercise some level of control to reduce the chances of it being stolen. Traditional host access protocols such as FTP, Telnet, and RSH, require passwords to be transmitted over the network in the clear (in unencrypted plain text). Although your local network may be secure, once packets leave your network, they travel through many other systems before reaching their ultimate destination. One of those systems may have had its security compromised. The thing a cracker usually does after breaking into a system is to set up a program called a sniffer to monitor all network traffic, searching for passwords. When a user logs into a Beowulf from across the country, all of his keystrokes might be actively monitored by some sniffer in an intervening network. For this reason, it is highly recommended not to allow Telnet, FTP, or RSH access to your Beowulf. A universally accessible machine should disable these services on all of the nodes, while a guarded Beowulf should only disable the services on the worldly node.

You clearly cannot turn off all possible ways to log in to your Beowulf, otherwise no one could use the machine. But you can use a new access method called SSH,[10] developed by a company in Finland, and intended to replace traditional remote login methods. SSH has become standard software at many Unix sites, and is quickly becoming standard on Beowulf systems. Many Beowulf clusters only allow system access via SSH. We highly recommend this setup because SSH encrypts all network communications between two endpoints, including the X Window protocol, eliminating the chance that your passwords or other information may be captured by an eavesdropper.

While there is much more to system security than we have presented, these tips should get you started. Beowulf systems can easily be made as secure as the policies of your institution require.

---

[10]SSH, or Secure Shell is a product developed by SSH Communications Security Ltd., offering both Win32 and Unix versions. The Unix version is available as open source software and can be downloaded from http://www.ssh.fi/

6.6   Job Scheduling

The task of managing a Beowulf cluster has been limited by the functionality of existing software. Few software packages have been tailored to cluster management, which as a result has largely relied on traditional LAN management software. Even though a large number of supplementary software systems, such as schedulers, have been created in research labs, none has emerged as standard software. As a result of the growing popularity of commodity clustered computing, it is inevitable that these software packages will be improved, redesigned, or supplanted by better implementations. As that happens. the tools and functions available for cluster management will become greatly enriched.

Many Beowulf administrators are interested in better job scheduling functions. Beowulfs usually start out with only a few users in a single department, but as news about the system spreads to neighboring departments, more users are added to the system. Once that happens, it becomes important to keep user-developed applications from interfering with each other. This is usually done by funneling all user programs through a job scheduler, which decides in what order and on what processors to execute the programs. At this time, we know of at least 10 different job schedulers that have been tried on Beowulf systems, none of which is entirely satisfactory to its users. Discussions at recent conferences and workshops indicate that this situation may be about to change. The importance of this class of software to managing a Beowulf cluster is now widely recognized, and work is in progress to improve the situation. Within the next year, it is possible that there will be one or two job schedulers favored as standard Beowulf system administration software. Work is also underway to improve the status of system monitoring support, cluster partitioning, and account management.

The world of Beowulf software development is about to start moving at the same rapid pace as general Linux development. You will have to be prepared to decide when you have a satisfactory and stable software environment to avoid playing the constant game of catch-up. It will help if you separate out one or two experimental nodes for software evaluation and testing. Before upgrading to a new kernel, make sure you've stressed it out on a single node for a week or two. Before installing that fancy new scheduler, test it extensively. The last thing you want is for your entire Beowulf to grind to a halt because a scheduler has a bug that swamps the entire system with more processes than it can handle. If your users demand a new compiler, install it in such a way that they still have access to the old compiler, in case the new one doesn't always do quite the right thing. If your production system is humming along just fine, don't mess with it. Users don't like system down time. If they can already do all the work they want, then you should think very carefully before perturbing the system configuration. These are recommendations, not hard-fast rules, but they tend to be useful guides in the course of managing a system. The future of Beowulf system software promises to be very exciting. If you pick and choose only those tools that do what you need, you will likely minimize problems and increase the productivity of your system.

7 Parallel Applications

Ultimately, the reason one buys, configures and assembles a Beowulf system is to run applications. Usually, the individuals or organizations assembling such systems already have an application, or suite of applications in mind prior to purchase and installation. In many cases, these applications have already been "parallelized" so that they work effectively and efficiently with one of the available parallel libraries, e.g., MPI or PVM.

In some cases, however, a Beowulf will be the user's first experience with parallel computing. The purpose of this chapter is to offer some guidelines, examples and advice in designing parallel applications suitable for Beowulf systems. This is just one approach to designing parallel applications. It is highly pragmatic and guided by the hardware and software available today on Beowulf systems. Other parallel computer systems have radically different characteristics and can support very different approaches to parallel application development.

7.1 Parallelism

The first step in designing a parallel application for a Beowulf system is to find suitable parallel algorithms. Parallelism is the ability of many independent threads of control to make progress *simultaneously* toward the completion of a task. Often, we refer to the amount of *available parallelism*, which is simply the maximum number of independent threads that can work simultaneously. In the rare case that the algorithms intrinsic to the application have little or no parallelism, there is little point in attempting to use a Beowulf (or any other parallel machine, for that matter). Fortunately, such problems are rare, but sometimes procedures simply cannot be parallelized—it takes one woman nine months to make a baby, but nine women can't do the job any faster.

Users usually consider Beowulfs because they have an application that is taking too long, or that is too large to run on other available machines. This suggests that there is something in the application space which is *large*. This is the place to look for parallelism. The large component may be the number of elements in some array or mesh, the size of a database, the size of a parameter space, the size of a task pool, the size of an image, the number of objects that need to be consumed or created, or something else entirely. Except in rare circumstances, these components offer a source of parallelism, and an opportunity to apply Beowulfs (or other parallel computing resources) to the problem. Whatever the large component, it can usually be updated, searched, analyzed, processed, rearranged or manufactured in parallel.

The typical Beowulf system today has between 4 and 40 processors. A few systems larger than 100 processors have been demonstrated, and it is likely that systems of several hundred processors will be constructed as research projects in the near future. These numbers provide reasonable guidelines as to how much parallelism is necessary in an application to be suitable for a Beowulf. It is important that the application developer not waste time exploiting more parallelism than is needed. The goal (usually) is to get work done, not to find the maximum amount of parallelism. If one is rendering a two-hour motion-picture at 24 frames per second, then one immediately has over 175,000 independent sub-problems. There is little point in parallelizing the individual renderers. Similar considerations apply to parameter searches and data reductions. If an instrument is delivering 100 frames per minute and each frame takes one minute to reduce on a single processor, then you can easily apply 100 processors to the job (assuming your network is up to the task)—without doing any recoding of the actual reduction procedure. You may not be able to write any papers for the parallel computing literature, but you'll be able to keep up with your data stream.

Occasionally, one encounters a large problem in which there is insufficient parallelism. This occurs when there is a causal relationship between the sub-tasks. For example, computing the time evolution of small systems over very long times can be difficult to parallelize. Understanding the long-term behavior of the solar system requires the computation of many billions of individual timesteps. However, since they are all causally related, it is difficult to obtain parallelism much greater than the number of bodies in the system—in this case ten. Even in this extreme case, there are alternatives, such as "waveform relaxation," which may be inferior in terms of overall operation count, but which allows one to exploit additional parallelism. Also, one should not overlook the desire to study the stability of the system, or the effects of different initial conditions, both of which offer avenues to parallelization simply by running several copies of the the same non-parallel or slightly parallel code.

Amdahl's law In a famous paper Amdahl[1] observed that one must consider an entire application when considering the level of available parallelism. If only one percent of a problem fails to parallelize, then no matter how much parallelism is available for the rest, the problem can never be solved more than one hundred times faster than in the sequential case. This observation has come to be known as Amdahl's law, and is widely used as an argument against parallel computation.

---

[1] Amdahl, G. M., Validity of the single processor approach to achieving large scale computing capabilities, AFIPS Proc. of the SJCC, v. 30, pp 483–485, 1967

Amdahl's law fails to apply in practice as much as one might think because to a large extent, computational problems grow in size through growth of their parallel components. For example, the sequential component of a finite element calculation is much the same regardless of whether the calculation involves one thousand or one million components. So that while Amdahl's law suggests restrictions on the amount of parallelism one can profitably apply to the one thousand element problem, the restrictions are much less severe for the one million element case.

Problems which have parallelism, but in a form difficult to exploit with a Beowulf are much more common. For example, problems with tightly coupled, fine-grained data structures may have substantial parallelism, but the overhead of frequently accessing small data elements over the network can overwhelm the benefit of performing the computation in parallel. Advanced (and expensive) hardware techniques can be used to mitigate the problem, but they are beyond the scope of this book.

There are two important reasons to actually "parallelize" an application code:

1. problem size demands a parallel solution
2. real time requirements demand a speedy solution

problem size   Problem size can be an issue for large-scale scientific and engineering applications. Individual commodity memory parts are difficult or impossible to purchase above a certain size. This limiting size is, of course, a function of time. In early 1999, memory prices rise dramatically above about 128MB per SIMM or DIMM. This effectively limits the size of cost-effective systems to about 512MB per processor. Problems that require more memory can only be solved by introducing parallelism, or by purchasing much more expensive systems and components. While 512MB is a substantial amount of storage, three-dimensional simulations can easily require orders of magnitude more. For such problems, it may be necessary to parallelize the problem in order to obtain a cost-effective Beowulf solution. This is the most compelling reason for parallelizing codes on Beowulf systems today.

real time requirements   Real time requirements come into play when the results of a program are time critical. The common usage of the phrase "real-time" refers to response in the millisecond or microsecond range. Optimizations necessary for such high-speed real-time applications are generally not available in commodity systems, so Beowulf systems are unlikely to have major impact where very rapid response is crucial. However, real time requirements can extend to time scales of minutes, hours or even months. In such cases, exploiting parallelism within an application can be worth the effort.

Examples of application domains with long real-time requirements, where Beowulf systems might be relevant include weather forecasting, financial modeling/prediction, and scientific and engineering simulations. The common feature of all these computational activities is that the importance of the result of a single computation may be strongly dependent on the passage of time, e.g., a weather forecast's value plummets dramatically as the forecasted hour approaches. A large scientific calculation may be important enough to invest a year of computation, but it would be considerably more valuable if the result were available in a month. A dedicated 16-processor Beowulf system could easily make that kind of difference.

It is important to separate the effects of throughput and response time. If the motivation for parallelizing an application is to improve response time, then one must carefully consider the effect of other users on the system. If a 16-processor Beowulf is shared with a dozen other researchers, it will have almost no effect on response time, i.e., the time for any one researcher to complete a problem. All other things being equal, it would probably have been easier, and just as effective, for the researchers to run their problems on individual workstations. Of course, if the problems don't fit on a single workstation due to size constraints, then parallelization is indicated anyway. However, that is a separate consideration from improving response time.

7.2 Broad Categories of Parallel Algorithms

Parallel algorithms can be categorized according to a number of criteria. While not strictly orthogonal, these criteria provide useful information about the structure and requirements of a particular method or algorithm. Some types of algorithms are more suitable for Beowulfs than others. Often, there are several algorithms or strategies available to solve any particular problem, and tradeoffs must be weighed to determine which is most appropriate.

7.2.1 Regular and Irregular

Regular algorithms use data structures that fit naturally into rectangular arrays. Irregular algorithms require more complicated data structures, e.g., indirect addressing, trees, linked lists, graphs, hash-tables, etc.. Regular structures are often easier to partition into separate parallel processes. For example, rectangular arrays can be split up into blocks and distributed to processors. The data residing in each processor is still a rectangular block, and hence the code that works on it often needs only minor modification to work in parallel.

Irregular structures often require careful consideration for parallelization. Usually, an irregular data structure is chosen to exploit or accommodate some feature of the underlying problem - sparseness, hierarchies, a need for unpredictable updates, etc. It is crucial that the parallel implementation continue to exploit or accommodate these features or overall performance may suffer tremendously. On the other hand, it is often the case that the precise form of a data structure chosen by a sequential implementation is not important - e.g., a tree may be implemented sequentially with pointers, but it may be possible to implement parallel tree search without implementing the full semantics of distributed pointers. This can require significant programming effort, as well as a deep understanding of both the computational methods, and the underlying problem domain.

7.2.2 Synchronous and Asynchronous

In a synchronous algorithm, the parallel parts of the calculation are required to remain in "lockstep." Conversely, in an asynchronous algorithm, different parts of the calculation may "get ahead" without adverse effect. Asynchronous algorithms often require less bookkeeping than synchronous. Because of the minimal bookkeeping, asynchronous algorithms are sometimes much easier to parallelize. They may be preferred, even when there is a slightly superior sequential alternative. If the performance penalty is not too great, this can allow one to save the most valuable commodity of all in parallel computing: programmer time. Although not always the case, genetic algorithms, data analysis, rendering of animations, and Monte Carlo methods often allow for asynchronous execution.

7.2.3 Coarse and Fine Grained

Grain size, when used in parallel computation, refers to how much work is performed by each process. There are often very elegant small-grain formulations of computational algorithms. For example, a vector dot-product can be formulated with one logical processor responsible for each pair of elements. The time required is proportional to the logarithm of the number of elements. While elegant, this formulation places very high demands on the communication network of the parallel computer. Alternatively, a large grain size formulation would follow the structure in Program 8.7 and assign many elements of the vectors to each logical process. If the grain size is large enough, then the interprocessor communication, `MPI_Reduceall` in this case, does not dominate the total time required by the algorithm.

Frequently, the relationship between grain size computation and communication can be understood in terms of the ratio of surface area to volume. Communication

occurs on the boundaries (suitably defined) of the computational volume assigned
to each logical processor. Operation counts, on the other hand, are proportional
to the volume of data assigned to each logical processor. Therefore, the relative
amounts of communication and computation are proportional to the ratio of surface
area to volume. Since large grains have a more favorable, i.e., lower, ratio of surface
area to volume, they reduce the relative importance of networking performance with
respect to computational performance.

7.2.4 Bandwidth Greedy and Frugal

Communication of data over a network takes time. While variations in system load,
interfering traffic, interrupt handlers, etc. make it impossible to exactly predict the
amount of time required to deliver a message, the following formula provides a
useful approximation:

$$t_{comm} = t_{latency} + \text{message length/bandwidth}$$

That is, the time to deliver a message is composed of a startup time, $t_{latency}$,
after which data flows at a relatively constant rate, the bandwidth. Beowulf systems employing fast Ethernet deliver network bandwidths in the neighborhood of
10 MByte/s, and latencies in the neighborhood of 200 μsec.

Now let's compare the rate at which data can be communicated with the rate
at which data can be processed by the CPU. For concreteness, consider a 300 MHz
Pentium II processor. If data is in registers, and if it is possible to keep pipelines
full, then the processor can perform an arithmetic operation involving two 8-byte
quantities every clock cycle. Such favorable situations are extremely rare in practice, and even the most carefully coded loops rarely exceed half this performance.
Therefore, we estimate the maximum rate at which data can be consumed from
registers to be about 0.5×300 MHz $\times 16$bytes $= 2400$ MBytes/s, about 240 times
faster than the network speed!

A processor's internal bandwidth is usually not the most important one for determining overall system performance. Modern microprocessors cannot deliver data
from main memory at anywhere near the rates required by the CPU. This simple
fact has driven a series of extremely complicated developments in microprocessor design over the last decade, including caches, wide memory buses, pipelined
architectures, speculative execution, out-of-order execution, etc. While these developments have mitigated the effect of memory bandwidth on overall performance,
there is no escaping the fact that memory bandwidth is often the limiting factor in
overall system performance. Partly because of the presence of so many advanced

architectural features, memory bandwidth is actually quite difficult to measure accurately. The widely used STREAMS benchmark[2] provides fairly reliable numbers for how much bandwidth is actually visible to an application that has not taken any special steps to enhance memory or cache performance. For our example system, a 300MHz Pentium II with SDRAM memory, the STREAMS benchmark reports memory bandwidths of approximately 128-182 MB/s. This is still more than an order or magnitude higher than the network speed in a Beowulf system.

Algorithms can place greater or lesser demand on network bandwidths. Some algorithms require almost no interprocessor communication. Brute force cryptographic attacks,[3] in which a very small amount of data initiates each long-running and completely independent calculation are an extreme example of bandwidth frugal algorithms. At the other extreme are algorithms in which every processor does little besides exchanging a large fraction of its total memory with other processors. The sorting problems discussed in Chapter 9.1 are bandwidth greedy algorithms in which there is relatively little computation for each datum transmitted.

Problems from the physical sciences can often be solved in parallel by applying "domain decomposition." That is, splitting the problem into domains and assigning each domain to a processor. In this case, the amount of data communicated between processors is typically proportional to the surface area of the domains, while the amount of computation to be performed by each processor is proportional to the volume of the domains. The ratio of surface-area to volume decreases as the domains become larger, i.e., as the grain size increases. Thus, one often finds that increasing the grain size in a physical problem leads to a more bandwidth frugal, and hence better performing algorithm.

7.2.5 Latency Tolerant and Intolerant

Latency is a property of the communication network in a parallel machine. It measures how long it takes for a message to *begin* to be delivered from one process to another. While usually reported in microseconds, latency is more useful when measured in units dictated by the rest of the system. A latency of $200\,\mu\text{sec}$ means little in isolation, but becomes meaningful when we compare it to a processor clock that cycles at 300 MHz. In this case, the network latency corresponds to 60000 ticks of the processor clock. Another useful comparison is with the network bandwidth. If we simply multiply network latency by bandwidth we obtain a number of bytes:

$$n_{\frac{1}{2}} = \text{latency} \times \text{bandwidth}.$$

---

[2] http://www.cs.virginia.edu/stream/
[3] http://www.certicom.com/sixth.htm

The time to send a message of length $n_{\frac{1}{2}}$ is about half latency and half bandwidth. Much longer messages may be said to be bandwidth-dominated, while much shorter messages may be said to be latency dominated. For fast Ethernet networks in Beowulf systems, $n_{\frac{1}{2}}$ is about 1500 bytes. It is no coincidence that this is close to the size of the fundamental units of transmission implemented by the underlying hardware.

High latencies are probably the most conspicuous shortcoming of Beowulf systems, and hence successful algorithms are usually latency tolerant. Such algorithms "don't care" about the high latency for one reason or another. There are several approaches to tolerating latency. First, the total number of messages should be minimized. Many short messages (shorter than $n_{\frac{1}{2}}$) are much more expensive than a few long ones (longer than $n_{\frac{1}{2}}$). In addition, one can work on some other task while the long-latency operation is under way. For example, overlapping communication and computation is supported by the asynchronous communication functions of MPI. Finally, results may be recomputed, or computed redundantly rather than communicated. Time to solution may be reduced even if the operation count increases. With a communication latency of 60000 clock cycles, there is plenty of opportunity to recompute rather than obtain a result from a distant processor.

7.2.6   Distributed and Shared Address Spaces

The MPI programming model discussed in Chapter 8 defines a distributed address space model with message passing. The only way for separate processes to share data is for them to communicate via explicit message passing procedure calls. In a shared address space system, there is a common, unified address space which may be accessed by any of the processors. In some cases, this can greatly simplify the design of parallel programs. With a shared address space, processes need not explicitly agree to transfer data, but may simply read and write a common address. On the other hand, there is considerable danger from race conditions and non-determinacy—special efforts must be made in both hardware and software to guarantee that when one processor writes to a location, and another reads from that location, that the desired ordering is preserved. Parallel compilers exist that can exploit (to some extent) shared address space architectures, while designing languages and compilers to exploit message passing systems has proven much more difficult.

7.2.7   Beowulf Systems and Choices of Parallelism

Communication networks in Beowulf systems have relatively long latencies and modest bandwidths. This argues for use of large-grain size algorithms with low ratios of surface area to volume, resulting in favorable ratios of communication to computation. Furthermore, Beowulf systems have relatively large latencies equal to tens of thousands of processor cycles or a few thousand bytes of network bandwidth. Investing more in hardware, e.g., Myrinet, can reduce these overheads by an order of magnitude or more, but even so, latency tolerant and bandwidth frugal algorithms will still be necessary. As with most parallel computing systems, regular and/or asynchronous problems are easier to implement than irregular and/or synchronous ones, but Beowulfs are not dramatically different from other parallel computers in this regard.

Once the fundamental issues of the existence of sufficient parallelism have been addressed, tuning applications for Beowulf consists primarily of minimizing communication and tolerating latency. While these same issues are important for the majority of parallel computing platforms, both commercial and non-commercial, loosely coupled Beowulf systems make it particularly necessary.

7.3   Process-level Parallelism

Beowulf systems are particularly well suited to, and may easily exploit process-level parallelism. That is, parallelism that is exposed by running multiple, independent processes. When applicable, process-level parallelism is often the easiest way to achieve speedup in parallel computation. It's so easy, in fact, that such tasks are often referred to disparagingly as "embarrassingly parallel." The only requirement for process-level parallelism is that there already exist a *sequential* code or codes that must be run many times. Parallel execution can be achieved by straightforward use of the standard remote execution command, `rsh`. If the process pool is large enough, then process-parallel applications can self-schedule and automatically load-balance across a Beowulf system.

7.3.1   Example: Ray Tracing Animation

Animation rendering is an excellent example of process-level parallelism. Fortunately, a well-optimized and extremely powerful rendering code already exists and is freely available for Linux, and hence Beowulf. The "Persistence of Vision" ray tracing program, `povray`. is available as precompiled binaries,[4] or in an easy-to-install rpm.[5] It also comes with a large number of demonstration and example scenes and extensive documentation. The example we will work here assumes that POV-ray has been installed on each of the nodes of your Beowulf system. One way to do this is to place the rpm file in a directory accessible by NFS, e.g., /shared, and to execute the following command (as root):

```
prsh `cat /var/run/bnodes-up` -- rpm -i /shared/povray-3.02-1.i386.rpm
```

Of course, you may have a more recent version of the rpm, or a different architecture, in which case the exact file name would be different.

Scenes and animations are rendered by POV-Ray by invoking the program and specifying a scene file (a .pov file) and list of optional command line arguments. POV-Ray has a complex and powerful syntax for describing scenes and controlling rendering options that are far beyond the scope of this book. For our purposes, we simply assume that we have encapsulated the necessary execution parameters of POV-ray into a a shell script that can render a subset of the scenes in an animation. A simple example is shown in Program 7.1.

```
#!/bin/bash
cd ~/rendering # EXAMPLE ONLY.  CHANGE TO SUIT ???
povray +i example.pov +SF $1 +EF $2 example.ini
```

Program 7.1:
doframes: takes two arguments specifying the starting and ending frame of a sequence. Notice also that the first command changes the working directory to the one where the .pov and .ini files will be found. This is because commands executed through the **rsh** utility always run in the user's home directory. Without the explicit change of working directory, povray would run in the user's home directory, and would probably fail because the expected files would not be present.

We are now ready to run POV-Ray in parallel, using only the remote execution and communication utilities supplied by NFS and rsh. There is no need to alter or recompile POV-Ray in any way. If we have four processors, named p00 through p03, we might type the following lines at a command prompt:

```
rsh p00 ~/rendering/doframes 0 74 > proc0.out  &
rsh p01 ~/rendering/doframes 75 149 > proc1.out &
rsh p02 ~/rendering/doframes 150 224 > proc2.out &
rsh p03 ~/rendering/doframes 225 299 > proc3.out &
```

---

[4]http://www.povray.org/
[5]ftp://contrib.redhat.com/libc6 and its many mirror sites

We have again inserted `~/rendering`, the current working directory, into the command before `rsh` ships it off to the remote node. Without this, it is likely that the remote node would not find the `doframes` script.

If all has gone well up to this point, after a few minutes, we will have 300 individual image files representing the frames of our animation. To view the animation, we need to convert the frames into a format recognized by one of the animation viewers. A dizzying array of animation formats exist, and readers may well have their favorite tools for creating and manipulating them. The `xanim` program,[6] which is included with most popular Linux distributions, can animate a sequence of GIF files named on its command line. While this is not a particularly fast or efficient way of storing or displaying animations, it does give instant gratification. The following very short shell script will convert the ppm files produced by POV-Ray into GIF files, allowing you to view them with `xanim`. You may save it in a file and run it, or simply type it at a shell prompt (assuming you are using the bash shell).

```
#!/bin/bash
for file in example*.ppm ; do
  ppmquant 256 $file | ppmtogif > `basename $file .ppm`.gif
done
```

It is now possible to run `xanim example*.gif` to see the results of the example animation.

A collection of separate PPM or GIF files is large and unwieldy. Readers interested in distributing animations over the web would be well advised to obtain the `mpeg_encode`[7] or `whirlgif`.[8] The MPEG format is highly compressed—compression ratios of 1000:1 are not uncommon—and is designed for relatively easy decompression. Plug-ins exist for popular web browsers which can decode MPEG files. In contrast, encoding of MPEG files is a slow and numerically intensive operation. Fortunately, `mpeg_encode` supports process-level parallelism through the PARALLEL parameter. The GIF89a format, created by `whirlgif`, is not as compact as MPEG, but is also easily decoded and is much easier to create. The result can be viewed directly with most graphical web browsers, as well as `xanim`.

---

[6]Home page: `http://xanim.va.pubnix.com/home.html`

[7]Home page: `ftp://mm-ftp.cs.berkeley.edu/pub/mpeg/encode/`
Precompiled rpm: `ftp://contrib.redhat.com/libc6/i386/mpeg_encode-1.5b-1.i386.rpm`

[8]Home page: `http://www.msg.net/utility/whirlgif`
Precompiled rpm: `ftp://contrib.redhat.com/libc6/i386/whirlgif-2.01-4.i386.rpm`

7.3.2 Utilities for Process-parallel Computing

A little experimentation with process-parallel computing using the techniques described above quickly reveals some major shortcomings. First, it is difficult to manually type all these commands accurately. Second, it is quite possible for different processes to take very different amounts of time, forcing one to wait for the slowest one, and significantly slowing down the overall execution. Third, we are exploiting POV-Ray's ability to loop over frames in a way that does not necessarily translate to other types of codes. For example, we might have a simulation that we wish to run many times with different input files. The existing simulation probably does not have controls analogous to POV-Ray's +SF and +EF flags. We may need a way to invoke this simulation hundreds or thousands of times, and it would be far too laborious to manually keep track of which processors are responsible for which invocations, etc. For these reasons, we have created a small "dispatcher" program that can take an arbitrary list of commands and dispatch them, one at a time, to a set of processors.

The Perl script in Programs 7.2 and 7.3 requires two arguments. The first is a filename containing a list of processor hostnames. These processors will be used as targets for remote execution commands. No more than one command will be run on any host at any one time, but the order in which commands are run, and the way they are dispatched to hosts is arbitrary. The second argument is a list of commands. One command is obtained from each non-blank line of the command file (following the conventions of shell programming, the '#' character is used to indicate comments that extend to the end of the line). Commands will be dispatched with the `rsh` utility, so absolute path names are still important. In the version of `prun` given, the standard input of the remote command is closed, and the standard output and standard error are redirected to files called `prun-NNN.out` and `prun-NNN.err` respectively, where NNN is the sequence number of the command in the script. In many cases, the remote commands themselves will be scripts which will perform suitable input and output redirection, in which case stdin and stdout could just as easily be closed.

For example, if we had a simulation that used daily weather data, and we created a script `dosim` to run it using the data for a given day, we might create a command file, `everyday` like:

```
~/model/dosim 01jan97
~/model/dosim 02jan97
~/model/dosim 03jan97
...
~/model/dosim 31dec97
```

```perl
#!/usr/bin/perl -w

use POSIX ":sys_wait_h";        # so we can do waitpid(-1, &WNOHANG);

$| = 1;                         # autoflush stdout.
$debug=1;
$seqno=0;
$list_of_procs=$ARGV[0];
$list_of_cmds=$ARGV[1];

sub debug{
    print STDOUT @_ if $debug;
}

open PROCS, "<$list_of_procs" || die "Could not open $list_of_procs\n";
while( <PROCS> ){
    s/#.*//;                # delete everything after '#'
    unshift @avail, split;  # split on white space and push values into avail
}
$nprocs = $#avail;
&debug("nodes: ", join(" ", @avail), "\n");

# Loop over commands in file $list_of_commands.  Give them to
# the first available processor for execution.
open CMDS, "<$list_of_cmds" || die "Could not open $list_of_cmds\n";
while( <CMDS> ){
    s/#.*//;                        # discard comments
    s/\s*$//;                       # discard trailing white space (newline too)
    next if /^$/;                   # skip if nothing left
    &debug("Command: $_, #avail=$#avail left\n");
    &wait_for_completion if  $#avail < 0; # wait if no available processors
    &run_remote_command($_);        # do it
}

# No more commands to run.  Wait for everything to finish.
while( $#avail < $nprocs ){
    &wait_for_completion;
}
debug("All done!\n");
```

Program 7.2:
Main body of a Perl script to dispatch commands to processors. The script accepts two arguments specifying a list of available processors and a list of commands to execute via rsh. The '#' character may be used as a comment character in either file. Note, however, that the command file parser does not "understand" the underlying shell syntax. Among other things, this means that commands containing embedded or quoted '#' characters will probably fail and line continuation with backslash-newline is not supported. These deficiencies could be repaired with some additional parsing in the while(<CMDS>) loop.

```perl
sub run_remote_command{
    local ($cmd) = @_;
    $proc = shift @avail;
    die "no proc to run $cmd on!\n" unless defined $proc;
    $STDOUT=">prun-$seqno.out";
    $STDERR=">prun-$seqno.err";
    @wholecmd = ('ssh', '-n', "$proc", "$cmd");
    $pid = &fork_exec( @wholecmd );
    $prochash{$pid} = $proc;
    $cmdhash{$pid} = join(' ', @wholecmd);
    $seqno++;
}

sub wait_for_completion{
    $pid = wait;
    while( $pid > 0 && defined $prochash{$pid} ){
        push @avail, ($prochash{$pid}); # This proc is available
        undef $prochash{$pid};   # Forget this pid,
        undef $cmdhash{$pid};    # avoid confusion later
        $pid = waitpid( -1, &WNOHANG); # Check for any other completions
    }
}

sub fork_exec{
    my @cmd = @_;
  FORK: {
        if( $pid = fork ){         # parent code
            return $pid;
        }elsif (defined $pid) {
            open(STDIN, "</dev/null");
            open(STDOUT, "$STDOUT");
            open(STDERR, "$STDERR");
            exec @cmd;
            die "Couldn't exec ", join(':', @cmd), "\n";
        }elsif ($! =~ /Try again/ && $ntry < 5) {
            print STDERR "fork: ", join(' ', @_), ": EAGAIN... retrying\n";
            sleep 5;
            $ntry++;
            redo FORK;
        }else{
            die "Can't fork: $!\n"; # wierd fork error
        }
    }
}
```

Program 7.3:
Subroutines used by the Perl script in Program 7.2. **run_remote_command** runs a command using
rsh on the first entry of the @avail list. It records the processor and command in hash tables
keyed by the process id. **wait_for_completion** waits for a command to complete. The processor
on which the command ran is found in the hash table keyed by process id. Finally, **fork_exec**
carries out the low-level work of forking and exec'ing a new process.

Now to run our simulation for every day of the year, we just run:

```
prun /var/run/bnodes-up everyday
```

It is no longer necessary to explicitly decide which processors will perform which simulations. The entire sequence is "load balanced" by `prun` because whenever a processor finishes one frame, it is immediately given another one.

7.3.3   Overheads—RSH and File I/O

The strategy of running a program on multiple machines via rsh is not without costs. Generally, it takes longer to run a job remotely than to run it locally. This is due to the startup costs of establishing a connection to the remote host, authenticating the user, and exec'ing the remote command. Furthermore, there are additional overheads associated with I/O. If the executable file is stored on an NFS mounted file system, then the program itself may be transferred on every invocation. Similarly, any NFS-mounted data files that it requires or produces must be transferred over the network.

The overhead associated with running a job remotely can be anywhere from a few tens of milliseconds to a few seconds. Anything more than that usually indicates that something is wrong with the system. NFS-based data transfers are usually limited by the performance of the server and its network connection. Even though the network switch might have an internal bandwidth in excess of 1 Gbps, the link to the NFS server is probably over a single 100 Mbps Ethernet connection. Thus, all simultaneous NFS accesses must contend for the shared 100 Mbps link to the server. In practice, these numbers should be compared with the typical time taken to run a remote job. Frequently the remote process performs a substantial computing task, taking anywhere from minutes to hours. In such cases, there is little point in worrying about a few extra seconds associated with startup and file transfer.

For those cases in which startup and data transfer overheads are important, it is possible to mitigate the problem by pre-staging data and executables and storing results on the disks that are physically attached to the processor doing the computation. This is a situation in which the transparency of and convenience of the NFS file system can cause unwanted surprises. Although we recommend against it, your system administrator may configure a Byzantine maze of symbolic links, NFS mount points and automounter settings which makes it difficult to determine exactly where a file is located. A pathname like `/usr/bin/foobar` looks local, but may, in fact be a symbolic link to `/packages/foo/bin/foobar`, which may, in turn be NFS mounted on the worldly node. If in doubt, the `-T` flag to `df` will tell you how a file is mounted, e.g., `df -T /shared/somefile`.

Consistent, system-wide naming conventions can help the user to recognize how files will be accessed. For example, in Chapter 6, it was suggested that all user home directories be shared under the file system `/home`. If this convention is followed, then one can be certain that any files in user home directories will require network I/O to be accessed by the internal nodes of the Beowulf. Similarly, the system files, `/`, `/usr` and `/tmp` are always on local hard disks. Thus, the examples using `povray` would not incur network traffic to copy the executable itself (assuming it is installed in the standard place in /usr/bin), but would incur network traffic to copy the files located in `~/rendering`. Unfortunately, NFS is a fundamentally sequential system. The NFS server on the worldly node will respond one-at-a-time to requests from internal nodes, even if those requests are all for the same file. It will not use any underlying broadcast mechanisms. On the other hand, NFS clients (i.e., internal nodes) can cache data that is unchanging, e.g., input data files and executables. Therefore, if there's enough swap space on the remote nodes, repeated requests for the same file objects, e.g., executables or common input files, from the same client will not cause significant network traffic.

In Chapter 6, we suggested devoting any extra disk space on internal nodes to a user-accessible file system called `/scratch`. If I/O performance over NFS is an issue, then output files can be written to `/scratch`, rather than back into the NFS-mounted user's home directory. While this can be an order of magnitude faster, it may require some additional bookkeeping for the user to keep track of his files.

7.3.4   Summary

Process level parallelism is often the easiest and most cost-effective way to utilize a Beowulf system. When it is applicable, it almost eliminates the time to "program" a parallel application. Essentially, all that is required is a few shell scripts to launch multiple copies of the application with suitable arguments. Optimizations are often unnecessary, but usually involve use of local file systems to reduce NFS traffic and improve I/O performance. The script shown in in Programs 7.2 and 7.3 allows for automatic load-balancing of process level parallelism across a Beowulf system. In many cases it is all that is needed. Nevertheless, it could be improved in several ways. A more sophisticated version might dynamically adapt to system load and could also allow commands to be dynamically added and deleted from the run queue. Multiple users could be accommodated with variable priorities and accounting and scheduling policies. Graphical user interfaces could display the state of the system, tailored to the needs of administrators and/or users. These features are typically found in large and complicated batch scheduling systems, which should be available for Beowulf systems in the near future.

In some cases, process parallelism is not appropriate. For example, if the problem of interest needs more memory than is available on a single processor, it becomes necessary to parallelize the application. The MPI library, discussed in the next chapter, provides a standard library interface that allows a programmer to implement a single instance of a program that executes in parallel on many processors.

8 MPI—A User-level Message-passing Interface

8.1 History

So far, we have shown how to set up a Beowulf that is little different from a network of independent workstations. Each of the workstations has network access via sockets, the standard BSD networking API.

A large variety of user-level utilities operate using this API including X windows, the r-commands: rsh, rcp, rlogin and their secure cousins: ssh, scp, slogin. File systems can be accessed remotely with NFS. The socket networking API is also available to application programmers, who may use it directly. However, experience has shown that although rich and powerful, it is difficult to use and not entirely appropriate for large scale distributed memory applications.

Through the 1980s, manufacturers of MPPs devised proprietary APIs which allowed more-or-less direct access to the underlying network hardware in their systems. For most purposes, these APIs were essentially the same, differing primarily in the names given to the routines and in subtle variations in the semantics of obscure and special cases. It was possible, but unnecessarily difficult, to write code that was portable between machines.

In April of 1992 a workshop on Standards for Message Passing in a Distributed Memory Environment was sponsored by the Center for Research on Parallel Computing. This workshop convened a working group and solicited input from industry and academia. A two-year process was begun which included meetings and extensive email discussions. The designers of MPI attempted to incorporate the best ideas from a variety of sources, including research projects such as P4,[1] and PVM,[2] and commercial systems from Intel (NX), IBM (EUI), Ncube (Vertex), Thinking Machines (CMMD) and others. The result was the MPI-1.0 Message Passing Interface,[3,4] released in May, 1994. In June 1995, the revised MPI-1.1 standard was released (most of the revisions were mere clarifications). Substantial revisions were deferred until the release of the MPI-2.0. In April 1997. MPI-1.2, another set of clarifications, and MPI-2.0, with several major new features, were released. Thus, the two principal branches of MPI are now version 1.2 and version 2.0. MPI-2 provides a richer set of functionality including I/O, and one-sided communication, but also incorporates all of MPI-1.2, again with some minor clarifications. Open source implementations of MPI-2 are expected to become available in 1999.

---

[1] P4 home page: http://www-fp.mcs.anl.gov/~lusk/p4/index.html

[2] PVM home page: http://www.eprm.ornl.gov/pvm/pvm_home.html

[3] All MPI documents may be found at http://www.mpi-forum.org/docs/docs.html

[4] *MPI, the Complete Reference*, Snir et al., MIT Press, 1996

MPI is designed to allow for efficient implementation on all existing distributed memory parallel systems. In some sense, it represents a lowest common denominator, but other protocols have been proposed which are closer to the actual hardware, e.g., Active Messages[5] and Fast Messages.[6] The ambitious goal that the MPI Forum set for itself was to design an API that could be implemented reasonably efficiently everywhere, but that did not preclude any implementation from making use of proprietary hardware features that might offer improved performance. This common interface can be confusing for the programmer. Some implementations do certain operations extremely quickly, e.g., global barriers, while others carry out the same logical operation much more slowly. Writing portable and correct code with MPI is straightforward. Writing portable and correct code that behaves optimally on a variety of platforms is much harder. Nevertheless, the situation is still better than it was before MPI existed.

8.2   MPI Basic Functionality

An MPI program consists of a number of processes running in multiple instruction/multiple data (MIMD) fashion. That is, each of the processes in an MPI program is independent with a separate and unshared address space. Data is communicated between processes by explicit invocation of MPI procedures at both the sending and receiving end. In MPI-1, processes are neither created nor destroyed, but this limitations is lifted in MPI-2.

An MPI process is just a "normal" program written in C or Fortran (C++ and Fortran90 bindings are specified in MPI-2) and linked with the MPI libraries. No special kernel, operating system, or language support is needed to run MPI programs on a Beowulf.

Although not required, it is most common for all the processes in a single MPI program to correspond to the same program text, i.e., to be the same executable file running in different address spaces. Less common, but perfectly legal is to create an MPI program in which the individual processes are instances of different executables, presumably compiled from different source files, but still linked with the MPI libraries. Similarly, it is possible to pass different command-line arguments to the different processes, but this too is not common.

If a single MPI program consists of multiple instances of exactly the same executable, with exactly the same command-line arguments one might wonder how

---

[5]Active Messages home page: `http://now.cs.berkeley.edu/AM/active_messages.html`
[6]Fast Messages home page: `http://www-csag.cs.uiuc.edu/projects/comm/fm.html`

one obtains useful parallelism, i.e., how does one prevent all these processes from computing exactly the same thing. The answer is for each process to ask the MPI library what rank it has in the `MPI_COMM_WORLD` communicator. Since each of P processes has a unique integer rank in the range [0, ... P-1], they can easily choose different parts of the problem to work on.

8.2.1   Example: "Hello World" in MPI

We begin our introduction to MPI by considering a program whose functionality should be familiar to all C programmers. Program 8.1 introduces several new concepts that occur over and over in MPI programs. The reader is encouraged to refer to Program 8.1 for an example of each of the concepts discussed in this section.

Initialization and Finalization   Since portability and ease of implementation were critically important criteria in the design of MPI, it was decided that the MPI library would not be allowed to "take over" the special behavior of C's `main` function or FORTRAN's `PROGRAM` statement. Instead, in order to use MPI, a program must first call `MPI_Init`. In C, `MPI_Init` should be passed the addresses of `argc` and `argv`. This mechanism allows for maximum flexibility—`MPI_Init` may obtain values passed on the command line by some implementations, and it may provide them in other implementations. Generally, it is unwise to rely on the values of `argc` and `argv` before a call to `MPI_Init` because the MPI environment is allowed to insert its own arguments into the list, which are then parsed and removed by `MPI_Init`. Naturally, it is necessary to call `MPI_Init` before calling any other MPI procedures. Similarly, `MPI_Finalize` terminates MPI. It is a good idea to explicitly call `MPI_Finalize` just before `exit` for normal program termination, so that MPI can gracefully release system resources, close sockets, etc. It is illegal to invoke any MPI procedure after calling `MPI_Finalize`.

Communicators   MPI is primarily a communications library. One of its major advances over earlier systems is the introduction of opaque communicator that provide a concise and modular way of referring to subsets of processes. Most of the MPI communication procedures require that the caller specify a communicator argument which defines the context in which the communication takes place. Every process within a communicator has a unique rank in the range from 0, .. , size-1. By inquiring about the number of processes with `MPI_Comm_size` and the process' rank with `MPI_Comm_rank`, it is possible to write parallel programs that dynamically adjust at runtime to the number of available processors. Communicators can be

```c
#include <mpi.h>
#include <stdio.h>
#include <string.h>

int main(int argc, char **argv){
  int rank, size, partner;
  int namelen;
  char name[MPI_MAX_PROCESSOR_NAME];
  char greeting[sizeof(name) + 100];

  MPI_Init(&argc, &argv);          /* Initialize MPI */

  /* How many processes are there? */
  MPI_Comm_size(MPI_COMM_WORLD, &size);
  /* Which one am I? */
  MPI_Comm_rank(MPI_COMM_WORLD, &rank);
  /* Where am I running? */
  MPI_Get_processor_name(name, &namelen);

  sprintf(greeting, "Hello world: rank %d of %d running on %s DEI!\n",
          rank, size, name);

  if( rank == 0 ){
    fputs(greeting, stdout);
    for(partner=1; partner<size; partner++){
      MPI_Status stat;
      MPI_Recv(greeting, sizeof(greeting), MPI_BYTE,
        partner, 1, MPI_COMM_WORLD, &stat);
      fputs(greeting, stdout);
    }
  }else{
    MPI_Send(greeting, strlen(greeting)+1, MPI_BYTE,
      0, 1, MPI_COMM_WORLD);
  }

  /* All done */
  MPI_Finalize();
  exit(0);
}
```

Program 8.1: A variation on everyone's favorite C program, using MPI.

created by MPI itself, by application programs, or by third-party libraries. In C, communicators have the opaque type `MPI_Comm`, while in Fortran they are `INTEGER`s. There is one distinguished communicator, `MPI_COMM_WORLD` defined in the header file `mpi.h` that refers to the entire collection of processes active in the current program.

MPI_Get_processor_name On Beowulf systems it is often useful for diagnostic purposes to determine what physical processor a process is running on. The procedure `MPI_Get_processor_name` tells the caller the name of the processor on which the process is running. The precise form of this name is unspecified by MPI, but on Beowulf systems it is usually the system's Internet hostname. See Section 6.2 for details of how Beowulf systems acquire a hostname.

MPI_Send and MPI_Recv Finally, we encounter our first MPI communication procedures. `MPI_Send` and `MPI_Recv` are the fundamental building blocks of MPI programs. Many other procedures are provided by the library, but in many cases, their behavior (but not necessarily their implementation) is defined in terms of `MPI_Send` and `MPI_Recv`. Their C and FORTRAN prototypes are shown in Program 8.2.

```
int MPI_Send(void* buf, int count, MPI_Datatype datatype,
             int dest, int tag, MPI_Comm comm)

MPI_SEND(BUF, COUNT, DATATYPE, DEST, TAG, COMM, IERROR)
<type> BUF(*)
INTEGER COUNT, DATATYPE, DEST, TAG, COMM, IERROR

int MPI_Recv(void* buf, int count, MPI_Datatype datatype,
             int source, int tag, MPI_Comm comm, MPI_Status
             *status)

MPI_RECV(BUF,COUNT,DATATYPE,SOURCE,TAG,COMM,STATUS,IERROR)
<type> BUF(*)
INTEGER COUNT, DATATYPE, SOURCE, TAG, COMM,
STATUS(MPI_STATUS_SIZE), IERROR
```

Program 8.2:
C and FORTRAN prototypes for the basic communication primitives, `MPI_Send` and `MPI_Recv`

`MPI_Send` and `MPI_Recv` are point-to-point communication primitives. That is, they cause the transmission of a message from a sender's memory to a receiver's memory. Logically, no other process is involved in the transaction. The MPI standard describes messages using a contents/envelope metaphor. The location, size and type of the contents of a message are specified by the first three arguments to `MPI_Send` and `MPI_Recv`. Note that the `count` argument is the number of elements of the given datatype, and is generally not equal to length of the message in bytes unless the data type happens to be `MPI_BYTE`. In `MPI_Send`, the last three arguments specify the message envelope which comprises the message's communicator (see above), an integer tag, and the source and destination ranks within the communicator.

An `MPI_Recv` call may then select messages based on their envelope. That is, the call to `MPI_Recv` specifies a communicator, a source and a tag, and the first message that matches all three, and whose destination matches the receiver's rank, will be received. Wildcard values may be used to receive messages from any source (`MPI_ANY_SOURCE`) and/or with any tag (`MPI_ANY_TAG`). The datatype and count arguments to `MPI_Recv` can be a source of confusion. They are not used for message selection. It is an error if the selected message exceeds the specified count, or has a different datatype from that specified by `MPI_Recv`. It is acceptable for the message to be shorter than the specified count, in which case, the message will be placed at the beginning of the receive buffer and any remaining space will be unmodified.

Blocking standard mode communication   `MPI_Send` and `MPI_Recv` are blocking procedures. That is, they do not return to their caller until the requested operation is complete. `MPI_Send` uses the standard mode of communication, which guarantees that upon return from the procedure, the buffer may be safely reused by the calling process. The MPI implementation may have copied the contents to internal storage, or it may have delivered the data without making intermediate copies. In short, standard mode neither promises nor guarantees anything about the state of the process executing the corresponding receive. In standard mode, the choice of whether to buffer or send directly is made by the MPI implementation, which can optimize behavior based on available resources.

The blocking procedure `MPI_Recv` does not return until the message has been completely received. Upon return, the initial contents of the receive buffer is a copy of the buffer on the sender's side.

Other communication modes (buffered, synchronous and ready) exist which give the programmer more control over buffering and the state of the receiving process. In addition, MPI provides non-blocking procedures (both send and receive) that immediately return an `MPI_Request` object, which can subsequently be used to enquire about or wait for completion of the request. We return to these variations in Section 8.4.1.

The MPI_Status structure   `MPI_Recv` also fills an `MPI_Status` structure with information about the actual message received. The `MPI_Status` structure can be examined to determine the source and tag of the message (for example, if the request used `MPI_SOURCE_ANY` or `MPI_TAG_ANY`). The actual length of the received message may be obtained from `MPI_Get_count`. Keep in mind that `MPI_Get_count` returns the number of items of the given `MPI_Datatype` that were delivered, which is generally not the same as the size in bytes.

Loosely synchronous operation   The blocking procedures above, as well as most of the other MPI communication procedures must be called loosely synchronously. A formal discussion of the meaning of loose synchronicity is given in the MPI Standard document. Roughly, it embodies the notion that all the processes engaged in a communication operation must call the corresponding MPI procedure at the same logical point in their execution, with respect to all other MPI communication calls. In Program 8.1, the sequence of MPI communication calls on the rank=0 processor is: `MPI_Init`, `MPI_Read(src=1)`, ..., `MPI_Read(src=nproc-1)`, `MPI_Finalize`. On other processors, the sequence is: `MPI_Init`, `MPI_Send(dst=0)`, `MPI_Finalize`. The sends and receives are balanced because exactly one `MPI_Recv` in process zero matches the one `MPI_Send` in every other process. Therefore, the program is correctly loosely synchronous. The fact that other non-MPI activity is performed asynchronously on different processors, e.g., only process 0 calls `fwrite` between calls to `MPI_Recv`, is immaterial to loose synchronicity.

Failure to abide by the loosely synchronous restriction often results in deadlock of the entire MPI program. The MPI standard recommends that implementations should provide diagnostics in cases that can be easily detected, but that overall performance should not be compromised by attempts to detect or correct such programming errors. This is not as bad as it sounds. Programs that violate the rules will probably deadlock, but they are usually easy to diagnose and repair. In Program 8.1 the calls to `MPI_Send` and `MPI_Recv` are nearby in the actual program source, so there is little possibility of introducing errors. It is possible, however, for matching loosely synchronous procedure calls to originate in different functions and source files. Programmers must pay careful attention to how communication procedures match up in different processes to avoid such deadlocks.

Balancing sends and receives   The requirement that sends and receives match up exactly is often a source of errors in MPI programs that use standard mode send functions. Program 8.3 shows three ways one might try to exchange data between two processors. The first and, unfortunately, most obvious way is prone to deadlock. The problem is that the calls to `MPI_Send` might not return until the corresponding `MPI_Recv` is called on **partner**. This kind of problem is particularly insidious because the program works correctly for small transfers (e.g., during testing), but

C elementary datatypes	FORTRAN elementary datatypes
MPI_CHAR	MPI_INTEGER
MPI_SHORT	MPI_REAL
MPI_INT	MPI_DOUBLE_PRECISION
MPI_LONG	MPI_COMPLEX
MPI_UNSIGNED_CHAR	MPI_DOUBLE_COMPLEX
MPI_UNSIGNED_SHORT	MPI_LOGICAL
MPI_UNSIGNED	MPI_CHARACTER
MPI_UNSIGNED_LONG	MPI_BYTE
MPI_FLOAT	
MPI_DOUBLE	
MPI_LONG_DOUBLE	
MPI_BYTE	

Table 8.1
MPI elementary data types in C (left) and FORTRAN (right). Note that the MPI_BYTE type treats binary data as raw and untyped, while the MPI_CHARACTER treats character arrays correctly as strings. MPI also allows for user-defined types, which are extensively used in the MPI-2 specification of I/O operations.

for large transfers (e.g., during production), the program hangs. There are at least three ways to fix it. In the second code block, we have explicitly guaranteed that one processor does the MPI_Send first and the other does the MPI_Recv first. This is a viable solution, but it can be tedious to locate every pairwise exchange in a program and carefully order the sends and receives. Another alternative (not shown) is to make one or both of the calls non-blocking. Finally, the most convenient solution is to use the MPI_Sendrecv procedure which combines a send and a receive as if they were executed in separate threads of control. This neatly solves the problem, makes the code shorter and more readable and even opens the possibility for optimizations by the library.

MPI Datatypes   MPI contains a sophisticated set of procedures for naming and manipulating data types. Most MPI communication routines require an argument that specifies the type of data being transmitted. This facility can be of considerable value when using MPI in heterogeneous environments, in which case the MPI communication procedures do automatic format translation. For a homogeneous Beowulf configuration this is largely superfluous. They elementary data types are shown in Table 8.1.

Use of standard libraries   MPI programs are free to use all the facilities of the programming libraries, e.g., stdio, X11, libc, etc., available on the system. MPI does not alter the libraries in any way, so that, one has a number of processes all

```
MPI_Comm comm;
MPI_Datatype type;
MPI_Status stat;
int count, tag, rank, partner;

MPI_Comm_rank(comm, &rank);
partner = rank^1;          /* toggle the lowest bit */

/* INCORRECT.  MAY DEADLOCK DEPENDING ON BUFFERING */
MPI_Send(out, count, type, partner, tag, comm);
MPI_Recv(in, count, type, partner, tag, comm, &stat);

/* CORRECT - SENDS MUST MATCH RECEIVES EXACTLY */
if(rank > partner){
    MPI_Send(out, count, type, partner, tag, comm);
    MPI_Recv(in, count, type, partner, tag, comm, &stat);
}else if(rank < partner){
    MPI_Recv(out, count, type, partner, tag, comm, &stat);
    MPI_Send(in, count, type, partner, tag, comm);
}else{ /* rank == partner */
    int sz;
    MPI_Type_size(type, &sz);
    memcpy(in, out, count * sz);
    /* contents of stat not set! */
}

/* ALSO CORRECT - USE THE MPI_SENDRECV PROCEDURE INSTEAD */
MPI_Sendrecv(out, count, type, partner, tag,
             in, count, type, partner, tag, comm, &stat);
```

Program 8.3:
A common error when using MPI standard mode blocking communication procedures is to
implicitly assume that sends are buffered, and hence that two processes may send to one another
and then receive the results. The first block of code works correctly for short messages when the
MPI library buffers the send, but hangs for longer messages when buffering is not used. One
solution is to explicitly balance sends and receives, e.g., higher numbered processes send first
and lower numbered ones receive first. Alternatively, one can use the convenient MPI_Sendrecv
procedure that correctly handles the case of the source and destination being the same processor,
as well as the common "bucket brigade" case in which source and destination are different.

making independent and asynchronous calls to the libraries. Often, calls to external libraries—especially I/O libraries—should be made only from one distinguished process, e.g., the one with rank 0 in `MPI_COMM_WORLD`. I/O is particularly problematical because the MPI-1 standard avoids all mention of I/O. The MPI-2 standard addresses issues of parallel I/O, but implementations are only just being released and even MPI-2 does not address output to `stdout` or `stderr`.

The safest and most portable assumption is that only the process with rank=0 in `MPI_COMM_WORLD` can do standard I/O (and even this is not actually guaranteed to work). In fact, both LAM and MPICH (the two implementations of MPI available on Beowulf) allow much more flexibility. This flexibility can be very powerful, but one should be aware of possible portability problems. The example in Program 8.1 invokes `fputs` only on process 0 of `MPI_COMM_WORLD`.

Errors in MPI   One of the principal features of MPI is that it shields the application programmer from issues of network errors, time-outs, etc. Usually, the MPI implementation or the networking layers upon which it is built have made reasonable, if not heroic, attempts to retry, wait, etc, so there is little that an application program can do to recover from internal networking errors.

The careful reader will have noted that `MPI_Send` and `MPI_Recv` both return an integer error code, usually equal to the defined constant `MPI_SUCCESS`, whereas Program 8.1 ignored the returned values. In fact, almost all MPI procedures return an error code, but it is usually a waste of time to check the value. After an error, the internal state of MPI is undefined and possibly inconsistent, and the standard document states that the behavior of subsequent calls to MPI procedures is "undefined." In fact, the standard goes further and defines a default error handler which immediately terminates the entire parallel process. While it is possible to install an alternative error handler which might, for example, flush data files prior to exiting, it is not possible to continue with message passing activity after an error. Therefore, there is little point in testing the value returned by MPI procedures.

Compiling an MPI program on Beowulf   The exact procedure for compiling and running an MPI program depends on which implementation of MPI is installed. In any case, it is probably best to check locally installed manual pages or documentation if the recipes presented here do not work.

MPICH is usually installed in a public location, e.g., `/usr/local/mpich`, which we call `<MPI_ROOT>`. All user-oriented MPICH utilities reside in `<MPI_ROOT>/bin`, so this directory should be in the user PATH before attempting to use MPI. `<MPI_ROOT>/bin` contains the scripts, `mpicc` and `mpif77` which can be used to compile and link MPI programs. There is nothing magic in these scripts—they do little more than pass their arguments through to cc or f77 with appropriate MPI-specific -I, -L and library arguments added. Nevertheless, it is a good idea to use them unless some specialized behavior is required. For those who prefer to call the C or Fortran compiler directly, header files are in `<MPI_ROOT>/include`, and on Linux Beowulf systems, libraries are in `<MPI_ROOT>/lib/LINUX/ch_p4/`. Both of the following commands should successfully compile a file called hello.c into an executable called `hello`.

```
> # the value of MPIROOT is site-specific
> MPIROOT=/usr/local/mpi
> mpicc -o hello hello.c
> cc -o hello -I$MPIROOT/include hello.c -L$MPIROOT/LINUX/ch_p4 -lmpich
```

One complication that can arise in Beowulf systems is the availability of several different compilers. Fortran programmers are particularly afflicted by the "blessing" of being able to choose from several compilers - both free and commercial. These compilers can and do have different conventions for capitalization, trailing underscores, etc., and mixing compilers can lead to obscure failures at link time. A simple, but not particularly elegant solution is to compile separate copies of MPICH for use with each compiler, and maintain them in different `<MPI_ROOT>` locations.

Running an MPI program   An MPI program is started with the `mpirun` utility. The most commonly used flag is `-np <number_of_processes>`, which starts the program with the specified number of processes. There is a system-wide default list of processors to use, but it is often necessary to supply a list explicitly. The `-machinefile <filename>` argument accomplishes this. By default, `mpirun` starts process 0 on the processor that called `mpirun`. This is undesirable in Beowulf installations where a worldly node is used for compiling, launching jobs, etc. In this case, the `-nolocal` flag will force the first process to execute on the first named processor in the `-machinefile` list. MPICH is extensively documented, and manual pages describing these and other flags and options are included with every installation. Program 8.4 is a log of a short session in which the example, Program 8.1, is compiled and run on four Beowulf processors.

8.3   Parallel Data Structures with MPI

Parallel data structures are crucial to the design of parallel programs. MPI provides a very simple memory model with which to construct parallel data structures.

```
$ mpicc -o hello hello.c
$ mpirun -np 4 hello
Hello world: rank 0 of 4 running on wealhtheow DEI!
Hello world: rank 1 of 4 running on wealhtheow DEI!
Hello world: rank 2 of 4 running on wealhtheow DEI!
Hello world: rank 3 of 4 running on wealhtheow DEI!
$ cat machines
y101 y102 y103 y104 y105 y106 y107 y108 y109 y110 y111 y112
$ mpirun -np 4 -nolocal -machinefile machines hello
Hello world: rank 0 of 4 running on y101 DEI!
Hello world: rank 1 of 4 running on y102 DEI!
Hello world: rank 2 of 4 running on y103 DEI!
Hello world: rank 3 of 4 running on y104 DEI!
$
```

Program 8.4: Log of a session compiling and executing Program 8.1 with MPICH.

Unlike other parallel programming systems, e.g., OpenMP,[7] Compositional C++,[8] MPI adds no language features at all. MPI programs can be compiled by any C or Fortran compiler and the semantics implied by those languages are unchanged. Parallel data structures in MPI are implicit in the fact that independent processes are running independently in each and every process. In an MPI program, *every* symbol is actually a parallel object that exists in every process. It is entirely up to the programmer how to treat this object. In some cases, it makes sense for every process to see the same value for the symbol. Alternatively, it may make sense for a value of a given symbol to be different in different processes.

8.3.1   Example: A Parallel Array

A parallel array is so simple that it often escapes notice as a parallel data structure. Program 8.5 shows a structure definition and constructor for a parallel array object.

In an MPI program, each process has a separate address space, so when an object, e.g., a `parray` structure, as in Program 8.5 is defined it automatically exists on every process. In order to use a `parray` as a parallel array, one need only adopt conventions about the meaning of the various fields. The choice of variable names suggests that `nelem_global` contains the total aggregate number of elements, including those on remote processes, while `nelem_local` contains the number in local memory. While this convention is reasonable, nothing in MPI enforces such a convention—it is entirely up to the programmer to maintain. The

---

[7]OpenMP home page: http://www.openmp.org

[8]CC++ home page: http://globus.isi.edu/ccpp/

```
#ifndef pa2DOTH
#define pa2DOTH

#include <stddef.h>

typedef struct {
  int nelem_local;
  void *data;
  MPI_Comm comm;
  int first_index_local;
  int nelem_global;
  size_t elem_size;
  int commrank, commsize;
} parray;

extern void pacreate(parray *pa, void *data, int nmine,
     size_t elem_size, MPI_Comm comm);

#endif
```

Program 8.5:
The header file "pa2.h", containing a structure declaration and function prototype for the
constructor of a parallel array. This declaration is assumed to be included in the following
program fragments by the directive #include "pa2.h".

integer `first_global_index` holds the global index of the first element of the local
data (whose local index is 0). It might be important, for example, if the array
is to be read from or written to a shared disk file. Obviously, there are implicit
relations between these values, e.g., `nelem_global` is the sum of `nelem_local` in
each process. Program 8.6 creates a self-consistent parallel array from a pointer
and a value of `nelem_local` on every process in a communicator. It must be called
loosely synchronously by all the processes in the communicator.

We have chosen to include the communicator explicitly in the data structure
defining the parallel array. This certainly improves modularity and generality, but
it is also common for MPI programs to implicitly assume that all communications
are with respect to `MPI_COMM_WORLD`. This is especially true of programs ported
from older communication systems, e.g., NX, which did not have a notion of communicators.

Collective communication   Program 8.6 illustrates two of MPI's collective communication procedures: `MPI_Scan` and `MPI_Broadcast`. Collective procedures perform operations that involve all the processes in a communicator. `MPI_Broadcast`
sends the contents of the buffer on one process (designated by the fourth argument)
to every other process in the communicator. `MPI_Scan` is more complicated, and

```
#include <stddef.h>
#include <mpi.h>
#include "pa2.h"

void
pacreate(parray *pa, void *data, int nelem, size_t size, MPI_Comm comm){
  int last_index;

  pa->nelem_local = nelem;
  pa->data = data;
  pa->comm = comm;
  pa->elem_size = size;
  /* My first element is the sum of the number of elements
     in lower ranked procs */
  MPI_Scan(&pa->nelem_local, &last_index,
   1, MPI_INT, MPI_SUM, pa->comm);
  pa->first_index_local = last_index - pa->nelem_local;
  MPI_Comm_size(pa->comm, &pa->commsize);
  MPI_Comm_rank(pa->comm, &pa->commrank);
  /* The global element count is the last index in the highest
     rank processor (commsize-1).  Use Broadcast to distribute it. */
  MPI_Bcast(&last_index, 1, MPI_INT, pa->commsize-1, pa->comm);
  pa->nelem_global = last_index;
}
```

Program 8.6:
A procedure to create a self-consistent parallel array from information provided by each process about its own local data.

performs an operation (in this case, arithmetic summation) on values supplied by each processor. The result returned on process i is the result of the operation applied to values supplied by every process of rank 0 through i. MPI's predefined reduction/scan operations include:

$$\texttt{MPI\_MAX, MPI\_MIN, MPI\_SUM, MPI\_PROD, MPI\_LAND, MPI\_BAND, MPI\_LOR, MPI\_BOR,}$$
$$\texttt{MPI\_LXOR, MPI\_BXOR, MPI\_MAXLOC, MPI\_MINLOC.}$$

The last two perform an operation that returns both the extremum, and an auxiliary value associated with that extremum (e.g., its array index or rank). In Program 8.6, `MPI_Scan` is applied to the individual values of `nelem_local`, and returns to each processor the global index of its last element. We then subtract `nelem_local` to get the first index.

Program 8.7 computes the mean of a parallel array, illustrating the use of `MPI_Allreduce`, which computes the result of an operation applied to a value supplied by every process. The result is returned to every process. `MPI_Allreduce` can perform the same operations as `MPI_Scan` (see above).

It is worth noting that most of **pamean** is identical to sequential code that would perform the same function. This phenomenon is common in MPI programs. A sequential "core" is modified only slightly to obtain a parallel program or function. Frequently, the modifications involve only very minor changes to loop bounds plus a preamble or epilog containing calls to MPI procedures.

```
#include <mpi.h>
#include "parray.h"

double
parraymean(struct parray *pa){
  double sum, sumall;
  int i;
  /* Compute the local sum of the elements */
  sum = 0.;
  for(i=0; i<pa->nelem_mine; i++){
    sum += pa->data[i];
  }
  /* use Allreduce to get the global sum */
  MPI_Allreduce(&sum, &sumall, 1, MPI_DOUBLE, MPI_SUM, pa->comm);
  return sumall/pa->nelem_global;
}
```

Program 8.7: A procedure to compute the mean of the elements in a parallel array.

Other collective communication functions are `MPI_Gather`, `MPI_Scatter` and various optimized combinations that are functionally equivalent to combinations of two or more operations, e.g., `MPI_Allreduce` is equivalent to `MPI_Reduce` followed by `MPI_Broadcast`.

In addition to the pre-defined reduction operations, programmers can provide external functions which `MPI_Reduce` will use to combine the values provided by different processors. For example, it is often convenient to obtain simple statistics on a single value supplied by each processor. The function `simpleStats` in Program 8.8 computes the min, max, sum and sum-of-squares of a value supplied by each process in a Communicator. This is achieved by defining an operator, `accumStats` in Program 8.9, that takes two pointers to `SimpleStats_t` structures, replacing the second one with their combination. The sum, sum-of-squares and number of samples are added, the maximum and minimum values are computed, and the rank of the process with the maximum or minimum value is copied. We will use `simpleStats` in Chapter 9 to process timing data.

```
void simpleStats(double value, SimpleStats_t *stats, MPI_Comm comm){
  SimpleStats_t in;
  static MPI_Datatype statstype;
  static int initized;
  static MPI_Op accumOp;
  if( !initized ){
    initized = 1;
    MPI_Type_contiguous(sizeof(SimpleStats_t), MPI_BYTE, &statstype);
    MPI_Type_commit(&statstype);
    MPI_Op_create(accumStats, 1, &accumOp);
  }
  Dbg("simpleStats(v=%g)\n", value);
  in.sum = value;
  in.sumsquared = value*value;
  in.min = value;
  in.max = value;
  in.nsamples = 1;
  MPI_Comm_rank(comm, &in.minrank);
  in.maxrank = in.minrank;
  MPI_Allreduce(&in, stats, 1, statstype, accumOp, comm);
}
```

Program 8.8:
A function, simpleStats, which takes a double precision argument (e.g., a time interval
measured by a stopwatch), and fills in the max, min, sum, maxrank and minrank fields of the
SimpleStats structure. Maxrank and minrank are the ranks of the processors that hold the
maximum and minimum values, respectively. This function illustrates the use of MPI's
user-defined types and user-specified reduction functions.

```
typedef struct {
  double sum;
  double sumsquared;
  double min;
  double max;
  int minrank;
  int maxrank;
  int nsamples;
} SimpleStats_t;

static void
accumStats(void *v1, void *v2, int *nptr, MPI_Datatype *tp){
  SimpleStats_t *s1, *s2;
  int n = *nptr;

  s1 = v1;
  s2 = v2;
  while( n-- ){
    s2->sum += s1->sum;
    s2->sumsquared += s2->sumsquared;
    if( s1->max > s2->max ){
      s2->max = s1->max;
      s2->maxrank = s1->maxrank;
    }
    if( s1->min < s2->min ){
      s2->min = s1->min;
      s2->minrank = s1->minrank;
    }
    s2->nsamples += s1->nsamples;
    s1++;
    s2++;
  }
}
```

Program 8.9:
Structure declaration for `SimpleStats_t` and the auxiliary function, `accumStats`, used by the `SimpleStats` function in Program 8.8. The structure fields, `sum`, `sumsquared` and `nsamples` are added to produce the result. The fields `max` and `min` are also combined in the obvious way. The `minrank` and `maxrank` fields are copied in much the same way that `MPI_MINLOC` and `MPI_MAXLOC` copy the auxiliary data. In Program 8.8 they are initialized with the rank of the calling process, so upon completion, they hold the rank of the process that supplied the minimum and maximum values, respectively.

8.3.2   Example: A One-dimensional Cellular Automaton

In the examples above, the order of the elements and the way in which they are assigned to processors was unimportant, so it was possible to do all communication using collective reductions, scans, broadcasts, etc. Now we consider an example in which the placement of data is meaningful, requiring us to use point-to-point communication routines. One-dimensional cellular automata (CA) are simple dynamical systems that can display surprisingly complex behavior. A CA with half-width `hw` is an array of values with an update rule that says the next value in location `i` depends only on the previous values in locations (`i-hw`, ..., `i`, ...`i+hw`). For simplicity, we consider finite CA with periodic boundary conditions, i.e., the location indices are computed modulo `ncells`, the number of cells in the array.

A wide variety of cellular automata have been studied. The values may be integers, or they may be restricted to a finite alphabet of size A. If A=2, the values are bits, and it is often possible to pack them very tightly and perform updates very rapidly. The update rule may be an arbitrary function of the $2\,\text{hw}+1$ input values. Special cases include linear functions and functions like "parity" which count the number of values of a particular type in the input domain. Program 8.11 shows some code from a simple sequential CA implementation designed to work with arbitrary functions of fairly small alphabets (each value must fit in a single unsigned char, i.e., A $\leq$ 256).

```
typedef struct ca_s{
  unsigned char *state; /* size ncells */
  int A;
  int hw;
  int ncells;
  unsigned char *old; /* size ncells + 2*hw */
  /* other fields that control updateRule */
} CA_t;
```

Program 8.10:
Structure definition for a 1-D cellular automaton with update rule implemented in Program 8.11.

The two distinct operations in the procedure `CAiterate` are important. The first operation, `CAcopystate` involves copying the contents of the `state` array to the `old` array so that we can write the new values into `state`. The second phase then computes the new state based on values in `old`. Notice that periodic boundary conditions are imposed by padding the `old` array on both ends by `hw` values, copied from the opposite end of `state`, as illustrated in Figure 8.1. Thus, when the new value of, e.g., `state[0]` is evaluated, `updateRule` uses values `old[-hw]` through

```
void
CAiterate(CA_t *ca, int ntimes){
  int i;

  for(i=0; i<ntimes; i++){
    CAcopystate(ca);
    CAupdate(ca);
  }
}

static void
CAupdate(CA_t *ca){
  int n = ca->ncells;
  unsigned char *oldcenter = ca->old;
  unsigned char *new = ca->state;
  while( n-- > 0 ){
    *new++ = updateRule(ca, oldcenter++);
  }
}

static void
CAcopystate(CA_t *ca){
  memcpy(ca->old, ca->state, ca->ncells);
  /* Now for periodic boundary conditions */
  memcpy(ca->old-ca->hw, ca->state+(ca->ncells-ca->hw), ca->hw);
  memcpy(ca->old+ca->ncells, ca->state, ca->hw);
}
```

Program 8.11:
Functions to update a 1-D CA, as declared in Program 8.10. Each iteration, implemented in
CAiterate is a two-step process. In the first step, CAcopystate copies the current state to an
array called old, and "boundary conditions" are used to fill in values in old that are beyond the
ends of the original array. In the second step, CAupdate creates a new state by evaluating the
update rule centered at every non-boundary element in the old copy.

old[hw], but the values with negative indices were copied from the last hw values
of state by the second memcpy in CAcopystate. To implement a different boundary
condition, all that is necessary is to change the last two lines of CAcopystate.

To parallelize Program 8.11, we again follow the guideline of keeping as much
as possible of the sequential code intact. Unlike the situation when computing the
moments of a parallel array, however, the order of elements in the CA, and the
relationship between elements stored in different processors is important. Instead
of performing a global reduction to exchange data between processors, boundary
data must be exchanged between neighbors. Most of the parallel code is exactly
the same as the sequential code. An MPI_Comm element has been added to the
structure in Program 8.12, and two calls to memcpy have been replaced by calls

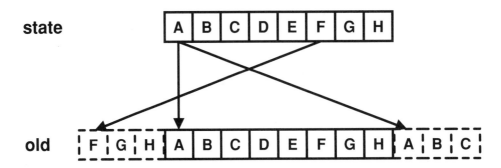

Figure 8.1
When the state of a CA is copied to old, it is padded at both ends so that the updateRule function always finds enough neighbors. Each arrow in the figure represents a call to memcpy in Program 8.11.

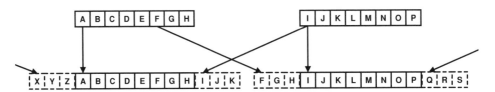

Figure 8.2
In the parallel version, when the state of a CA is copied to old, it is padded at both ends by data from neighboring processors. Two processors are shown. The diagonal arrows represent data transfers by MPI_Sendrecv, and the vertical arrow represents a memcpy.

to MPI_Sendrecv in CAcopystate. Figure 8.2 illustrates the data communication pattern in Program 8.13. All processes simultaneously transfer data to their higher-numbered neighbor in the first call to MPI_Sendrecv and to their lower-numbered neighbor in the second call to MPI_Sendrecv. Data is transferred downward (left-ward in the figure) in the second call. Periodic boundary conditions are enforced by setting the down_neighbor in process 0 to be nproc-1, and similarly for the up_neighbor in process nproc-1.

MPI_Sendrecv combines a send and a receive into a single blocking operation that "does the right thing" in most cases. The first five arguments describe the outgoing data, its destination and tag, and the second five arguments describe the incoming buffer. Using it is much easier than carefully balancing sends and receives to avoid the possibility of deadlock. A different procedure, MPI_Sendrecv_replace, should be used if the incoming and outgoing buffers overlap.

```
typedef struct ca_s{
  unsigned char *state; /* size ncells */
  int A;
  int hw;
  int ncells;
  unsigned char *old; /* size ncells + 2*hw */
  MPI_Comm comm; /* parallel version only */
  /* other fields that control updateRule */
} CA_t;
```

Program 8.12:
Structure definition for a parallel 1-D cellular automaton with update rule implemented in
Program 8.11. The ncells field refers to the number of local cells, not the total number on all
processes. We assume that the total is stored elsewhere, or, if not, it can be computed with a
call to MPI_Reduce, as in Program 8.7.

Domain decomposition and boundaries It is often possible to formulate a
parallel version of a problem as a collection of near-copies of a sequential implementation with special boundary conditions derived by communication with neighbors.
This is most often true for problems that have an underlying spatial structure, e.g.,
finite-difference or finite element discretizations of differential equations. In the
case of the CA, the underlying spatial structure was one-dimensional, and we were
able to retain the majority of the sequential code by making a small modification
to the boundary generating code in CAcopystate.

Start with a good sequential implementation The parallelization of this
example was particularly simple because we started with a relatively clean sequential code. In most cases, this is how parallel programs are written. Fundamental
numerical or computational algorithms are designed and implemented sequentially.
Changes required for parallelization should be as small as possible, and should be
isolated in the "periphery" of the sequential code. For the CA, it was a matter
of obtaining boundary conditions from neighboring processors. Whenever possible,
it is a very good practice to avoid changing the fundamentally local parts of a
parallel code. In many cases, these local operations, e.g., matrix operations, have
been heavily optimized and carefully debugged, and it would adversely affect both
development time and execution time to alter them. In the CA, it is possible that
the updateRule may have been heavily optimized, but since we did not modify it
in any way, it should perform just as well in parallel as sequentially.

Treating communication as a separate phase from local computation has a second
benefit, particularly on Beowulf systems. If all the communication is done at once,
multiple logical messages can be merged into a smaller number of actual messages.

```
#define CA_UPTAG 1
#define CA_DOWNTAG 2

CAcopystate(CA_t *ca){
  int up_neighbor, down_neighor, myrank, nproc;
  memcpy(ca->old, ca->state, ca->ncells);
  MPI_Comm_rank(ca->comm, &myrank);
  MPI_Comm_size(ca->comm, &nproc);
  up_neighbor = (myrank+1)%nproc;
  down_neighbor = (myrank+nproc-1)%nproc;
  MPI_Sendrecv(ca->state + (ca->ncells - ca->hw), ca->hw, MPI_BYTE,
      up_neighbor, CA_UPTAG,
      ca->old, ca->hw, MPI_BYTE, down_neighbor, CA_UPTAG,
      ca->comm, &stat);
  MPI_Sendrecv(ca->state, ca->hw, MPI_BYTE, down_neighbor, CA_DOWNTAG,
      ca->old+(ca->ncells+ca->hw), ca->hw, MPI_BYTE, up_neighbor,
      CA_DOWNTAG, ca->comm, &stat);
}
```

Program 8.13:
The parallel version of CAcopystate. The rest of the parallel 1-D CA is identical to
Program 8.11. In the parallel case, "boundary conditions" are imposed by communication with
neighbors rather than by copying data from elsewhere in the same processor. When **nproc** is one
there is only one processor and **rank**, **up_neighbor** and **down_neighbor** are all zero. In this case,
the **MPI_Sendrecv** calls are identical to the **memcpy** calls in Program 8.11.

Recall that with Ethernet networks, each message takes at least 200 or so microseconds, even if it is only one word long. Therefore, sending one large message can be much faster than sending several short messages of the same aggregate length. It is much easier to apply this type of optimization if communication is logically separated from computation.

Performance There is one overriding fact that governs the performance of parallel programs on Beowulfs: *Communication is slow.* One advantage of programming in MPI is that all communication is explicitly exposed. While this can be a burden for program development, it is a tremendous benefit for performance tuning. In the CA code, we can see that exactly two send/receive communications are necessary for each timestep. Furthermore, unless the half-width of the update rule is very large, the messages sent are very short (a few bytes). Therefore communication latency will dominate the time and for Fast Ethernet networks, this will amount to a few hundred microseconds spent in communication on each timestep. If the local **CAupdate** is much faster than that, we will be disappointed by the performance of our parallel implementation because it will spend most of its time in communication.

We can derive the same result analytically by estimating the time to complete an iteration with N cells and P processors as:

$$
\begin{aligned}
t_{step} &= 2t_{latency} + (N/P)t_{update} \\
&= \left(\frac{Nt_{update}}{P}\right)\left(1 + \frac{2t_{latency}}{(N/P)t_{update}}\right)
\end{aligned}
$$

The first term is just the time it would take on one processor, Nt_{update}, divided by P, i.e., it is the perfect speedup result. The last term, therefore, represents how much worse than perfect is the actual implementation. It is the ratio of the time spent by one processor in communication, $2t_{latency}$ to the time spent in `CAupdate`, $(N/P)t_{update}$. If this ratio is small, then the overall speedup will be near perfect, while if this ratio is large, the overall speedup will be disappointing. The sample implementation performs about 4 million updates per second on a 200MHz PentiumPro processor. On a Fast Ethernet network with $t_{latency}$ of $200\,\mu$sec, N/P would have to be larger than 1600 or so to obtain good speedups. Of course, all these numbers are very rough estimates. Nevertheless, a quick analysis like this one can be extremely useful when designing, implementing, and debugging an MPI program. It allows one to estimate how times will scale with N, P, etc., and also to determine how communication latency and/or bandwidth affect overall performance. One obtains a quantitative expectation about real performance which can be compared against actual behavior. If they differ, further analysis and investigation may uncover an unexpected source of overhead, or an opportunity for improvement. One must be careful about factors not accounted for by this analysis. Graphical output and user interfaces, in particular, can be a significant overhead, especially if one tries to display the result of every iteration.

8.4   MPI Advanced Features

So far we have only covered the most basic procedures in the MPI library. MPI incorporates many of the best ideas that were implemented in the older research and proprietary systems that constitute its heritage. In this section we briefly review some of the more important advanced features. Programmers intending to use these features will need to consult the reference manual either online or in print form for details.

8.4.1   Blocking and Non-blocking Calls and Alternative Sending Modes

Blocking calls blocking communication calls, discussed in Section 8.2.1, always wait for the requested action (send or receive) to complete before returning control to the caller. When a blocking call is used, MPI does not return until it is safe for the calling program to use (or re-use in the case of send) the data buffer that was communicated.

Non-blocking calls Non-blocking communications are initiated with a start procedure, and completed with a completion procedure. After the start call, the MPI system may cause the communication to take place in the background. On some systems this provides a mechanism for overlapping communication and calculation. On today's Beowulfs, however, there is little to be gained by using non-blocking sends because the available MPI implementations do not invoke background communications. Nevertheless, it is not safe to read or write the communicated data after a start call has returned. It is only after a corresponding completion procedure returns that one can be confident that the data is safely copied, either into internal MPI buffers, or to its final destination. One important reason to use non-blocking communications is to avoid unnecessary copying between system buffers and user memory, thereby increasing overall bandwidth. Since MPI communications are sender-initiated, an additional memory copy can sometimes be avoided by posting a receive before the corresponding send is issued. A non-blocking receive can be used in this case to allow the caller to post the receive well in advance of the send and then continue with other work. has been posted. Non-blocking communications can also be used to implement asynchronous servers that respond to messages of a given type by performing some computation. Such services can be implemented by posting a non-blocking read, and then occasionally testing its status to see if any messages have arrived.

MPI offers four different sending modes that can be either blocking or non-blocking.

Standard mode sends In this, the most common case, buffering is left to the discretion of the MPI library. Data may be buffered internally by the library, in which case a blocking send call may return when the buffer has been copied, but (possibly) before the recipient has received the data. However, there is no guarantee that buffering will be employed, so the send call may also block until the corresponding receive has been issued at the receiving end. Thus, the completion of standard calls may depend on activity on the receiving processor.

Buffered mode sends In buffered mode, MPI always attempts to buffer the messages. Buffer space must be supplied in advance by the user, and the procedure will fail if there is insufficient buffer space. Completion in this case is local because there is never a need to wait for the availability of remote resources.

Buffered sends could also be used to avoid the problem illustrated in Program 8.3, but the user would then be responsible for allocating buffer space. Buffering also requires additional copying, which can impact performance.

Ready mode sends Ready communication procedures imply a promise by the caller to the MPI library that the receive has been posted before the send is initiated. Under this assumption, the library is free to perform optimizations that would be difficult or impossible otherwise.

Synchronous mode sends A synchronous send does not return until the corresponding receive has been posted. Blocking synchronous sends and receives can be used to implement a two-process barrier. They may also be used as a debugging aid. In a correct program, all standard mode sends can be replaced by synchronous mode sends without altering the behavior. On the other hand, if the standard mode sends in Program 8.3 were replaced by synchronous sends, the program would immediately deadlock regardless of buffer sizes or other considerations. This can be used to quickly verify the absence of such incorrect constructs.

8.4.2   Virtual Topologies and Attribute Caching

In addition to defining contexts for communication based on groups of processes, communicators can also support virtual topologies, which allow applications to work in terms of logical Cartesian groups of processes, regardless of the underlying hardware network or architecture. Attribute caching allows libraries to attach arbitrary pieces of information to a communicator. This information might be used, for example to optimize subsequent library calls.

8.4.3   Derived Data Types

In the examples above, we restricted ourselves to a few of MPI's primitive data types. In fact, MPI includes a powerful set of procedures for defining and manipulating complex data types. These procedures can be used to refer to non-contiguous data, e.g., a sub-block of a matrix, and to refer to data of inhomogeneous type, e.g., an integer count followed by a sequence of floating point values.

Communication in parallel computations is frequently latency dominated. This means that the cost of sending a message is primarily in the startup overhead at both ends, and the actual transfer of data is relatively inexpensive. On Beowulf systems employing Fast Ethernet, messages below about 1.5 kbytes are generally latency dominated. Under such circumstances, it is advantageous to pack multiple logical messages into a single physical message, and to incur the startup cost only once. MPI's derived data types can be helpful in such packing and unpacking tasks.

8.4.4   Intercommunicators

Normal communicators (see Section 8.2.1) are constructed by elimination. That is, one begins with MPI_COMM_WORLD, the group of all active processes, and communicators are derived by selecting subsets from this communicator or its descendents. Objects constructed this way can only become smaller, never larger. Occasionally one finds that this logical structure is insufficient, and it is desirable to construct a new communicator from the union of two existing communicators. These are called inter-communicators, and are used primarily in applications that display functional parallelism.

8.4.5   MPI-2

The MPI-2 standard was released in April 1997, and defines support for several new features. The most important of these are:

Process creation and management   MPI-1 programs consist of processes that are statically allocated at runtime and that exist through the life of the program. MPI-2 also allows processes to be dynamically created and destroyed. Much of this functionality is derived from the extensive experience with the PVM research effort.

One-sided communications   In some dynamic applications it can be useful for either the sender or receiver of a communication to specify all the parameters of the transfer, i.e., both the source and destination. This relieves the other party of needing to know the identity or timing of requests or replies. There is also the possibility of exploiting very fast communication mechanisms such as the direct memory access capabilities that exist on shared memory processors.

Extended Collective Operations   MPI-1 does not allow for collective operations involving intercommunicators. This restriction is relaxed in MPI-2, along with the introduction of new procedures for the creation of intercommunicators, and two new collective operations.

External interfaces   Features are provided so that users and library designers can access the internals of MPI's opaque objects. This allows for new functionality to be layered on top of MPI's internal data structures. The relationship between MPI and generic thread libraries is also defined.

New language bindings   MPI-2 defines language bindings for C++ and FOR-TRAN90 applications.

I/O   MPI-IO describes the application side of an abstract model of parallel I/O, in which processes may work either collectively or independently to describe parallel I/O operations. MPI-IO does not define how a parallel file system should actually commit the data to permanent store. That is left entirely to the implementation. It is concerned solely with the very complex issue of how to define requests to a parallel (or sequential) abstract I/O device from a distributed memory parallel program. Strided, blocked and more complex operations are defined in terms of MPI derived data types.

9 Programming with MPI—A Detailed Example

As discussed in the previous chapter, MPI presents the programmer with a distributed address space model. The programmer must therefore *partition* or *decompose* the data so that individual computational objects are assigned to individual processors. This decomposition can be either static, i.e., fixed once and for all, or dynamic, i.e., changing in response to the simulation or the system on which it is running.

In the CA example in Chapter 8 the state of the system was described by a vector of integers. We partitioned that vector over a set of MPI processes so that each process was responsible for a contiguous block of data. The important feature of that partitioning was that it *minimized communication*. The only data that needed to be shared between processors were the end-points of every block.

In this chapter we give a detailed example of an approach to implementing high performance, parallel applications with MPI. The basic approach to designing a good parallel application is as follows:

- Choose an algorithm with sufficient parallelism and a favorable ratio of communication to computation;
- Optimize a sequential version of the algorithm. This may mean finding library implementations of key steps, e.g., well tested and extremely fast implementations of Fourier transforms[1] and linear algebra[2] are widely available. High quality software archives[3] are an excellent starting place for locating both sequential and parallel implementations of key algorithmic components;
- Implement the parallel version using the simplest possible MPI operations—usually blocking, standard mode procedures;
- Profiling and analysis. Find what operations or activities are taking the most time;
- Attack the most time-consuming components. Be selective. Remember the corollary to Amdahl's law: if something takes 10% of the time, then no matter how much you optimize it, your overall speed will never increase by more than 10%.

Experience has shown that the most effective way to improve the performance of a parallel program is to improve the single-node performance. This is at odds with a

---

[1] The FFTW library at http://theory.lcs.mit.edu/~fftw/
RPM at: ftp://contrib.redhat.com/libc6/i386/fftw-2.0.1-3.i386.rpm
[2] LAPACK home page: http://www.netlib.org/lapack/
RPM at: ftp://rhcn.redhat.com/pub/rhcn/RPMS/i386/lapack-2.0-12.i386.rpm
[3] http://netlib.org/ and http://www.nhse.org

widespread desire to report near linear "speedup" or near unity "parallel efficiency." More often than not, increases in single-node performance lead to decreases in efficiency and speedup. Avoid the temptation to target good speedup numbers, and focus instead on overall performance (time to execution).

Furthermore, it is important to avoid the trap of equating performance with "Megaflops". Performance should be measured as time-to-solution. The algorithm or implementation that delivers the highest Megaflops rate is not necessarily the one that gets the solution fastest. As an extreme example, one could use high-megaflops dense-matrix methods to solve a problem where sparse methods would work just as well. The $O(N^3)$ dense methods deliver outstanding Megaflops numbers due to the regular structure of the algorithms and the considerable efforts that have gone into designing optimized libraries. Sparse methods, on the other hand, deliver significantly fewer Megaflops, but only require $O(N^2)$ operations. The sparse methods would obtain results more quickly, but would report lower Megaflops rates.

The examples of parallel programs we have seen so far have been very small. They have been presented as more-or-less finished products. The purpose of this chapter is to illustrate some of the analyses and thought processes that go into designing, implementing and tuning a parallel program using MPI. It is obviously impossible to survey all possible approaches to the design and implementation of parallel programs. We have chosen a non-trivial problem, and explored its implementation on a particular machine. The thought processes, and to some extent, the tools used, are common across the space of problems. Roughly in both chronological order and in decreasing order of importance, the steps to a good parallel implementation are:

- Understand the strengths and weaknesses of sequential solutions of the same problem;
- Choose a good sequential algorithm to form the core of a parallel implementation;
- Design a strategy for parallelization;
- Develop a rough semi-analytic model of how the parallel algorithm should perform;
- Implement using MPI or other primitives for interprocessor communication;
- Carry out measurements and verify that the performance is as expected;
- Identify bottlenecks, sources of overhead, etc., and minimize their impact;
- Iterate as necessary, as long as substantial improvement is still possible.

9.1 Example: Sorting a List of Uniformly Distributed Integers

We have chosen to investigate *sorting* to illustrate some of these processes. Sorting is a multi-faceted problem. It is fundamental to many basic problems in computer science and engineering. According to Knuth,[4] program was the first major "software" routine ever developed for automatic programming. Today, sorting, and its closely related cousin, searching, are perhaps most widely used in database servers.

There is no single "best" sorting algorithm on sequential computer hardware, and if anything, the situation is even more complicated in parallel. Issues that affect the choice of a sorting algorithm include:

- the size of the elements to be sorted;
- the form of the desired result, e.g, is a permutation sufficient, or must the data actually be rearranged;
- does each element have a corresponding, known integer key, or is the order implied solely by a comparison function;
- the cost of comparing two objects relative to other operations (exchanging elements, interprocessor communication, pointer dereference, etc.);
- availability of auxiliary primary storage, i.e., must the algorithm work "in-place," or may it allocate temporary storage;
- limitations on primary storage and availability and characteristics of secondary storage, i.e., out-of-core or tape-based sorts;
- the distribution of keys;
- non-random structure in the input data, i.e., is the input data likely to be pre-sorted or almost pre-sorted;
- the relative importance of worst-case vs. average-case behavior;
- stability - the property that the ordering of elements that compare equal is preserved from the input to the output.'

While these considerations make it difficult or impossible to devise a universally optimal sorting algorithm, they also allow for constant refinements tailored to changing hardware, usage patterns, and the demands of specific applications.

Sorting is also an example of an irregular, non-grid-based problem. As such, it illustrates techniques and algorithms rather different from those in Chapter 8. While it is widely believed that large, regular, numerical applications run well on Beowulf systems, good performance of irregular, non-numerical algorithms is less

---

[4]D. E. Knuth, *The Art of Computer Programming volume 3: Sorting and Searching* Addison Wesley, 1973, [pg 386]

widely reported. In this section we discuss two possible approaches to parallel sorting. The first one addresses a fairly restricted domain, while the second one is more general and builds upon the experiences and shortcomings of the first.

We begin with a simple formulation of the problem, and assume all the "easiest" answers to the issues mentioned in the previous section. In particular:

- the elements are positive integers, and hence they are their own corresponding integer key, and comparing and exchanging elements is extremely fast;
- they should be rearranged;
- secondary storage (disk, tape) will not be used;
- auxiliary primary storage is available;
- the input data are uniformly distributed over the range of integers;
- average-case behavior is of primary concern.

Parallel algorithms and applications almost always have well-studied sequential analogs. That is, it is rare to encounter a problem for parallel computation that has not already been solved, to one degree or another, for more traditional sequential architectures. Often, such sequential solutions exist as libraries, system calls, or language constructs which can be used as building blocks for a parallel solution. This approach - building on a sequential solution to a similar problem - is extremely powerful, as it leverages the design, debugging, and optimization that has been performed for the sequential case. Our approach to ray tracing in Chapter 7 invoked this method by using a sequential ray tracing package with no modifications whatsoever. Here we take a slightly less extreme approach, but we do assume that the programmer has at his disposal an optimized, debugged, sequential `isort` function that sorts an array of integers in the memory of a single processor. An implementation `isort` using the standard library `qsort` function is shown in Program 9.1.

Frequently, among the most difficult decisions in designing a parallel library function like sort is the API. How much structure should be assumed by the library, and how much should be specified by the caller? In Section 8.3.1 we developed a parallel array data structure which will be convenient to use for input and output from our sorting routines. Recall that a `parray` represents an array of objects distributed over a group of processes designated by an MPI communicator. Our sort functions will take a `parray` argument as both input and output. The parray succinctly specifies the number and location of elements in each processor, as well as the communicator that describes the ensemble of cooperating processes. For convenience, we will assume that the `data` field in the input `parray` was obtained from `malloc`, and that we can use `free/malloc` to obtain a new buffer if the

```
static int cmpints(const void *vp1, const void *vp2){
    int i1 = *(int *)vp1;
    int i2 = *(int *)vp2;
    return (i1>i2)? 1 : ((i2>i1)? -1 : 0);
}

static int cmpposints(const void *vp1, const void *vp2){
    return *(int *)vp1 - *(int *)vp2;
}

void isort(int nelem, unsigned int *data){
    qsort(data, nelem, sizeof(unsigned int), cmpints /* or cmpposints */);
}
```

Program 9.1:
An implementations of the sequential integer sort function, isort, using the standard library
function qsort and an auxiliary comparison function, cmpints. There are faster techniques for
sorting integers, e.g., radix sort, but it is unlikely that any can be implemented as succinctly in
C. If one can assume that all input data are positive signed integers, then the slightly faster
comparison function, cmpposints may be used in lieu of cmpints.

amount of data on each processor changes. The C language provides no entirely
satisfactory solution to the memory allocation problem, and other approaches are
certainly possible.

One way to use isort in parallel is to partially pre-sort the elements so that all
elements in processor p are less than all those in higher-numbered processors and
are greater than all those in lower-numbered processors. At this stage we disregard
the order of elements within any given processor because the internal ordering will
be fixed by calling isort.

Recall that on Beowulf systems, the high latency of network communication
favors transmission of large messages over small ones. It would be terribly inef-
ficient to transfer individual words between processors. Therefore, we must devise an algorithm that will move data in large blocks. The first task is to determine the range of values that will be delivered to each processor. For this,
we rely on the restrictions imposed by the problem statement: the input data
are uniformly distributed over the range of integers. Therefore, it is safe to assign integer values to processors so that processor p will receive all values between p*(INT_MAX/commsize) and (p+1)*(INT_MAX/commsize)-1, inclusive. Conversely, we can quickly determine the processor to which an element belongs by
dividing the element by INT_MAX/commsize.

Every processor scans its own list of elements, and for each element, it determines a destination processor. The element is then placed in a buffer specific

to that processor. The eventual size of these buffers is not known in advance, so to avoid nasty surprises (segmentation violations, bus errors, etc), it is necessary to implement a dynamic array data structure to be used for this purpose (the functions `DAcreate`, `DApush`, `DAnelem`, `DAbase` and `DAdestroy` comprise the API). If the input data is truly uniformly distributed, then the size of each per-processor array will be a random value with mean $\mu = nelem/commsize$ and variance $\sigma^2 = \mu * (commsize - 1)/commsize$. It is very unlikely that more than $\mu + 4*\sigma$, elements will be assigned to each processor, so this can be used as an initial guess for the size of the dynamic arrays, minimizing any overhead associated with dynamically extending the arrays. Program 9.2 shows the initial decomposition of the unsorted array into a set of per-process dynamic arrays.

Once all the elements have been scanned we are ready to communicate data between processors. MPI provides several collective communication routines that eliminate the need for the programmer to explicitly write a loop that communicates with all processors. On some platforms (but unfortunately not on Beowulfs), these routines can exploit hardware features that may make certain types of operations particularly fast. In the case at hand, every processor has a different amount of data for every other processor. This particular case is handled by the MPI routine `MPI_Alltoallv`. It is straightforward to determine how much data must be sent to each partner simply by checking the length of the associated dynamic array. On the other hand, `MPI_Alltoallv` also requires that each processor provide arguments describing how much data is *incoming* from every partner, and exactly where it should go. One way to obtain this information is to first distribute the lengths with a call to `MPI_Alltoall`. In addition, the interface to `MPI_Alltoallv` requires that all outgoing data be stored in the same array, so it is necessary to allocate contiguous space for all outgoing elements, and to copy each of the dynamic array buffers into that space. Once the dynamic arrays have been copied, they are no longer needed, so they are immediately destroyed to free up auxiliary storage. The code fragment Program 9.3 shows the steps required to call `MPI_Alltoallv`

After `MPI_Alltoallv` has been called, the array `allinbuf` contains all elements that fall within the range assigned to each processor. All that remains is to call `pacreate` to initialize the returned structure and `isort` to return a completely sorted array to the caller.

```
void
sort1(parray *pa){
  unsigned int per_proc_range, nproc, p, nguess, i;
  DA *darrays;
  int *nout, *nin, *odisp, *idisp, ninall;
  int *alloutbuf, *allinbuf;

  nproc = pa->commsize;
  assert(pa->elem_size == sizeof(int));
  if( nproc == 1 ){
    /* Special case for the nproc=1 case.  Avoid lots of unnecessary
       copies and computations, making the one-processor timings
       more meaningful. */
    goto endgame;
  }

  swStart(&swDecomp);
  darrays = alloca(nproc*sizeof(DA));
  nin = alloca(nproc*sizeof(int));
  nout = alloca(nproc*sizeof(int));
  odisp = alloca(nproc*sizeof(int));
  idisp = alloca(nproc*sizeof(int));

  nguess = pa->nelem_global/nproc + 1;
  nguess += 4. * sqrt( nguess * ((nproc-1.0)/nproc) );

  for(p=0; p<nproc; p++){
    Dbg("Call DAcreate(%p)\n", &darrays[p]);
    DAcreate(&darrays[p], nguess, sizeof(int));
  }

  per_proc_range = ((unsigned)INT_MAX/nproc) + 1U;
  for(i=0; i<pa->nelem_local; i++){
    unsigned int value;
    value = ((int *)pa->data)[i];
    assert(value >= 0);
    p = value / per_proc_range;
    assert( p < nproc );
    Dbg("Call DApush(%p)\n", &darrays[p]);
    DApush( &darrays[p], &value );
  }
  swStopStartv(&swDecomp, NULL, &swAlltoall, &swComm, NULL);
```

Program 9.2: Code fragment showing the initial steps in a parallel integer sort.

```
for(p=0; p<nproc; p++){
  nout[p] = DAnelem( &darrays[p] );
}

MPI_Alltoall(nout, 1, MPI_INT, nin, 1, MPI_INT, pa->comm);
swStopStart(&swAlltoall, &swAlltoallv);

alloutbuf = pa->data;

odisp[0] = 0;
idisp[0] = 0;
for(p=0; /* break from middle */; p++){
  memcpy(alloutbuf + odisp[p], DAbase(&darrays[p]),
         nout[p]*sizeof(*alloutbuf));
  DAdestroy( &darrays[p] );
  if( p == (nproc-1) ) break;
  odisp[p+1] = odisp[p] + nout[p];
  idisp[p+1] = idisp[p] + nin[p];
}
ninall = idisp[p] + nin[p];
allinbuf = malloc(ninall*sizeof(*allinbuf));
MPI_Alltoallv(alloutbuf, nout, odisp, MPI_INT,
              allinbuf, nin, idisp, MPI_INT, pa->comm);
swStopStart(&swAlltoallv, &swPacreate);

free( pa->data );                /* assume it was obtained with malloc */

pacreate(pa, allinbuf, ninall, pa->elem_size, pa->comm);
endgame:
swStopStartv(&swPacreate, &swComm, NULL, &swQsort, NULL);
isort(pa->nelem_local, (int*)pa->data);
swStop(&swQsort);
}
```

Program 9.3:
Code fragment from sort1.c showing the steps necessary to construct the arguments for
MPI_Alltoallv, and the final call to isort which finishes the local sort.

9.2   Analysis of Integer Sort

The conventional way to assess the quality of a parallel implementation is by measuring its speedup, or one of the algebraically related quantities, efficiency or overhead. If $T(P)$ is the time to execute a particular problem on P processors, then

$$\text{speedup} \quad s(P) \quad = \quad T(1)/T(P) \tag{9.2.1}$$

$$\text{efficiency} \quad \epsilon(P) \quad = \quad T(1)/(P * T(P)) = s(P)/P \tag{9.2.2}$$

$$\text{overhead} \quad \nu(P) \quad = \quad (P * T(P) - T(1))/T(1) = (1 - \epsilon)/\epsilon \tag{9.2.3}$$

In these formulae, $T(1)$ should be understood to measure the best available implementation on a single processor. This is not necessarily the same as running the parallel code with, e.g., `mpirun -np 1`. Overhead is particularly useful because it is roughly additive. That is, the overhead in an implementation is approximately the sum of distinct contributions. Total overhead measures the difference between the time on P processors from the time one would expect from perfect-speedup of a single-processor implementation. If one can identify and measure a time interval in a parallel implementation that is not present in a sequential case, that time is a contribution to overhead. The sum of all of such times, normalized to the overall single-processor time is the total overhead. Thus, one can independently assess different kinds of overhead in a parallel implementation to develop a predictive model for how that implementation will perform. The most important sources of parallel overhead are:

9.2.1   Communication

Interprocessor communication does not take place in a sequential implementation, so any time spent communicating in the parallel code contributes to overhead. Fortunately, it is easy to estimate, and is also very likely the largest contribution to the overhead in the sort example. Each processor calls `MPI_Alltoall` to communicate an array of `nproc` integers, and then calls `MPI_Alltoallv` to transmit and receive arrays approximately equal to `nelem_local` in size. While the underlying implementation of `MPI_Alltoall` is hidden, the interested Beowulf users can pierce the veil and examine the source code. In MPICH at least, `MPI_Alltoall` and `MPI_Alltoallv` are implemented fairly naively as loops over point-to-point communication calls. Therefore, we can estimate the total time in communication as:

$$T_{comm} = 2 * P * t_{latency} + \text{sizeof(local arrays)}/\text{bandwidth}$$

9.2.2   Redundancy

Sometimes a parallel algorithm performs the same computations on many processors. Although this can often be faster than computing the result once and broadcasting, $P-1$ of the processors are nevertheless not carrying out useful work. This is accounted as redundancy overhead. Such redundant calculations are negligible in the sort1. A few O(1) operations are performed redundantly, e.g., calling malloc to obtain temporary space, but these should not impact performance.

9.2.3   Extra Work

Extra work is parallel computation that does not take place in a sequential implementation. For example, sort1 computes the processor destination of every input element. This computation is not required by the sequential algorithm. As implemented, an extra integer division and dynamic array assignment is performed for every element.

On the other hand, the in-memory sort that every processor performs is smaller by a factor of P. Since sorting (using the library qsort at least) is $O(N \log N)$ in time, there are actually fewer cycles spent in qsort in the parallel case. These two effects tend to cancel, and it is even possible for the overhead from extra work to be negative. Such situations are fairly common in practice and are often met with skepticism because they can lead to the counterintuitive phenomenon of "superlinear speedup," the situation where P processors may solve a problem more than P times faster than just one processor. In this case (and in fact, generally), superlinear speedup results from using a non-optimal sequential algorithm. The sequential sort would be faster if its behavior was closer to the parallel algorithm, i.e., first categorize the input into bins, and then sort the bins.

9.2.4   Load Imbalance

Load imbalance measures the extra time spent by the slowest processor, in excess of the mean over all processors. If we assume that every processor starts with an equal number of unsorted elements, then there is negligible load imbalance in the initial decomposition phase of the algorithm. The final isort, however, can become imbalanced if different numbers of elements are delivered to every processor. The problem assumptions guarantee that the data are uniformly distributed, which implies that the number of elements in any given processor is a random variable with a binomial distribution with $p = 1/P$. For large N, the number of elements assigned to any given processor will be approximately a Gaussian distribution with mean N/P and standard deviation $N/P * \sqrt{(P-1)/N}$. As such, it is very unlikely that any given processor will be more than a few standard deviations away from the mean, so the load imbalance should satisfy:

$$\text{imbal} \approx (n_{largest} - n_{mean})/n_{mean} \gtrsim O(1) * \sqrt{(P-1)/N}$$

9.2.5 Waiting

Overhead associated with waiting can be difficult to disentangle from load imbalance. Waiting occurs when there is fine-grained imbalance even though the overall load may be balanced. For example, if processes must synchronize frequently between short computations, there is a possibility of substantial waiting overhead even if the computation on each processor is balanced in aggregate. In the sort algorithm the only synchronization occurs during the calls to `MPI_Alltoall` and `MPI_Alltoallv`, and they occur immediately after the initial decomposition, which should not suffer from load imbalance. Therefore, waiting overhead is negligible. It is also possible that waiting overhead could appear *inside* the implementation of `MPI_Alltoallv`.

9.3 Measurement of Integer Sort

Now that we have a general idea of sources of parallel overhead, we can instrument the code to ascertain how much overhead is actually present in practice. Overhead is usually a complicated function of hardware, implementation details, problem size, software environment, etc. Even on a particular machine, the relative importance of different operations depends on the size of the problem and the number of processors employed. The presence of other users and non-determinism due to cache effects, swapping, etc., further complicates the problem. It is easy to become overwhelmed with data when trying to understand the behavior of a parallel program. One solution to this problem is to use graphical tools to render a visual representation of the behavior of a parallel program. One such tool is `upshot`, which is part of the MPICH package. A screen shot is shown in Figure 9.1.

Upshot reads an event log which is automatically generated if the program is compiled with the `-mpilog` argument to `mpicc`. By default, the log records the start-time and finish-time of most of the basic MPI primitives. It is possible to add user-defined, application-specific elements to the trace, and to view them along with the communication routines using `upshot`. Consult the man pages for `MPE_Log_event`, `MPE_Describe_event` and `MPE_Describe_state` for details. Upshot has a sophisticated user interface that allows zooming, panning scrolling, etc., so that fine detail can be viewed within a much larger context.

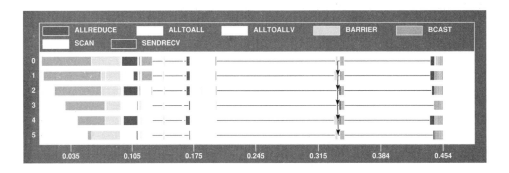

Figure 9.1
Screen shot of upshot. The log file shown is from a six processor sort of 300000 integers. Details
are easier to read on a color monitor. Even in monochrome it is apparent that the ALLTOALL
segment is the dominant communication task following the BARRIERS that separate the
calculation from diagnostic I/O and problem setup at approximately t=0.13s.

Tools like `upshot` are particularly useful when a program exhibits very complicated or counter-intuitive behavior. In such cases, they can often provide a clue
to what is really happening. However, one should not underestimate the amount
that can be learned by simply recording the time spent in different phases of a
computation.

It is not difficult to add explicit instrumentation to a code like `sort1`. Timing
is done with a simple *stopwatch* abstraction, as in Program 9.4, where we also call
`MPI_Barrier` to guarantee that every processor starts at the same time, and that
every process is finished before we stop the timer. The observant reader will also
have noted the calls to `swStart`, `swStopStart`, etc. in Programs 9.2 and 9.3.

With these simple tools it is very easy to record a large amount of data. It
is important not to lose sight of the ultimate goal: improving the performance
of `sort1` over an interesting range of input sizes. It may not be necessary to
understand every bump and wiggle in every plot of time (or a derived quantity) vs.
number of processors and/or problem size.

The first graph to produce is, of course, time-to-sort vs. problem size and number
of processors. In order to make the plots fit nicely on the same axes, we actually
plot time-to-solution divided by the number of integers sorted. This is shown in
the upper plot in Figure 9.2. Also on this graph, a line with logarithmic slope -1 is
shown. Any line with this slope indicates time inversely proportional to the number
of processors, i.e., *perfect speedup*.

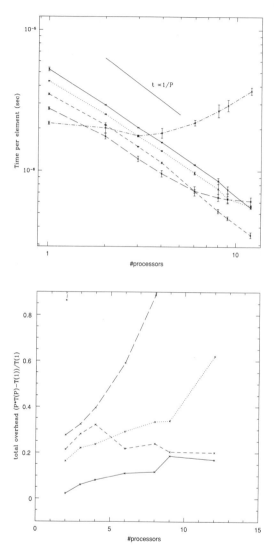

Figure 9.2
Plot of time per element vs. number of processors to sort arrays of 30M(solid), 3M(dotted), 300k(short dash), 30k(long dash) and 3k(dot-dash) random integers. All measurements were performed on a Beowulf system with 300 MHz Pentium II processors and a 100baseT Ethernet network. Communication used the MPICH implementation of MPI. Error bars indicate the maximum and minimum times observed over six runs on otherwise unloaded machines and network. The lower graph is shows the same raw data algebraically rearranged to represent the parallel overhead.

```
StopWatch swSort;
SimpleStats_t sortStats;
...
MPI_Barrier(MPI_COMM_WORLD);
MPI_Barrier(MPI_COMM_WORLD);
swStart(&swSort);
sort1(pa);
MPI_Barrier(MPI_COMM_WORLD);
swStop(&swSort);
simpleStats(swRead(&swSort), &sortStats, MPI_COMM_WORLD);
if( rank == 0 ){
  printf("Sort: mean: %g, max: %g, min: %g",
          sortStats.sum/sortStats.nsamples, sortStats.max, sortStats.min);
}
```

Program 9.4:
A few lines of instrumentation surrounding the call to `sort1` that generate the raw data for the plot in Figure 9.2. The functions `swStart` and `swStop` and `swRead` are part of a stopwatch package, and the function `simpleStats` was introduced in Section 8.3.1. Additional instrumentation would require the addition of four more lines of code: calls to `swStart` and `swStop` to measure the time interval, a call to `simpleStats` to accumulate the results, and a call to `printf` to report it.

Several facts are immediately apparent from Figure 9.2:

- There is a point of negative returns for any given problem size, beyond which adding more processors actually slows the time to solution. In Figure 9.2 this occurs where the curve begins to turn upwards.
- Before the point of negative returns is a region of diminishing returns, where adding more processors has less and less effect on the time to solution. To sort 3k integers, even two processors offers marginal improvement. The curve begins to bend upward (indicating diminishing returns) around 6 processors for 30k integers.
- For 300k and 30M integers, adding processors improves performance up to the maximum size in the experiment, 12 processors. This is usually stated succinctly as "the problem scales well up to 12 processors." The curve for 3M integers appears to have diminishing returns above 9 processors. This curious lack of monotonicity going from 300k to 3M to 30M will be addressed below.
- The error-bars are not completely negligible, especially for the smaller problem sizes where the sort completes in a fraction of a second. Isolating and understanding time differences comparable to the error bars will be extremely difficult.

While a plot of times gives some quantitative information, it does not immediately convey how well the parallel implementation is performing. It is instructive to also plot the same data as overhead rather than time. The lower plot in Figure 9.2 highlights different aspects of the same raw data. In particular, it gives us a much clearer idea of how well the implementation is utilizing multiple processors. Figure 9.2 shows the total overhead as defined in Equation 9.2.3. This plot provides quantitative confirmation of the observations above. Sorting 30 million integers incurs a parallel overhead less than 20% up to 12 processors, whereas 12 processors is past the point of diminishing returns for sorting 3 million integers (overhead of 0.65). The curve for N=300k contains a surprising feature at P=4. The overhead actually drops dramatically between four and six processors and stays low through 12 processors. It is very uncommon for the overhead to decrease as the number of processors increases, and this feature suggests that one should look more closely at individual sources of overhead. Perhaps this feature can be exploited to improve performance elsewhere, or perhaps other overheads are anomalously high.

To understand the cause of the overhead decrease at P=4, N=300k, we first checked the "obvious" candidates:

- The timings are repeatable;
- They persist through a complete system-wide reboot;
- There is no other activity on the system;
- They are not affected by selecting a different subset of processors.

To understand the behavior of the implementation in more detail, it is necessary to introduce some additional instrumentation to time the data partitioning, i.e., the code in Program 9.2, as well as the execution of `qsort`, `MPI_Alltoall`, `MPI_Alltoallv` and `pacreate`. The decomposition and `qsort` times added, and the time spent in `qsort` on one processor subtracted to give the overhead due to additional work. The other three constitute the communication overhead. Analysis at this level of detail cannot distinguish between load imbalance and communication overhead, but the problem specification (input consists of random, uniformly distributed integers) suggests that load imbalance should be negligible. Figure 9.3 shows the overhead due to communication and extra work incurred by the program.

The feature at P=4, N=300k is clearly visible in the graph of communication overhead. Therefore, we suspect some idiosyncrasy in the communication libraries. As further confirmation, we have measured the time spent in `MPI_Alltoallv`, and used it to compute an effective per-processor communication bandwidth. The result is plotted in Figure 9.4. We made an educated guess, and plotted bandwidth against the volume of data transmitted in or out of a single processor. While the curves are

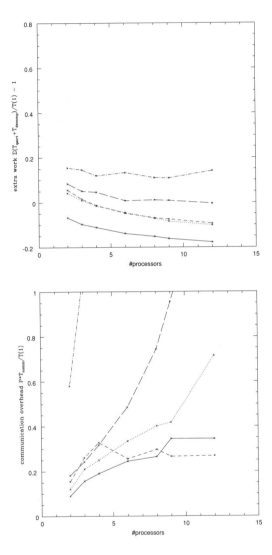

Figure 9.3
Overheads for sorting arrays of 30M(solid), 3M(dotted), 300k(short dash), 30k(long dash) and 3k(dot-dash) random integers. The upper graph shows the overhead from extra work, $\Sigma_{procs}(T_{qsort} + T_{decomp})/T(1) - 1$, In many cases, the overhead is negative because binning the data into P separate bins, and then applying the library qsort to the bins is less work than applying the library qsort to the entire array. This implies that the library qsort is not the best way to sort large arrays of integers! The lower graph shows overhead from communication, i.e., time spent in MPI_Alltoall, MPI_Alltoallv and pacreate, scaled by the time for a single-processor execution.

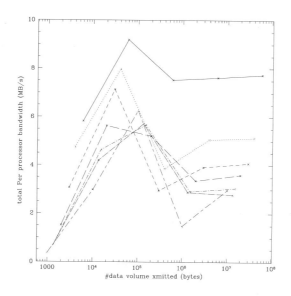

Figure 9.4
Bandwidth plotted against volume of data transmitted for different numbers of processors,
P=2(solid), P=3(dotted), P=4(short dash), P=6(long dash), P=8(dot-long dash),
P=9(dot-short dash), P=12(short-long dash).

not coincident, there is a pronounced peak between 10k and 100k bytes. Another
source of worry is that the bandwidths fall below 3 MB/s for several of the large data
transfers. Other measurements on this machine, and many other similar machines
using fast Ethernet switches, indicate that bandwidths for large messages should
be 8 MB/s or more. Therefore something is wrong with the communication library
and/or its interaction with the underlying network.

The fundamental cause of the problem is not clear. Nevertheless, the dominant
feature in Figure 9.4 does suggest a workaround. We implemented a simple wrapper
that calls `MPI_Alltoallv` several times in a loop with each iteration limited to a
maximum of 64 Kbytes of data. The external interface is exactly the same as
`MPI_Alltoallv`. With this routine substituted for the library routine, the timing
and overhead results are much better behaved. They are shown in Figure 9.5.
Bandwidths (not shown) are uniformly above 5 MB/s, which is much closer to
what one would expect from a 100 Mbit/s Ethernet network.

The total overhead is actually negative for N=30M, P=12 implying superlinear
speedup. As discussed above, this is a result of the fact that `qsort` is not optimal for

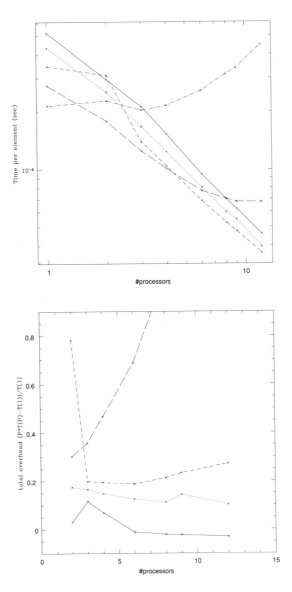

Figure 9.5
Time per element and total parallel overhead sorting arrays of 30M(solid), 3M(dotted), 300k(short dash), 30k(long dash) and 3k(dot-dash) random integers. Similar to Figures 9.2 and 9.3 but the data were taken using an alternative implementation of `MPI_Alltoallv` that works around the performance degradation observed with large transfers.

sorting integers, and its sequential performance could be improved (for this special case) by emulating the behavior of the parallel program, i.e., first pre-sorting the data into bins of fixed width and then sorting the bins.

9.4   Example: Sorting with User-supplied Comparator

The integer sort function discussed in the previous section performs reasonably well on a Beowulf. Performance improvements are most likely to come from use of a faster sequential sort routine. While this is a fascinating topic, it is not particularly relevant to programming Beowulfs. The interested reader can consult any of the standard texts on algorithms.[5,6]

Another way to improve the sort routine would be to relax some of the restrictions that it imposes on the input data. In particular, an interface more like the standard ANSI C `qsort` function would be far more flexible. The caller can still specify the input and output data with a **parray**, but now one also specifies a comparison function similar to that passed to `qsort` to define the order relationship between objects.

Since it was successful for integers, it seems reasonable to adopt the same overall strategy for sorting more general objects. There will be an initial scan in which objects are categorized only to the extent of deciding in which process they belong. Then a call to `MPI_Alltoallv` will shuffle the data between processes so that every process has its final compliment of objects. Finally, a call to `qsort` will finish the procedure. The crucial difference between this problem and the previous one is that it is no longer obvious how to decide which objects belong to which processors. We cannot simply divide an integer key by a range to get a target processor number. In fact, there is no integer key at all. The only way to determine the ordering of objects is to call the `compar` function. This suggests an approach based on somehow selecting a set of ordered, uniformly spaced elements, "fenceposts," and using them to define the range of elements destined for each processor. When each element is tested, we perform a binary search over the fenceposts to determine which processor the element is destined for.

We are still left with the problem of choosing the fenceposts. We could just choose one element at random from each processor, but that runs the risk of introducing very bad load imbalance. There is no guarantee (or even likelihood) that the

---

[5]D. E. Knuth, *The Art of Computer Programming volume 3: Sorting and Searching*, Addison Wesley, 1973

[6]Aho, Hopcroft and Ullman, *Design and Analysis of Computer Algorithms*, Adison-Wesley, 1974

selected fenceposts will be evenly distributed in the space of all objects, in which case some processors will end up with considerably more work than others.

One solution is to oversample, i.e., to partition the data into more than `nproc` distinct bins with fenceposts chosen at random. The bins are just a set of dynamic arrays, as in Program 9.3, so there is no problem having as many of them as we like.

The first step is to select `nfence` objects to use as dividers between partitions. In general, the larger the value of `nfence`, the better the ultimate load balance. On the other hand, larger `nfence` results in more work because the binary searches are over a larger space. The optimum value of `nfence` is difficult to determine a priori. We shall return to it in Section 9.5.1. For now, we just note that Program 9.5 contains code that randomly selects fenceposts from each processor, gathers them by calling `MPI_Allgather`, and then calls `qsort` to order them in preparation for binary search.

Once an ordered array of `fenceposts` has been created by `find_fenceposts`, we can pre-sort the elements into dynamic arrays in much the same way that we did for integer sorting. This time, however, selecting the bin is more complicated, and requires a binary search to find the right pair of elements in the `fenceposts` array that bracket the element under consideration. Many systems (including Linux) provide a `bsearch` function, but its API is not suitable for this purpose (it finds exact matches, not intervals). Fortunately, the complete source to the C library is available on Linux systems, so we can modify the library's `bsearch` implementation to solve the problem at hand. A function to perform interval searches is shown in Program 9.6

At this point, we have divided the data into more bins than we have processors. We can now look at the populations of these bins and send one or more of them to each processor, with the number chosen to achieve an approximate load balance. Program 9.8 calls `MPI_Allreduce` to compute the sum over all processors of the (byte) counts in each bucket. Upon completion, every processor has exactly the same values in `bktcountall`.

We now have enough information to decide which elements are destined for which processors. We loop over the bins (more than `nproc` of them), and assign them to processors more-or-less equally using a greedy algorithm that tries to allocate a fair portion to process 0, then process 1, etc. This does not necessarily achieve the best possible load balance, but it takes time linear in the number of processes, and should be fine in practice. The code is shown in Program 9.9

Finally, we can complete the task and deliver the elements to the correct destinations. `MPI_Alltoallv` requires some additional arguments, which must be assem-

```
static void *fenceposts;
int nfence;

static void
find_fenceposts(parray *pa, int (*compar)(const void *, const void *)){
  void *myfenceposts;
  int nfence_local, i, qskip;
  char *p, *q;

  swStart(&swExtra);
  if( argv_nfence_local ){
    nfence_local = argv_nfence_local;
    /* But handle one annoying special case with very small sorts */
    if( nfence_local >= pa->nelem_global/pa->commsize )
      nfence_local = 1;
  }else{
    nfence_local = (int)ceil(3.0*lg2((double)pa->nelem_global
                                     /pa->commsize));
  }
  Dbg("nfence_local=%d, pa->nelem_local=%d\n",
      nfence_local, pa->nelem_local);
  assert( nfence_local <= pa->nelem_local && nfence_local > 0 );
  myfenceposts = malloc(nfence_local*pa->elem_size);
  /* Choose nfence_local equally-spaced elements */
  p = myfenceposts;
  q = pa->data;
  qskip = pa->elem_size * ( pa->nelem_local/nfence_local );
  for(i=0; i<nfence_local; i++){
    memcpy(p, q, pa->elem_size);
    p += pa->elem_size;
    q += qskip;
  }
  fenceposts = malloc( nfence_local * pa->commsize * pa->elem_size );
  /* Resets nfence! */
  swStopStart(&swExtra, &swComm);
  MPI_Allgather(myfenceposts, nfence_local * pa->elem_size, MPI_BYTE,
                fenceposts, nfence_local * pa->elem_size,
                MPI_BYTE, pa->comm);
  swStopStart(&swComm, &swExtra);
  nfence = nfence_local * pa->commsize - 1;
  free(myfenceposts);
  Dbg("After EzMPI_Allgatherv: nfence=%d\n", nfence);

  qsort(fenceposts, nfence, pa->elem_size, compar);
  swStop(&swExtra);
}
```

Program 9.5:
The function find_fenceposts that selects nfence elements at random, distributes them so that
every process has the same set using (MPI_Allgather), and calls qsort to sort them so that
binary search can be used on them.

```
static int
intervalsearch(const void *key, const void *fenceposts, size_t nfence,
               size_t elem_size, int (*compar)(const void *, const void *)){
  int l, h;

  l = 0;
  h = nfence;
  while( l<h ){
    const void *post;
    int i;
    i = (l+h)/2;
    post = (const char *)fenceposts + i*elem_size;
    if( (*compar)(key, post) < 0 )
      h = i;
    else
      l = i+1;
  }
  return l;
}
```

Program 9.6:
A function to perform a binary search for an interval. The binary search converges by iteratively testing the midpoint between a lower bound l and an upper bound h, and updating one of the bounds accordingly. The value returned is zero if key<fenceposts[0], or it is nfence if key>=fenceposts[nfence-1], or it has the property that key>=fenceposts[answer-1] and key<fenceposts[answer].

bled by first calling `MPI_Alltoall`, and looping over the processes one more time. After that, all that remains is to reset the fields in the `parray` structure and to call the C-library `qsort` to complete the local sort within each process' local memory.

9.5   Analysis of a More General Sort

The program described in the previous section is considerably more complicated than that of Section 9.1. It invokes more MPI collective communication routines, and is subject to statistical fluctuations in the resulting load balance based on the details of the randomly chosen `fenceposts`. In fact, there is a complex tradeoff between the cost of selecting more `fenceposts` and the benefit of improving the load balance by using more samples.

Nevertheless, the times and overheads shown in Figure 9.6 are still very encouraging. The problem scales well up to twelve processors for N=3M and above. It may well be sufficient to stop here and live with overheads of 30% or less. It is unlikely that overall performance can ever be improved (for these problem sizes and machine parameters) by more than 30%, which may not justify additional

```
void
sort2(parray *pa, int (*compar)(const void *, const void *)){
  int nproc = pa->commsize;
  int nelem_local = pa->nelem_local;
  int nguess, nintervals, i, p, s, b;
  DA *darrays;
  int ninall, noutsofar, sumcountall, first_idx;
  int target, nleft, nelem;
  char *cptr;
  int *bktcount, *bktcountall;
  int *nout, *nin, *odisp, *idisp;
  void *alloutbuf, *allinbuf;

  if( pa->commsize == 1 ){
    goto endgame;
  }

  find_fenceposts(pa, compar);
  nintervals = nfence+1;
  darrays = alloca(nintervals*sizeof(DA));
  nguess = pa->nelem_global/nintervals + 1;
  for(i=0; i<nintervals; i++){
    DAcreate(&darrays[i], nguess, pa->elem_size);
  }
  cptr = pa->data;
  for(i=0; i<pa->nelem_local; i++){
    int bin;
    bin = intervalsearch(cptr, fenceposts, nfence,
                         pa->elem_size, compar);
    Dbg("%u into interval %d\n", *(unsigned int *)cptr, bin);
    DApush( &darrays[bin], cptr );
    cptr += pa->elem_size;
  }
  free(fenceposts);
```

Program 9.7:
Excerpt from the beginning of a general parallel sort that uses a comparison function to determine the order of elements...

```
  bktcount = alloca(nintervals*sizeof(int));
  bktcountall = alloca(nintervals*sizeof(int));
  for(i=0; i<nintervals; i++){
    bktcount[i] = DAnbytes( &darrays[i] );
  }
  MPI_Allreduce(bktcount, bktcountall,
                nintervals, MPI_INT, MPI_SUM, pa->comm);
```

Program 9.8:
Code fragment showing the steps necessary to invoke MPI_Allreduce in the implementation of sort2.

```
noutsofar = 0;
cptr = pa->data;
b = 0;
nleft = pa->nelem_global * pa->elem_size;
odisp = alloca(nproc*sizeof(int));
nout = alloca(nproc*sizeof(int));
sumcountall = 0;
first_idx = 0;
for(p=0; p<nproc; p++){
  int one_taken;
  odisp[p] = noutsofar;
  target = nleft / (nproc - p);
  nout[p] = 0;
  one_taken = 0;
  if( p == pa->commrank )
    first_idx = sumcountall/pa->elem_size;
  while( b<nintervals
         && (!one_taken /* always take at least one bucket */
              || (target > 0 && (target-bktcountall[b]) > -target)) ){
    memcpy(cptr, DAbase(&darrays[b]), bktcount[b]);
    target -= bktcountall[b];
    nleft  -= bktcountall[b];
    nout[p] += bktcount[b];
    cptr += bktcount[b];
    Dbg("copied interval %d (%d bytes), target = %d, nleft=%d\n",
         b, bktcount[b], target, nleft);
    DAdestroy(&darrays[b]);
    sumcountall += bktcountall[b];
    one_taken = 1;
    b++;
  }
  Dbg("send bucket %d to processor %d, odisp[] = %d, nout=%d\n",
       b-1, p, odisp[p], nout[p]);
  noutsofar += nout[p];
}
assert( sumcountall == pa->nelem_global * pa->elem_size );
```

Program 9.9:
Loop over bins and assign them to processes according to a greedy load-balance strategy. That
is, assign bins to processes until a target count is reached, and then move on to the next process.
At the same time, copy data from the dynamic arrays associated with each bin back onto the
original input data, free the storage used by the dynamic arrays, and fill in the arrays nout and
odisp which will subsequently be passed to MPI_Alltoallv.

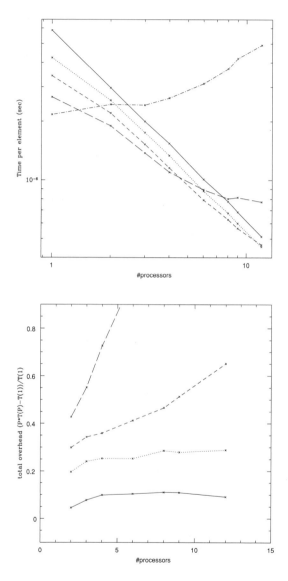

Figure 9.6
Time per element and total parallel overhead sorting arrays of 30M(solid), 3M(dotted), 300k(short dash), 30k(long dash) and 3k(dot-dash) random integers using the more general `sort2` routine. Times are not much worse than in Figure 9.2 despite the added generality of the algorithm. Data were taken using an alternative implementation of `MPI_Alltoallv` that works around the performance degradation observed with large transfers.

```
  nin = alloca(nproc*sizeof(int));
  idisp = alloca(nproc*sizeof(int));
  MPI_Alltoall(nout, 1, MPI_INT, nin, 1, MPI_INT, pa->comm);
  ninall = 0;
  for(p=0; p<nproc; p++){
    idisp[p] = ninall;
    ninall += nin[p];
  }

  allinbuf = malloc(ninall);
  MPI_Alltoallv(pa->data, nout, odisp, MPI_BYTE,
                allinbuf, nin, idisp, MPI_BYTE, pa->comm);
  free(pa->data);
  nelem = ninall/pa->elem_size;
  pa->data = allinbuf;
  pa->nelem_local = nelem;
  pa->first_index_local = first_idx;
  /* elem_size, comm, commrank, commsize, and nelem_global are unchanged */
  Dbg("qsort(%p, %d, %d, %p)\n", allinbuf, nelem, pa->elem_size, compar);
 endgame:
  qsort(pa->data, pa->nelem_local, pa->elem_size, compar);
  swStop(&swQsort);
}
```

Program 9.10: Code fragment showing the final steps in the general sort function `sort2`.

investment in analysis and coding. However, the purpose of this chapter is to illustrate techniques for optimization, so we persevere and try to locate places where improvements might be made.

One approach is to follow the course set out in the previous chapter and create a series of plots of overheads vs. number of processors. Another possibility is to choose a representative case and study it in more detail. There is little point in studying a case which obviously works well because there is no possibility for improvement. Similarly, there is little point in studying a case that works very poorly because it is unlikely that deeper understanding will improve the performance enough to be worthwhile. Therefore, we choose an intermediate case: P=12, N=1M. Also, since this version sorts objects of arbitrary size, we conveniently choose to study the case with objects of size 32 bytes.

9.5.1   Choosing the Number of Fenceposts

In the design of `sort2`, we had little or no theoretical justification for choosing the number of presort-bins, so this is a potential source of improvement. In Figure 9.7, we plot the total overhead as a function of the number of fenceposts chosen per

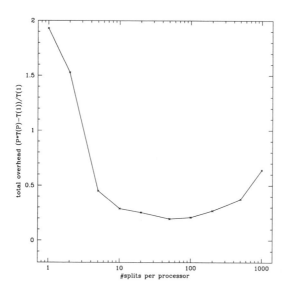

Figure 9.7
Total overhead vs. the number of fenceposts for P=12, N=1M elements of size 32 bytes.

processor. The curve has a minimum near 50, which is thus the optimal choice for this particular set of parameters. Fortunately, the bottom of the curve is very flat. There is little difference between 10 and 200 fenceposts per processor, so the penalty for deviating from the optimal value of **nfence** is not very large. A more thorough study would measure the position of the bottom of the overhead curve for different problem sizes, numbers of processors, etc. An alternative is to just guess at a solution guided by intuition and a few measurements. For the general case, we chose the number of fenceposts per processor to be $3 * \log_2(N/P)$. This has the right value for N=1M, P=12, and is a slowly varying function of N/P, with generally the right derivatives (fewer fenceposts when there are fewer objects, more fenceposts when there are more processors). With this function for the number of fenceposts, the times and overheads for a series of problems similar to those shown in Figure 9.2 were computed. This time, the data objects were 32 bytes in length, making the very largest problem (N=30M) too large for the memory of a single processor. The results are plotted in Figure 9.6, but the overheads for N=30M are computed by assuming the P=2 case had an overhead of 10%.

9.6   Summary

The implementation of sorting functions in this chapter has exposed a number of important techniques and guidelines that are generally useful when working with high-performance computers. We may wish it were otherwise, but parallel computers are difficult and idiosyncratic. This is equally true of Beowulfs and their more expensive commercial cousins. The following is a synopsis of a few of the lessons exposed in this chapter.

Trust no one   Libraries, compilers, device drivers and operating systems were all written by mere mortals. Occasionally, one finds genuine bugs, but more frequently, one encounters unexpectedly poor performance for certain inputs or environmental conditions. In this chapter, we saw that the performance of `MPI_Alltoallv` could be improved by the counter-intuitive step of issuing a sequence of smaller requests. Presumably even better performance could be obtained by diagnosing and repairing the cause rather than the symptom. The existence of open source implementations of critical system components makes this latter course conceivable.

A performance model   It is crucial to have a qualitative model of how the program should behave with different problem parameters, system parameters, etc. Without such a model, one cannot identify sources of inefficiency or effectively tune or improve performance.

Instrumentation and graphs   Program instrumentation allows one to compare the actual behavior of the program with the model. Plots of overhead with respect to problem size and machine size should be studied for deviations, anomalies, unexpected bumps, wiggles, etc. If available, quantitative comparisons should be made, e.g., we found that the bandwidth delivered by `MPI_Alltoallv` was far below what we expected based on previous measurements of point-to-point communication performance.

Graphical tools   Graphical tools can be helpful in certain cases, but they are no substitute for a semi-analytic performance model. Graphical performance analysis tools can give a good overview of what is happening in a single run, but usually cannot offer assistance with trend analysis, e.g., how does the performance change as one changes problem parameters, machine size, etc.

Superlinear speedup   It is not impossible, but it probably means there's an opportunity for further sequential optimization. The fact that we see super-linear speedup in sorting is indicative of the fact that our sequential sort is non-optimal.

Enough is enough   At some point, it is not worth the effort to optimize or tune any more. A few percent improvement probably does not justify a major rewrite. Keep in mind that programmer time is more valuable than CPU time.

10 Conclusions and Views

This book has explored a new computational opportunity that delivers the capabilities of earlier supercomputers into the hands of small laboratories, groups, or even individuals. Beowulf-class computing systems have enabled a revolution by breaking the price/performance barrier and by putting control of system configuration and operation directly in the hands of the end-user. The possibilities implied by Beowulf, some of which have largely gone unexplored, are breathtaking, although several factors conspire to impede broader usage of Beowulf-class systems in the work place. In the concluding comments to this book, these issues are considered as they relate to the practical capabilities and limitations of Beowulf-class systems and their future evolution.

10.1 New Generation Beowulfs

Changes are occurring almost daily in the core technologies used to implement Beowulf-class systems. The earliest Beowulfs could sustain less than 5 Mflops per node on favorable (but real) applications with 10 Mbps communication links. As this book goes to print, the 500 MHz Intel Pentium III processor and the 533 MHz DEC Alpha processor are being incorporated into Beowulf systems. The AMD K-7 and Intel's Merced chip are on the horizon, promising performance between two and four times the last generation of systems. Although costs have yet to drop sufficiently, both Myrinet and Gigabit Ethernet communications technologies (aided by the new PCI-2 bus which is wider and runs at a higher clock rate) will provide a near-term path to 1 Gbps communication channels. Several companies, including Cisco, 3Com, Extreme and Lucent offer Ethernet switches supporting a mix of Fast and Gigabit links and backplanes with many Gbps of internal bandwidth, all at commodity prices. All these trends broaden the domain of applications and algorithms that may be effectively performed on Beowulf-class systems and will permit larger configurations to be implemented with off-the-shelf components.

By the end of 2001, Gflops performance, GByte memory capacity, and Gbps network bandwidth Beowulf nodes will be commonplace. Processor nodes of 2 Gflops peak performance will be achieved shortly thereafter by employing the newest processors in symmetric multiprocessor node configurations. Peak performance to cost will approach $1/Mflops, enabling Teraflops peak performance Beowulfs at a cost of about a million dollars by the year 2002 or earlier. That is well within the budget range of many moderate sized computing centers. In 1999, machines of that capacity qualify as the fastest in the world.

The deployment of very large Beowulf systems will require evolutionary advances in software. Historically, Beowulf have been modest in size, and were used almost exclusively as single-user systems; that is, one user and one application at a time. Some primitive space division methods were employed so that more than one user could do development at a time. This was ordinarily coordinated by word of mouth or email without elaborate scheduling tools. However, the management challenge grows with the size of the system and the number of users. Large Beowulf class systems will be distinguished as much by new, more sophisticated software as by improved hardware. This emerging software environment will present a virtual distributed machine to multiple users, providing automatic resource allocation and job scheduling similar to that on high-end commercial systems. Several research groups are already developing such packages.

As discussed in Chapter refchap:Hardware, the "lots of boxes on shelves" system packaging methodology has been the dominant means of assembling Beowulf systems and is effective for a couple of hundred processors. Beyond that scale, factors come in to play which favor alternative concepts. While straightforward, the conventional technique results in low-density installations that can consume substantial machine room floor space for larger Beowulfs. Such space is at a premium in many computer centers. Cabling can be unwieldy with very large systems making maintenance more difficult. Access to a given node within a very large system is not always convenient using the shelves-of-towers approach. To get to a motherboard or disk drive requires that the unit be extracted from the assemblage of like boxes, the correct cables disconnected from the tangle of wires, and the unit then opened up. Future systems are likely to employ packaging methods that are better suited to Beowulf requirements. Rack mounted hardware developed around PC motherboard form factors, memory boards, controllers, and so forth provide cleaner structuring, superior maintenance accessibility, and enhanced packaging density.

To date, custom packaging, including rack mounting, for such installations would have constituted a significant overhead in terms of cost. As the role of PC based products in corporate environments expands, commercial grade mass-market packaging for multiple PCs in a modular extensible form should become available. Inexpensive rack mounting will facilitate the deployment of physically smaller Beowulf systems.

10.2   New Opportunities

Historically, Beowulf-class computers have been used primarily for science and engineering applications or as experimental test beds in educational settings. But their low cost, scalability, and generality provide a wide array of opportunities for new domains of application. Some of these can be accomplished now with existing hardware and software technology. Others require the development of new and innovative software infrastructure. Some examples of these new application opportunities follow.

10.2.1   Databases

Commercial software relies heavily on the management and manipulation of data in complex databases. At the time of writing, major vendors of widely used commercial database software systems including Oracle, Sybase, Informix and Objectivity have announced their support of the Linux operating system. Beowulf presents the opportunity to support distributed databases for coarse grain searches and multiple transaction processing tasks for multiple simultaneous users.

10.2.2   Web Servers

One of the most rapidly growing responsibilities of local systems is hosting World Wide Web pages and servers including search engines. In the last few years, the web alone has caused Internet bandwidth usage to increase by more than an order of magnitude in certain areas. This is due, in part, to the heavy emphasis on image data that is a significant component of many web sites. With appropriate server support software, Beowulf can provide a low cost, high performance, scalable platform for future web servers.

10.2.3   Dynamic Interactive Simulation

Dynamic interactive simulation (DIS) is a class of applications that present multi-user shared simulated environments with real-time response. DIS systems have been applied to everything from war gaming to multi-user video games. DIS requires complex scenario simulation, fast response time and sophisticated user interfaces. Beowulfs can be a low-cost, scalable platform to stage complete simulations or they can act as computational elements in larger, more dispersed simulations.

10.2.4   Virtual Reality

Full immersion synthetic environments can be generated by exploiting Beowulf's parallel nature. This will require extensive software development, and may also benefit from hardware advances, such as new graphics engines with explicit support for parallel rendering. Different parts of the virtual space can be manipulated and visually rendered on separate nodes with overall synchronization and final image assembly coordinated across the system. It is likely that with proper partitioning of the simulated space, the I/O bandwidth to drive large, immersive visual presentation devices can be parallelized across the Beowulf nodes as well.

10.2.5   Process Control

Process control in manufacturing has long been a key application area for distributed systems. Process control is often achieved with a mix of specialized embedded processors and larger more rugged computers integrated with a LAN. Beowulf-class systems could be applied to this important domain of application. However, additional requirements that have not been satisfied to date would be imposed on the Beowulf. These include fault tolerance and real-time response. Both require additional capabilities to be developed as part of the Linux-based software infrastructure.

10.2.6   Artificial Intelligence

The use of symbolic processing for the emulation of cognitive processes is the domain of artificial intelligence (AI). Although quite different from more conventional numerical computation in that it manipulates encodings of relationships rather than numbers, AI can be very compute intensive. Structures such as semantic webs describe the complex interrelationships of objects, actions, qualities, and concepts. These and other symbolic data are processed to solve puzzles, play chess, control robots, analyze images, and perform speech analysis. The dominant language for the AI community is LISP and the premiere commercial Common LISP package, Allegro Common LISP is available for Linux systems. Porting AI applications to Beowulf, while not trivial, may be feasible in many cases where large symbolic data structures can be searched in parallel.

10.2.7   Genetic Programming

Writing programs that write programs is the purview of genetic programming, a rapidly evolving discipline that is dedicated to devising means of automatic or declarative programming. Genetic programming searches an abstract space of possible methods using specially crafted heuristics. Genetic algorithms typically require the execution and measurement of many programs that make up a population. This embarrassingly parallel computation is ideally suited for the loosely coupled Beowulfs.

10.3 True Costs

The costs of creating and maintaining a Beowulf exceed the price of its constituent components. Besides the space, power, and cooling which can be nontrivial for the larger systems, there are the personnel costs involved with the maintenance and management of Beowulfs. Beowulfs go through a three-phase life cycle: the burn-in phase, the application phase, and the upgrade phase.

The burn-in phase involves both hardware and software. Components are most likely to fail during the first few weeks of operation. The most likely components to fail will be fans, power supplies, disk drives, and network control cards, in that order. While these parts will be under warranty, it may be desirable to initially purchase a spare so that one does not suffer extended down-times due to the delays in obtaining replacements. For a 32 node Beowulf system, a single spare would add only 3% to the total cost and provides significant additional reliability. In addition to hardware burn-in, there will be some inevitable reconfiguration of software systems as users and administrators become familiar with Beowulf operations.

The application phase is the steady-state condition for most Beowulfs and can last for months or years. There can be very long periods of stability with system uptimes measured in months. The personnel costs incurred during this phase are related to application program development and are essentially the same as those associated with ownership of comparable commercial parallel systems.

The third stage of the Beowulf life-cycle involves upgrades to both system software and hardware. For hardware upgrades, new nodes or components may be added, or old nodes may need to be taken off line, powered down, etc. Almost all software upgrades can be done on running systems without the need for a reboot. The only real exception is a kernel upgrade, i.e., replacing the most central component of the OS. Such upgrades are rarely needed. Linux "production" kernels are extremely stable, and rarely require upgrades. Development kernels, on the other hand, can be extremely volatile and should only be used where there is some compelling need.

All three phases of the Beowulf life-cycle incur the costs of the personnel required to attend to the system, the physical infrastructure required to support it, and the disruption in productivity due to changes. Assembling the hardware and software configurations of a Beowulf system, whether the nodes are pre-assembled or constructed from parts, can be time consuming but should not be over-estimated. Assembly of a node from shrink-wrapped, component parts takes less than an hour for an experienced technician. Even if this labor cost is added to the capital cost of the components, the price/performance still exceeds commercial MPPs by a large factor. Software configuration requires planning and experience, but it is only weakly dependent on the size of the system. That is, configuring the file systems, networks, user accounts, etc. on a 4 node system is little different from doing so on a 20 node system.

Programming a Beowulf, especially fine tuning the performance of codes, even if already operational on other parallel systems can be labor intensive. The longer latencies and reduced bandwidths with respect to more tightly coupled MPPs, even when employing the same message passing programming model, demand added diligence in managing the spatial and temporal locality of the application program and its working data set.

Upgrades, repairs, software patches, and reconfigurations with new, usually more capable, nodes all involve direct labor to carry out the required changes. One last form of cost is the learning curve required by personnel to perform the needed tasks implied by the life-cycle three phases. Expertise in the use of Linux, network configuration, and system maintenance as well as backups and other routine chores has to be acquired by on-site personnel.

Fully loaded, turnkey commercial systems can require less on-site hands-on personnel time than a Beowulf. However, experience at large computer centers with such commercial high end computers exposes many sources of additional costs as well. For one thing, the maintenance contract can be very expensive. One such center a few years ago de-installed a moderate sized commercial system because the annual maintenance budget for that machine exceeded the entire replacement cost of a Beowulf providing superior performance. They could buy a complete, new Beowulf every year for the cost of their MPP's service contract. Large commercial systems will routinely require on-site operators and systems administrators, with significant recurring costs. Hardware maintenance will usually be done by the vendor's own technical staff. On the other hand, software patches and upgrades are often performed by computer center staff. One unique advantage of commercial systems is that there is someone to call (or sue) when everything goes wrong. Sometimes, the support team is even helpful and knowledgeable, and they can significantly enhance a system's utility for sites that lack in-house expertise.

Parallel systems are tricky beasts, whether you bought the full package or put it together from a kit, and applications programming is always time consuming. The difficult issue then is the relative additional costs of a Beowulf with respect to the commercial offering. This often depends on the environment in which the system is to be used and the culture/talent base available. Sites that already have the necessary talent usually know it, and hence have been more likely to adopt the Beowulf approach. While efforts are being made to reduce the required level of expertise, it is unlikely that Beowulf systems will ever be any more turn-key than, say, an equivalently powerful commercial system. Nobody thinks twice about investing in the talents of an experienced sysadmin to manage or program a million dollar commercial MPP. Although a great deal cheaper to purchase, an equally powerful Beowulf system will probably need equally talented staff.

10.4   Total Work versus Peak Performance

A perception exists that large and compute-intensive applications need supercomputers to carry them out. This is the peak-performance argument. But such machines are rarely made available to a single dedicated problem for long periods because they must be shared among many contending users. Beowulf-class systems may be more readily dedicated to individual tasks for a longer period of time than their mainframe/supercomputer/MPP counterparts because of their low cost. While the normal operational mode of a large expensive tightly-coupled system is as a shared resource, a moderately sized Beowulf may be devoted to the needs of a single computational experiment for a significant duration. The important issue is the total aggregate work performed on the problem, not the peak performance applied to the problem. With large systems in shared environments users get a small portion of the total machine or the entire machine for a short period of time. With a Beowulf, the user may get the entire machine for an indefinite period. Over an interval of time, say a week, the total work accomplished by the Beowulf on the problem is many times that available to a specific user of a major system shared among many users. Thus, from the standpoint of a computational scientist a moderate sized Beowulf can actually outperform a large shared system from the standpoint of the time between program submission and program completion.

10.5   Big Memory versus Out-of-core

Large shared systems have one crucial advantage over dedicated Beowulfs. Even
if access to the machine is limited to only a few hours per week, the user with a
500GByte data set will accomplish more on the large shared system than on the
dedicated Beowulf. The reason is simple. The problem simply does not fit in the
Beowulf's memory so the Beowulf can make no progress at all. Purchasing enough
memory would be prohibitively expensive for a dedicated system. On the other
hand, the large capital investment in the large system's memory can be shared by
all its users.

One way for Beowulf systems to sustain their price/performance advantage, even
for large memory problems, is out-of-core techniques, i.e., exchanging utilizing disk
space as dynamic memory. In a sense, this is doing explicitly from the application
program what virtual memory is supposed to do. The advantage of controlling
secondary storage from the application is that the access patterns may be well
understood and therefore can be exploited. As noted in other sections of this book,
almost nothing is cheaper than a spinning bit (a bit of disk storage). When data can
be partitioned, operated upon, and replaced, disk storage can be used in place of
main memory. The programming methodology for application management of disk
storage is similar to that of programming loosely coupled clusters; they both require
that latency tolerant algorithms be employed. Thus, once an application has been
crafted to perform well in the presence of latency, it may be able to exploit disk
storage to hold large data sets. For such applications, a moderately scaled Beowulf
dedicated to a single problem for a significant period of time can perform large
applications in less time, and for far less money than a heavily shared large high
end computer. Returning to the scenario above, if the application can be recoded
to effectively use out-of-core storage, then there is no reason at all why a modest
Beowulf could not address a 500GByte data set.

10.6   Bounding Influences on the Beowulf Domain

While Beowulf-class computing affords great opportunity for many applications and
contexts, its innate properties limit its ultimate scope. The success of Beowulf is due
primarily to the wide availability of its components. But Beowulf's limitations can
be found in the same market forces that drive the development and distribution
of those components. The market, while friendly to the needs of spreadsheets,
word processors, and video games, is indifferent to the integrity of 3-D plasma

simulations of controlled fusion reactors or molecular modeling for future medical drug design. The Beowulf community is small, providing at most an incidental market share when compared to the general PC-buying public. It can exploit what is available but has little influence on the direction of hardware product development. However, it can and has impacted software development. The needs of clusters had a strong influence on the development of both the PVM and MPI message passing libraries. Beowulf has also contributed directly to the development of the Linux operating system. The Beowulf model has been fortunate in the simultaneous development of both high performance mass-market microprocessors and high bandwidth networking technology at an appropriate price/performance to support clustering in the Beowulf style.

It is often stated that Beowulf-class systems and other families of PC clusters are "market driven." This is an error and confuses the role of the market versus the motivating factors. Beowulf is "market enabled." The technology is created for other purposes allowing mass production and encouraging competition, leading to aggressive pricing and exceptional price/performance. But this does not directly drive the creation of Beowulfs. Rather, Beowulf is "user-driven." The creation of Beowulfs has relied solely on the motivation of the users to apply the potential of PC clusters to real-world applications or to employ them as test beds for computer science and education. Often, Beowulfs have been assembled by teams of scientists outside the computer science arena who wish to bring more power to their specific scientific challenges while operating with restricted budget.

The timing of the various Beowulf activities around the country has been lucky so far in the rapid improvement of both floating point performance and local area network bandwidth utilizing what the commodity market has needed (and therefore produced) for other reasons. Storage capacities have increased and prices have dropped for both main memory and hard disks over the same period. The Beowulf model also has benefited from the base of experience developed in using distributed memory, parallel architectures such as the Intel Paragon and IBM SP-2 as well as earlier research with workstation clusters such as the projects at the University of Wisconsin and UC Berkeley. The development of standardized message passing libraries for those systems has provided a ready methodology for exploitation of Beowulf systems. Finally, the two decade-long Unix experience leading to FreeBSD and Linux again fortuitously provided a robust, sophisticated, and well understood software environment.

But the Beowulf vision has its own limiting horizon. Within these many complementing opportunities are the constraints that bound Beowulf's utility. The loosely coupled nature of Beowulf clusters dominates the operational capabilities and characteristics of Beowulf-class systems, now and in the future. The range of applications that may be suitably hosted by Beowulfs will be strongly determined by this aspect of the system class. Some applications are sufficiently regular and employ minimal communications that they are natural targets for Beowulfs. A second group of applications, if captured with appropriate latency-tolerant algorithmic techniques, can also be supported, although with greater program development effort. Important examples of these have already been demonstrated. But a third, hopefully small, class of applications that exhibit substantial intrinsic communications demands requiring frequent global synchronization may never be served adequately by future Beowulf-class systems. The performance and generality of Beowulf systems are likely to be communications limited even as faster networks become commodity products. The performance advances of the emerging Gigabit per second commodity networks are being offset by the increase in demand resulting from faster processors and I/O buses.

10.7   New Programming Models

The limitations imposed by communication latency go beyond performance issues. As indicated above, managing latency even influences the programming model adopted by most Beowulf applications. While efforts have been made to devise distributed shared memory systems on top of Beowulf-like systems, they have been unable to hide the latency from the programmer. Because of this, programmers of Beowulf are always conscious of the need to manage locality of data and program flow in order to mitigate the effects of latency. Techniques include data partitioning, static and dynamic task distribution and load balancing, message buffering and other means of reducing communication and taking best advantage of existing resources. But the fragmented name space imposes the additional burden of working with a non-unique mapping between variable names and physical locations. Some attempts to minimize this particular consequence of distributed computing have been made with implicit programming models such as BSP and HPF. But even these require careful attention to data partitioning and distribution. An added complication is the possibility of non-uniform access times resulting from complex caches and networks. New approaches to programming are needed that strike the right balance between expressiveness and abstraction. The programmer wants to specify what he knows about the data structures, control flow, etc, and then leave the rest to the compiler or runtime system. It is easy to err in on direction or another, i.e., either allowing so much abstraction that good performance cannot be obtained, or requiring so much specificity that programming is difficult. The programmer should to be cognizant of memory hierarchies, bandwidths and latencies, but should not necessarily control them directly. Devising and implementing new programming models is a major research effort which may bear fruit in the coming years.

10.8 Will Linux Survive the Mass Market?

There is much discussion today about the future of Linux and its vulnerability to the "juggernaut" of the dominating PC operating system. How can Linux survive when Windows NT is taking over the world? Or so goes one of many forms of the argument. But the argument is fallacious because it is based on the underlying assumption that Linux and other operating systems are in competition. With the possible exception of BSD, this is essentially untrue. Linux and NT serve two different communities. Linux is no threat to NT. It has a tiny installed base compared to Microsoft's products, and does not support the same base of shrink-wrap applications.

The key point in determining the outcome of this non-competition is how Linux was created. It did not result from some corporate board room decision or the plans of some marketing department. It was created by and for people who wanted it. Today, it matures and evolves driven by that same community. No external influence is going to kill Linux. As long as the people who make up the Linux community continue to want it, Linux will continue to prosper, even to the point of spawning support companies. If Linux dies, it will do so because that same community finds something better to meet their needs. Perhaps this will be some future descendent of the current Microsoft offerings. Perhaps not. In any event, the decision will be based on capability, not on the decisions of corporate CIOs. Today, Linux continues the Unix tradition, making Unix-like systems more widely available than ever before. Today, Microsoft continues to develop the set of software environments and tools that serve the needs of its customers. Both have a place and serve a useful purpose. Neither is in conflict with the goals and market of the other. This chapter is being typed on a current generation laptop computer that hosts both Windows 95 and Linux as co-resident operating systems; there is plenty of room for both.

10.9   Final Thoughts

Beowulf is a phenomenon, perhaps even a unique phenomenon. When the original
Beowulf project was initiated, its goals were modest, its anticipated lifetime limited. It was not even known if effective scientific computation could be performed
on clusters of personal computers. But the answer was "yes" and the timing proved
auspicious. Many researchers at diverse locations and organizations were considering similar approaches; the idea was in the air. The Beowulf project provided some
of the earliest demonstrations and quantitative test results as well as supplying
some of the necessary software. But today, with hundreds of sites, Beowulf-class
computing no longer belongs to any one group or project. It is a tool of the
computational science community, providing one alternative approach for high end
computing. Its attraction to many is its flexibility, low cost, and user control. A
number of efforts are underway across the country and around the world to develop
new software tools that will enhance its utility and improve its ease of use. While
many of these tools are under development for a broad range of system classes,
Beowulfs are among the intended targets. Other such tools are being developed
expressly to assist in using Beowulf clusters. A community of Beowulf users and
developers has emerged, sharing results and tools, and contributing to the general
understanding of the means and value of this model. The future of Beowulf-class
computing is in the hands of its users. As new roles are discovered and explored,
the world of Beowulf will continue to grow. But if the many challenges still con-
fronting useful and robust application of this technology are not met in the near
future with innovative tools and techniques, then the Beowulf revolution will stall.
This book has been offered as one step in advancing the objectives of Beowulf-class
computing and facilitating their exploitation by new users for an increasing range
of applications.

Index of Acronyms

EUI End User Interface, 163

EXT linux EXTended file system, 70

EXT2 second linux EXTended file system, 70

FDD Floppy Disk Drive, 62

FDDI Fiber Digital Device Interface, 103

FFTW Fastest FFT in the West, 191

FHS File system Hierarchy Standard, 133

FIFO First In First Out, 72

FIPS Federal Information Processing Standard, 78

FORTRAN FORmula TRANslator, 77

FSSTND File System Standard, 133

FTP File Transfer Protocol, 142

GCC GNU C Compiler, 77

GIF Graphics Interchange Format, 155

GNAT GNU-NYU Ada Translator, 77

GNU GNU's Not Unix, 69

GUI Graphical User Interface, 69

HDD Hard Disk Drive, 62

HP Hewlett Packard, 63

HPC High Performance Computing, 2

HPCC High Performance Computing and Communications, 2

HPF High Performance Fortran, 77

HPFS High Performance File System, 70

HTML Hypertext Markup Language, 90

I/O Input/Output, 28

IBM International Business Machines, 119

IDE Integrated Drive Electronics, 47

IDL Interface Definition Language, 116

IEEE Institute of Electrical and Electronics Engineers, 63

IP Internet Protocol, 105

IPv4 Internet Protocol, version 4, 105

IPv6 Internet Protocol, version 6, 105

IRQ Interrupt Request, 60

ISA Industry Standard Architecture, 31

ISDN Integrated Services Digital Network, 69

JDK Java Development Kit, 77

JIT Just In Time, 117

JPL Jet Propulsion Laboratory, 3

JVM Java Virtual Machine, 117

LAM Local Area MPI, 172

LAN Local Area Network, 93

LANL Los Alamos National Laboratory, 3

LDP Linux Documentation Project, 91

LED Light Emitting Diode, 36

LILO LInux LOader, 88

LINPACK Linear algebra Package, 51

Lisp LISt Processing language, 77

LOBOS Lots of Boxes on Shelves, 51

LPT Line Printer, 54

M²COTS Mass Market Commodity Off The Shelf, 9

MAC Media Access Controller, 98

MAU Medium Attachment Unit, 99

MIMD Multiple Instruction Multiple Data, 164

MIME Multipurpose Internet Mail Extensions, 72

MIPS MIPS Technologies, 67

Index